China's Four Modernizations

Other Titles in This Series

The Medieval Chinese Oligarchy, David G. Johnson

Women in Changing Japan, edited by Joyce Lebra, Joy Paulson, and Elizabeth Powers

The Chinese Military System: An Organizational Study of the People's Liberation Army, Harvey W. Nelsen

Mineral Resources and Basic Industries in the People's Republic of China, K. P. Wang

Mineral Economics and Basic Industries in Asia, K. P. Wang and E. Chin

The Problems and Prospects of American–East Asian Relations, edited by John Chay

The Politics of Medicine in China: The Policy Process, 1949–1977, David M. Lampton

Intra-Asian International Relations, edited by George T. Yu

Chinese Foreign Policy after the Cultural Revolution, 1966–1977, Robert G. Sutter

Huadong: The Story of a Chinese People's Commune, Gordon Bennett

China's Oil Future: A Case of Modest Expectations, Randall W. Hardy

A Theory of Japanese Democracy, Nobutaka Ike

Perspectives on a Changing China: Essays in Honor of Professor C. Martin Wilbur on the Occasion of His Retirement, edited by Joshua A. Fogel and William T. Rowe

Technology, Defense, and External Relations in China, 1975–1978, Harry G. Gelber

Encounter at Shimoda: Search for a New Pacific Partnership, edited by Herbert Passin and Akira Iriye

China's Quest for Independence: Policy Evolution in the 1970s, edited by Thomas Fingar and the Stanford Journal of International Studies

Military Power and Policy in Asian States: China, India, Japan, edited by Onkar Marwah and Jonathan D. Pollack

Westview Special Studies on China and East Asia

China's Four Modernizations: The New Technological Revolution
edited by Richard Baum

With the death of Mao Tse-tung and the subsequent purge of the "Gang of Four," China's new pragmatic leaders have embarked on a crash program of national development known as the Four Modernizations. This program is geared to the primary objective of turning China into a major world economic and military power by the year 2000.

In this book, the outgrowth of a major international conference on China's post-Maoist development, ten distinguished analysts examine one of the core issues in China's current modernization drive: the acquisition and use of modern industrial science and technology. The authors address the politics of China's technological modernization, the institutional structure of technological research, the purchase of foreign technology, constraints on technological absorption, the growth potential of China's critical energy sector, and the modernization of China's military establishment. Supplemented with brief commentaries by leading academic, government, and private sector contributors, their chapters provide an in-depth look at the process, problems, and prospects of China's widely heralded technological revolution.

Richard Baum is professor of political science at the University of California, Los Angeles.

China's Four Modernizations: The New Technological Revolution

edited by Richard Baum

Westview Press / Boulder, Colorado

Cover photograph and text photographs courtesy of Richard Baum.

Westview Special Studies on China and East Asia

Published in 1980 in the United States of America by
Westview Press, Inc.
5500 Central Avenue
Boulder, Colorado 80301
Frederick A. Praeger, Publisher

Library of Congress Cataloging in Publication Data
Main entry under title:
China's four modernizations.
(Westview special studies on China and East Asia)
Based on a workshop held in St. George, Bermuda, in January 1979.
Includes index.
1. Technology and state—China. I. Baum, Richard, 1940— II. Series.
T27.C5C552 338.951 79-23496
ISBN 0-89158-673-3
ISBN 0-89158-755-1 pbk.

Printed and bound in the United States of America

For Barry M. Richman
(1936–1978)

an esteemed colleague
and a good friend

In Memoriam

Contents

Tables and Figures

Tables

Figures

Abbreviations

Abbreviations in Text

CAS	Chinese Academy of Sciences
CCP	Chinese Communist Party
NPC	National People's Congress
PLA	People's Liberation Army
P.R.C.	People's Republic of China
R & D	Research and Development
SSTC	State Scientific and Technological Commission
S & T	Science and Technology
STA	Science and Technology Association
STCND	Science and Technology Commission for National Defense
UNESCO	United Nations Educational, Scientific, and Cultural Organization
U.S.S.R.	Union of Soviet Socialist Republics
VTOL	Vertical Take-Off and Landing
WHO	World Health Organization

Abbreviations in Notes

BR	*Beijing Review*

CBR	*China Business Review*
FBIS	Foreign Broadcast Information Service
FBIS-P.R.C.	Foreign Broadcast Information Service, Daily Report—People's Republic of China
HC	*Hung-ch'i*
JMJP	*Jen-min jih-pao*
JPRS	Joint Publications Research Service
KHSY	*K'o-hsüeh shih-yen*
KMJP	*Kuang-ming jih-pao*
NCNA	New China News Agency
NYT	*New York Times*
OECD	Organization for Economic Cooperation and Development
PR	*Peking Review*
SCMP	*Survey of China Mainland Press*
SPRCM	*Selections from P.R.C. Magazines*
SPRCP	*Survey of People's Republic of China Press*
SWB	*Summary of World Broadcasts*

Preface

In January 1979, fifty-seven informed observers of contemporary China—including in roughly equal proportion academic specialists, U.S. government policy analysts, and representatives from the private sector of industry and commerce—met in St. George, Bermuda, to assess the programs, policies, problems, and prospects of China's current, post-Maoist modernization drive.

For four days the participants brought their diverse multidisciplinary experiences, ideas, and insights to bear on a common set of questions concerning the technological dimension of this new developmental revolution: What are the programmatic goals and priorities of the P.R.C.'s so-called Four Modernizations? What are the major technological and institutional strengths and weaknesses affecting Peking's ability to attain these goals? How is technological innovation promoted and organized in China? What types of foreign technology are the Chinese currently importing, and for what purposes? To what extent does China's large-scale acquisition of foreign plant and machinery tend to compromise the long-standing Maoist goals of maintaining technological independence, initiative, and "self-reliance"? How is modern technology absorbed, assimilated, and disseminated within China? What problems have arisen as a result of the P.R.C.'s current "quick fix" approach to modernization, and what measures have been adopted to deal with these problems? And finally, what are the long-term economic, social, political, and strategic implications of China's new technological revolution for China, the United States, and the world at large?

Given the divergent professional backgrounds, institutional affiliations, and value preferences of the fifty-seven men and women who attended the Bermuda workshop, it is small wonder that there was less than universal agreement among those present on the answers to these questions. Where some participants viewed the Chinese technological glass as half-full, others saw it as half-empty; where some were optimistic about China's ability to succeed in its modernization campaign, others were more pessimistic; and where some viewed the emergence of a "strong and secure" China with favor, as a potentially cooperative U.S. partner in world affairs, others regarded the P.R.C.'s growing industrial and military strength with alarm, as posing an eventual threat to U.S. national security interests. Like the various protagonists in the Japanese psychodrama *Rashomon*, each participant brought his or her unique perspective to bear on the achievements, shortcomings, and broad implications of China's modernization program.

This diversity of views is fully reflected in the present volume, which is a direct outgrowth of the Bermuda workshop. In the following pages, seven of the eighteen topical papers originally presented at the workshop are reproduced (with minor revision and updating), along with three newly commissioned essays. In order to capture the full flavor of the discussion and debate that took place at Bermuda, many of the individual chapters in this volume are followed directly by one or more brief topical commentaries, transcribed and edited from the taped proceedings of the workshop. The result is a wide-ranging, free-wheeling assemblage of ideas, insights, interpretations, and information concerning China's post-Maoist technological transformation.

For proprietary reasons, several of the papers originally presented at Bermuda were not available for publication in this volume. Four of these papers—on the state-of-the-art in Chinese agricultural engineering (by Jon Sigurdson), mechanical engineering (by C. L. Tien), electronics (by Bohdan Szuprowicz), and energetics (a more detailed version of the chapter by Vaclav Smil)—will appear, under the editorship of Leo Orleans, in a forthcoming multivolume series on Chinese science and technology, to be published by Stanford University Press under the auspices of the Committee on Scholarly Communication with the P.R.C. of the National Academy of Sciences. In addition, a paper on industrial manpower training and utilization (by Pierre Perrolle) will be published in a forthcoming volume on engineering education in the P.R.C., also under the auspices of the Committee on Scholarly Communication, Pierre Perrolle, editor. Finally, a paper on the strategic implications of China's technological modernization (by Lucian Pye) appears in the summer 1979 issue of *International Security.*

Partially to compensate for these unavoidable deletions from the present collection and partially to fill in a few gaps in the original proceedings, three new essays were written especially for this volume: a general editorial introduction (by Richard Baum), an analysis of China's recent industrial performance (by Chu-yüan Cheng), and a summary discussion of the socioeconomic and commercial implications of China's modernization drive (by Jeffrey Schultz).

Throughout this volume, Chinese terminology and the names of individuals are rendered in the traditional Wade-Giles system rather than in China's official pinyin system—an adoption arising from the editor's belief that Wade-Giles, though far from perfect as a guide to Chinese pronunciation, is nevertheless more widely recognized and understood by non-Chinese-speaking readers. The names of provinces and major cities are rendered in the familiar postal system; smaller places are spelled in the Wade-Giles system.

The editor would like to acknowledge the generous financial and administrative support provided by three cosponsors of the Bermuda workshop: the Henry Luce Foundation, the Social Science Research Council, and the Committee on Scholarly Communication with the P.R.C. of the National Academy of Sciences. I am particularly indebted to Martha Wallace and Robert E. Armstrong of the Henry Luce Foundation, Mary Brown Bullock and Leo Orleans of the Committee on Scholarly Communication, and Patrick Maddox and Anne Thurston of the Social Science Research Council for their personal efforts in helping to bring this project to fruition.

A strong debt of gratitude is also owed to William Clarke, Hans Heymann, Jr., Rensselaer Lee, III, and my late esteemed colleague, Barry M. Richman, for providing valuable ideas and suggestions during the formative stages of this project; to Jeffrey

Schultz, who performed heroically as rapporteur for the Bermuda workshop; to Helyn Bebermeyer, Adgerean Calhoun, Antoinette Botsford-Epstein, and Mary McMahon of the UCLA Committee on International and Comparative Studies, for patiently attending to the myriad administrative details involved in preparing for the workshop; to Urs Jakob, for his valuable editorial assistance; and last, but far from least, to all the workshop participants, without whose sharp insights and diligent efforts this volume would not have been possible.

Needless to say, the opinions expressed in this volume are solely those of the individual authors and commentators and do not necessarily reflect the views or policies of either the sponsoring organizations, the U.S. government, or any other institution, public or private.

Richard Baum
Los Angeles, California

The Contributors

Richard Baum is professor of political science at the University of California, Los Angeles. He is editor of *China in Ferment: Perspectives on the Cultural Revolution* (1971) and author of *Prelude to Revolution: Mao, the Party, and the Peasant Question, 1962–66* (1975). He is currently working on a long-term study of U.S.-China trade and technological relations under a grant from the Henry Luce Foundation. He organized and chaired the January 1979 Bermuda workshop on China's technological development.

Shannon R. Brown is associate professor of economics at the University of Maryland, Baltimore County. He has written extensively on the late nineteenth century transfer of technology to China and is currently working on a study of technology transfer to the P.R.C., with special reference to the chemical fertilizer industry.

Chu-yüan Cheng is professor of economics and chairman of Asian studies at Ball State University. His recent publications include *China's Petroleum Industry: Output Growth and Export Potential* (1976) and *The Machine-Building Industry in Communist China* (1971). He is now working on a new book on China's economic development, to be published by Westview Press.

Genevieve C. Dean, formerly research associate with the Stanford University U.S.-China Relations Program, is currently a Peking-based representative of Fluor Mining and Metals, Inc. She holds a Ph.D. in the history and social study of science from the University of Sussex. She is author of the bibliographic study, *Science and Technology in the Development of Modern China* (1974), and has written extensively about science policy in the P.R.C.

Thomas Fingar is assistant director of the Stanford University U.S.-China Relations Program. He is coeditor of *China's Quest for Independence: Policy Evolution in the 1970s* (Westview Press, 1980).

Jonathan Pollack is a member of the social science department of the Rand Corporation, Santa Monica. He was previously affiliated with the Harvard University Program for Science and International Affairs. He is coeditor of *Military Power and Policy in Asian States: China, India, Japan* (Westview Press, 1980).

Jeffrey Schultz, formerly affiliated with the National Council for U.S.-China Trade, is currently a staff member of Chase Pacific Trade Advisors. He is author of two recent monographs, *China's Foreign Trade Corporations: Organization and Personnel* (1979) and *China's Petroleum Industry* (1979), both published by the National Council for U.S.-China Trade.

Vaclav Smil is professor of geography at the University of Manitoba. His recent writings include *China's Energy* (1976) and *Energy and the Environment* (1974). He is editor of a forthcoming volume, *Energy in the Developing World.*

Richard P. Suttmeier is associate professor and chairman, Department of Government, Hamilton College. He is author of *Research and Revolution: Science Policy and Societal Change in China* (1974) and *Science, Technology and China's Drive for Modernization* (1979).

Rudi Volti is associate professor of sociology at Pitzer College. He is currently completing a major study of technology and society in contemporary China, to be published by Westview Press.

China's Four Modernizations

1
Introduction

Richard Baum

A Pierre Cardin fashion show opens in the shadow of Tien An Men Square; disco dancers gather at Peking's International Club; U.S. businessmen in Shanghai negotiate plans for a chain of modern tourist hotels and joint ventures in petroleum exploration; Chinese students openly discuss the virtues of Western-style democracy, Coca Cola, and Laurel and Hardy. Had Chairman Mao lived to see it, he might well have been moved to inquire, "Where am I?"

In the three years since Mao's death and the related purge of his radical ideological minions, the so-called Gang of Four, the winds of change have blown strongly across China. A new, pragmatic leadership headed by Mao's hand-picked successor, Hua Kuo-feng, and the twice-purged, twice born-again Vice Premier Teng Hsiao-p'ing, has embarked upon a bold, comprehensive program of long-term industrial, agricultural, military, and scientific/technological development. The goal of this program, termed the Four Modernizations, is to transform China into a "powerful, modern socialist country by the end of this century."[1]

In order to accomplish this ambitious objective, the Hua/Teng regime has jettisoned much of the revolutionary rhetoric and political dogma of the Maoist era and has substituted for it the highly pragmatic, instrumental ethos of "efficiency first." As Teng Hsiao-p'ing himself once put it, "it does not matter if the cat is white or black, so long as it catches mice."

To Mao and the Gang of Four, on the other hand, the color of the cat was always of prime significance. As one erstwhile mem-

A statue of Mao at the Shenyang Metals Research Institute (September 1978).

ber of the Gang reportedly said, "It is better to have a socialist train run late than a capitalist train run on time."

Since 1977, the cat has perceptibly changed color and the Chinese train has begun making up lost time. In line with the pragmatic philosophy of the new leaders of the People's Republic of China (P.R.C.), a wave of major policy changes has been initiated, the cumulative result of which has been to effectively dismantle the radical egalitarian legacy of Mao's turbulent Great Proletarian Cultural Revolution (1966–1969). Where once, a short decade ago, youthful Red Guards roamed the streets of Peking and Shanghai denouncing and abusing scientists, technicians, and teachers as "stinking bourgeois intellectuals," today the Red Guards have been banished and the erstwhile "stinking intellectuals" have been placed in charge of China's modernization program.

In education, academic achievement is now being emphasized over such traditional Maoist criteria as class background and political behavior in the recruitment and promotion of high school and university students. Nationwide unified college entrance examinations have been reinstituted after a hiatus of more than a decade, with primary emphasis on mathematics, physics, chemistry, and foreign languages. Postgraduate education has been restored; thousands of Chinese research scientists and technical specialists are being sent abroad to study advanced Western techniques and methods.

In industry, the technical and managerial authority of experts has been reasserted vis-à-vis Red political cadres and ordinary workers, and scientific management (once eschewed as an insidious form of worker enslavement) has been introduced in an effort to improve the efficiency of industrial operations. In order to stimulate increased labor enthusiasm, productivity bonuses and technical innovation bonuses (once condemned as revisionist) have been restored throughout the industrial sector.

In agriculture, peasants are being permitted an expanded role for their private plots, and government price supports for grain purchased by the state have been raised by 20 to 50 percent, giving farmers a direct, visible incentive to produce more food.

Along with these attempts to stimulate labor productivity, the Hua/Teng regime has also sought to provide China's workers and peasants with a tangible stake in the performance of the national economy by expanding the production and distribution of a wide variety of consumer goods—from color television sets, radios, and cameras to soft drinks and fashionable clothing.

Finally, with the adoption of a new state constitution in 1977 and the subsequent political rehabilitation of tens of thousands of individuals previously suppressed as counterrevolutionaries and rightists, China has embarked on a process of political liberalization unprecedented in its modern history. Legal safeguards have been introduced to protect citizens from arbitrary arrest and harrassment; freedom of speech and assembly—albeit limited in scope—have been introduced through such vehicles as Hyde Park–style "democracy walls"; and the Chinese court system has been overhauled to provide at least a modicum of due process to those accused of committing crimes. Though China has not by any stretch of the imagination become a democracy in the Western sense (the ruling Communist party is still omnipotent and tolerates no organized opposition), the political climate in Peking is more relaxed and tolerant today than at any time since the founding of the People's Republic of China some thirty years ago.

The Four Modernizations

China's current modernization drive is centered around the Ten-Year Plan (1976–1985) belatedly promulgated by Hua Kuo-feng in February 1978 (and therefore sometimes called the Eight-Year Plan). This economic plan originally called for the construction of 120 large-scale industrial projects, including 10 major iron and steel complexes, 9 nonferrous metals facilities, 8 large-scale coal combines, 10 new oil and natural gas fields, 30 major hydropower stations, 6 new trunk railways, and 5 key harbors. Major sectoral targets of the Ten-Year Plan included a projected doubling of steel production to 60 million tons per year, a 125 percent increase in gross industrial output, and a 50 percent increase in annual food production.[2]

Putting aside for the moment the question of the technical feasibility of these targets, it has been observed that in order to meet the original objectives of the plan, China's GNP growth would have to average almost 8.5 percent per year over the life of the plan—a rate almost 50 percent higher than the average growth rate of the previous twenty-five years. Similarly, in order to achieve the projected grain production target of 400 million tons annually by 1985, output would have to increase around 4.3 percent annually—almost twice the growth rate of the previous decade. And to attain the regime's projected target of 60 million tons of steel, the growth rate of the previous half decade would have to be almost doubled.[3]

In part because these original targets appeared excessively ambitious and in part because they stressed too heavily large-scale capital investments in a few key sectors of heavy industry (at the expense of augmented investment in the chronically sluggish agricultural sector as well as in the critical, growth-inducing sector of light industry), the initial programmatic objectives outlined by Hua Kuo-feng in February 1978 were substantially readjusted and scaled down a year later. Thus, in the spring of 1979 the projected 1985 target for steel production was lowered by almost 50 percent to a more modest 45 million tons and the projected industrial growth rate was reduced from more than 10 percent annually to a more manageable 8 percent. At the same time, it was announced that industrial investment would be cut from 54.7 percent of the state capital investment budget to 46.8 percent, while agricultural investments would correspondingly rise from 10.7 percent to 14 percent.[4]

Such intersectoral readjustments notwithstanding, however, the Four Modernizations campaign continues to represent an unprecedented commitment to the wholesale upgrading of China's economic and technological capabilities. Assuming that no major new political traumas occur over the next few years, the attainment of the P.R.C.'s ambitious developmental objectives will depend largely upon two closely related factors: the ability of the Chinese economy to generate the requisite amounts of investment capital, and the rapid acquisition and effective absorption of a wide variety of advanced productive technologies.

China's leaders have estimated that their modernization program will require capital investments totaling at least $600 billion between 1978 and 1985. This figure is roughly equal to the P.R.C.'s total industrial investments over the entire twenty-eight years of its prior existence, from 1949 to 1977.[5]

Where is this investment capital to come from? And how will it be allocated? One major source lies in the rapid expansion of export-oriented light industries, including textiles, clothing, and handicrafts. With their relatively low capital requirements, short gestation period, and high foreign exchange earnings potential, these industries are being counted on to generate quick profits for reinvestment in longer-term heavy industrial construction. Tourism is another industry being counted on to provide substantial foreign exchange earnings, as is the export of moderate amounts of China's abundant energy resources—principally coal and crude oil. Indeed, the strategy of using energy exports to finance technology acquisition from abroad is the essence of an eight-year, $20 billion trade agreement signed between China and Japan in 1978.

In the short run, then, the generation of investment capital to underwrite the Four Modernizations will depend largely upon China's ability to earn foreign exchange. It is for this reason that, in the course of China's economic readjustment of 1979, highest priority was placed on the rapid expansion of light industrial capacity (including the attraction of foreign capital through compensatory trade and joint stock ownership schemes), while the originally projected plans for new heavy industrial construction were temporarily scaled down until the light industrial investment pump could be sufficiently primed. In the meantime, heavy industrial expansion will occur primarily through renovating existing plants and equipment, rather than through the construction of expensive new facilities.[6]

In the long run, however, the P.R.C.'s goal of becoming a modern, socialist country by the year 2000 clearly depends on expanded economic production made possible by the acquisition of modern high technology. This technology will, it is hoped, facilitate the exploration and development of China's vast energy resources; upgrade China's iron, steel, and machine-building industries; mechanize, fertilize, and irrigate China's 500,000 rural villages; and modernize China's antiquated infrastructure of transportation and communications.

If technology acquisition is the key to the ultimate success of China's modernization program, it is apparent that foreign trade will play an increasingly important role in that program. It is thus hardly accidental that a prominent feature of the current Ten-Year Plan is the P.R.C.'s wholesale reentry into the mainstream of the world market. Where once the Gang of Four eschewed foreign economic entanglements as a betrayal of the Maoist ethos of self-reliance, Teng Hsiao-p'ing and Hua Kuo-feng now advocate the acquisition of "necessary foreign techniques and equipment" in the interest of "hastening China's socialist construction."[7] Indeed, China's post-Maoist leaders have turned rapidly outward to import everything from computers and steel mills to Coca Cola and Pierre Cardin fashions.

Recent estimates project that upwards of 10 percent of China's total investment budget for 1978–1985—roughly \$60 to \$70 billion—will be spent on the purchase of foreign technology, plant, and equipment. In 1978 alone, China and foreign technology suppliers concluded (or initialed) contracts for more than \$10 billion in product sales and whole plant imports.

Although some of these contracts were briefly frozen by the P.R.C. during the early stages of the spring 1979 economic retrenchment, there is no indication that Peking's overall plan for accelerated technology acquisition has been scrapped or even substantially cut back; it has only been temporarily delayed in the interest of securing more favorable financial terms and credit arrangements.[8]

At the second session of China's Fifth National People's Congress, held in June 1979, Premier Hua Kuo-feng reaffirmed the broad goals of the Four Modernizations and personally approved the revised priorities and targets announced previously. In his opening speech at the Congress, he acknowledged that there were "still quite a few difficulties and many problems waiting to be solved." Among these, he singled out for special attention shortcomings in several key economic sectors:

> The development of China's agriculture, light, textile, coal, petroleum and power industries, and transport and communications services still lagged behind what was required, the Premier said. There was imbalance in many respects within and among industrial departments. In capital construction, far too many projects were being undertaken all at the same time, and there were obvious shortcomings in the management of the economy and enterprises.[9]

Despite such shortcomings, however, Hua confidently predicted that China would "be able to expand its agriculture, light and heavy industries, and various other branches of industry in a harmonious way and maintain a rational proportion between accumulation and consumption."[10]

Additionally, the premier reaffirmed that, during the current three-year readjustment period and in the future, China would "continue implementing the set policy of actively importing up-to-date technologies and making use of foreign funds." And, finally, he indicated that, in order to finance costly foreign technology purchases, China would "adopt various reasonable practices now being used internationally to absorb foreign funds."[11]

In the following chapters, the technological component of

China's Four Modernizations campaign is examined from a variety of perspectives and with respect to a variety of specific problem foci. In Chapter 2, Chu-yüan Cheng presents a general economic assessment of the recent performance and current growth prospects of Chinese industry. After examining the major policy objectives of the Four Modernizations, he analyzes recent developments in certain key industrial sectors: iron and steel, petroleum, coal, electric power, and agricultural machinery. Based on this analysis, he concludes that many of the specific industrial objectives embodied in the original Ten-Year Plan were unrealistic insofar as they underestimated the costs, tradeoffs, technical constraints, and time lags involved in generating new industrial capacity.

Detailing some of the recent problems encountered by P.R.C. policy makers in such areas as industrial planning, enterprise management, organizational structure, and work incentives, Cheng relates these problems to the broader issues of capital formation and investment, absorptive capacity, and overall industrial efficiency.

Finally, Cheng analyzes in depth some of the various readjustments made in the Four Modernizations program in the first half of 1979. He observes that the recent scaling down of Chinese capital investments in heavy industrial construction will inevitably result in slower overall economic growth rates than originally envisioned (a point officially conceded by P.R.C. leaders at the National People's Congress in June 1979). Nevertheless, he views such readjustments as being rational over the long run, since they will ostensibly lead to better overall balance in the economy.

Three supplementary commentaries are appended to Chapter 2. K. C. Yeh first discusses some of the economic ramifications of China's modernization program, after which Thomas Wiens analyzes the problems and prospects of agricultural mechanization in the P.R.C. Finally, William Clarke assesses China's steel industry from the perspective of technological development.

In Chapter 3, we turn from a general assessment of Chinese industrial performance and capabilities to a more detailed examination of some of the primary institutional and behavioral constraints on technological modernization. Elaborating on themes raised by Chu-yüan Cheng, Thomas Fingar notes six basic problem areas—attitudinal, organizational, technical, educational, managerial, and financial—that have obstructed Chinese modernization efforts in the past. He then examines a number of recent policy initiatives that have been specifically designed to ameliorate these problems.

Characterizing the P.R.C.'s current developmental approach as a "maxi-max" strategy, which involves taking high risks in order to secure maximum benefits, Fingar argues that the quick-fix approach to technological modernization represents a substantial gamble, insofar as long-term solutions to current technical, institutional, and behavioral problems and bottlenecks cannot simply be purchased "out of the box" from abroad. While noting that it is still too early to assess the probable efficacy of recent policy changes in substantially accelerating the pace of China's technological transformation, he concludes that the success or failure of the Four Modernizations will ultimately hinge upon the ability of China's present leadership to create and coordinate the manifold infrastructural supports necessary to promote the development of industrial science and technology.

Placing China's Four Modernizations in historical perspective, Genevieve Dean examines the roots of China's current technology policies in Chapter 4. She is particularly interested in two earlier periods of P.R.C. development: the First Five-Year Plan, 1953–1957, and the economic retrenchment of the post–Great Leap Forward era, 1961–1965. Noting many basic similarities between the developmental strategies of the current stage and those adopted in these earlier periods, she argues that Chinese planners, for all their manifest commitment to the rationalization of scientific and technological processes, have thus far failed to resolve a fundamental, endemic problem that has severely constrained China's technological modernization in the past: the absence of institutionalized innovativeness.

Dean traces this shortcoming to the ostensibly prevalent Chinese belief that the processes of technological innovation and development are culturally and socially neutral, i.e., that innovativeness is embodied in technology itself and is thus inherently transferable in machines, managerial techniques, and associated software imported from advanced countries. The problem with this concept, in her view, is that it gives rise to a static and mechanistic view of technological innovation, one that fails to take into account the dynamic, systemic qualities of self-sustaining technological growth.

In a commentary appended to Chapter 4, C.H.G. Oldham discusses some of the central themes contained in the Fingar and Dean chapters and raises the additional key issue of how China's current developmental policies differ from those being pursued by other developing countries.

Elaborating on the theme of innovativeness raised by Dean, Richard P. Suttmeier looks at the institutional structure of China's technological research and development programs in Chapter 5. Echoing the distinction made by Dean between technology and innovation, he notes that a key problem for Chinese leaders has been the articulation of an appropriate institutional setting for stimulating and sustaining innovation. He observes that China's current leaders have inherited a philosophical legacy premised on the belief that discovery and innovation could be rationalized and promoted through centralized planning and administration, and he argues that one major difficulty with this premise has been its inhibiting effect on the development of a strong tradition of autonomous, basic scientific and technological research.

As a result of this lack of an institutionalized tradition of basic research, Suttmeier argues, Chinese industrial science and technology have evolved in an essentially "Edisonian" fashion, wherein solutions to immediate production problems are sought through a trial and error approach rather than through attempts to gain systematic insight into the nature of the problem at hand.

Tracing the evolution of Chinese research and development (R & D) institutions in the 1960s and 1970s, Suttmeier concurs with Dean that the major policy changes of the post-Mao era have been in the direction of restoring pre–Cultural Revolution institutional structures. Detailing the organization and operations of such R & D institutions as the Chinese Academy of Sciences, the State Scientific and Technological Commission, and various professional societies and specialized research institutes, Suttmeier assesses the strengths and weaknesses of China's current system of technological R & D, noting that the Chinese view of R & D as an administratively centralized "planned activity" is substantially at variance with Western notions of the innovation process.

Appended to Chapter 5 is a brief commentary by David M. Lampton, who notes that the division of China's technological R & D sector into three separate, vertically controlled hierarchies (the Academy of Sciences, the central government ministries, and institutions of higher education) may create severe problems with respect to the overall integration and coordination of research efforts, with the attendant risks of operational redundancy and duplication of effort.

In Chapter 6 we move from consideration of R & D policies and institutional structures to an examination of China's current program of technology acquisition from the advanced industrial nations of the West. In this chapter, Shannon Brown traces briefly the evolution of Chinese attitudes toward technological borrowing, from the initial self-strengthening movement of the late nineteenth century to the present post-Maoist era. He notes a substantial similarity between China's current attempt to maintain its cultural and institutional autonomy in the face of expanded foreign technological contacts and the late nineteenth-century ethos of "Chinese learning as the essence [*t'i*]; Western learning for practical use [*yung*]."

Arguing that China's economic development depends largely upon its capacity to absorb and assimilate foreign technology, Brown searches for clues to the probable impact of massive transfers of foreign technology. He first examines the record of the 1950s, when the P.R.C. was almost wholly dependent on Soviet technical assistance. He then traces the Maoist rejection of extreme technological dependency in the self-reliance ethos of the Cultural Revolution, noting that during that period China's acquisition of modern technology declined "in an often chaotic atmosphere characterized by strong xenophobic overtones."

In the aftermath of the Cultural Revolution, a basic decision was made in China to resume large-scale technological imports from abroad—principally from the industrially advanced nations of the West. But in the mid-1970s, Brown notes, political opposition to this decision among radical "nativist" elements of the Chinese leadership—in particular the Gang of Four—led to a sharp cutback in foreign technology purchases on the grounds that such purchases allegedly manifested a "slavish comprador philosophy" and a tendency to "worship things foreign." With the death of Mao and the downfall of the Gang, however, the stage was set for the resumption of large-scale technology purchases.

After recounting these developments, Brown goes on to assess current P.R.C. priorities in technology acquisition. He details China's recent contract signings (and ongoing negotiations) for the import of Western plant and equipment. Like Fingar and Suttmeier, Brown believes that the long-run contribution of such purchases to the P.R.C.'s overall modernization will ultimately depend not simply on the types or quantities of plant and machinery purchased, but also on the effectiveness of Chinese institutions in absorbing, assimilating, adapting, and internally disseminating the acquired technologies.

In a commentary appended to Brown's paper, Robert F. Dernberger emphasizes that foreign technology "must inevitably be grafted onto a Chinese base." In his view, it is imperative to first consider domestic Chinese technological capabilities before assessing the probable impact of foreign plant and equipment. Dernberger thus stresses more strongly than Brown the distinction between technology *acquisition* and technology *transfer.* (The former is achieved through simple business transactions, while the latter requires the ability to integrate acquired plant and machinery into the domestic economy. And this, in turn, requires the acquisition of technical expertise, indigenous design capability, managerial skills, and a host of related infrastructural capabilities.)

Taking up this question of technological absorption and assimilation, Rudi Volti in Chapter 7 examines the social/organizational impact of technology acquisition. Raising once again the distinction between Chinese "essence" (*t'i*) and Western "use" (*yung*), Volti notes that in pre-Communist China the absorption of foreign technology gave rise to a tendency for *t'i* to be devoured by *yung*, resulting in the virtual obliteration of what he terms "the last of the great preindustrial civilizations."

Taking as his point of departure the contemporary Chinese desire to restore a suitable balance between imported technology and indigenous culture and institutions, Volti focuses on the question of what constitute appropriate technological choices for the P.R.C.—i.e., what types of technology are most directly and immediately suitable for China's needs under present socioeconomic and demographic conditions? Given the fact that China remains an overwhelmingly agrarian society with an overabundance of unskilled and semiskilled rural labor (and a chronic shortage of investment capital and technically skilled manpower), Volti argues that the headlong pursuit of the most up-to-date capital-intensive technologies for use in a few key urban industries may not be an optimal strategy for promoting China's overall development. Such a strategy, he observes, tends to create a few isolated enclaves of modernity and may thereby exacerbate existing gaps between urban and rural labor productivity, technical skills, incomes, and life styles. In this regard, Volti sees much of value in the earlier Maoist developmental approach of "walking on two legs," with its emphasis on low-cost, labor-intensive intermediate technologies and local self-reliant economic diversification in the countryside.

Noting that "technologies do not diffuse automatically, nor are they assimilated by atomized individuals and economic units," Volti next examines the organizational characteristics of the various agencies involved in technology transfer and diffusion in the P.R.C. He argues that the Maoist organizational model, with its stress on multipurpose organizations, popular decision-making initiative, and an "open door" approach to technological R & D, constitutes an apparently effective method of harnessing technological growth to desired patterns of general social change. By way of contrast, he observes that recent trends toward the encapsulation of technological development within highly specialized, exclusive single-purpose organizations may result in a narrowing of social perspective and a one-sided stress on technical efficiency at the expense of broader social and cultural objectives. He thus sounds a note of caution concerning the potentially counterproductive side effects of post-Maoist changes in P.R.C. organizational policies governing technological R & D.

Elaborating on Volti's theme of a rural-urban technological dichotomy, Jack Baranson comments on the linkage between the two sectors, noting that in the course of rural development, "something that was a [village] blacksmith shop may eventually become an automotive parts manufacturer." He nevertheless observes that China's current leaders appear to believe that the key to modernization lies not in the rural economy but rather in the urban industrial sector, which he characterizes as the "leading edge" of technological change. Noting that China is attempting to solve its technological problems by training a vast army of scientists, engineers, and technical workers in Western methods of research and production, he argues that the P.R.C.'s current approach to industrialization closely resembles that of late nineteenth century Japan.

In Chapters 8 and 9, we take a closer took at two sectors destined to play a key role in China's technological transformation: energy and national defense. In Chapter 8, Vaclav Smil presents a comprehensive review of Chinese energetics. He notes that the development of Chinese energy technology over the past three decades has been fairly impressive on the whole, but he nevertheless points to the existence of certain chronic "weak links." The first of these is the coal industry, which he characterizes as highly dispersed and undermechanized. Although China will soon become the world's second ranking producer of raw coal, Smil finds the mining-machinery industry to be chronically short of high quality steel. He also observes that transportation facilities are grossly inadequate to handle China's expanding coal production.

A second weak link, in Smil's view, is China's electric power industry. He notes that much of China's power-generating equipment is obsolete, overloaded, and in bad repair. As a result, the P.R.C. is currently unable to produce adequate amounts of electricity to support its modernization program, which has been slowed down by chronic power shortages and brownouts in various parts of the country.

Smil finds the picture to be somewhat brighter in the area of hydrocarbon production (petroleum and natural gas), which he calls "the most successful extractive branch of Chinese energetics." Though he is relatively optimistic about the long-term prospects of China's petroleum industry, he does not believe that the P.R.C. will be able to export substantial quantities of crude oil in the near future.

Finally, Smil assesses China's prospects for large-scale development of alternative energy sources—including nuclear energy, biogas, solar, and the like. Although he sees some hope here (particularly in the current proliferation of small biogas digesters in the countryside), he concludes that the technological level and overall performance of China's energy sector will continue to lag substantially behind the most advanced world levels for some time to come.

Smil's analysis is followed by three brief commentaries covering various aspects of Chinese energetics by William Clarke, Alfred H. Usack, Jr., and K. P. Wang. In the first commentary, William Clarke is generally optimistic about current Chinese efforts to rapidly develop new power-generating capacity through the construction of a blend of small-scale hydropower projects and large-scale efforts, such as the Yangtze River dam at Kochoupa near Ichang. He acknowledges that China's electric power industry has been plagued by serious problems in the past, but he believes that many of these problems have been substantially corrected in the current Ten-Year Plan.

Usack reveals a more pessimistic point of view in his commentary. He observes that there currently exists an "installation gap" in China's power industry, as a result of which most of the new generating equipment produced in the P.R.C. goes to replace obsolete or faulty equipment already in service, rather than to create new capacity. In the area of natural gas, he notes that, although China is well endowed with this important energy source, the location of major natural gas deposits in remote Szechwan Province renders the efficient use of this resource problematic, at least in the short run. Turning to the petroleum industry, Usack suggests that, although several new oil fields are being opened in China, their production "may not be sufficient to meet Chinese needs in the future, much less leave a surplus for export." Finally, he suggests that China's current plans for hydropower development may be poorly conceived, since they are too costly, too slow in terms of construction lead times, and too dependent upon expensive advanced transmis-

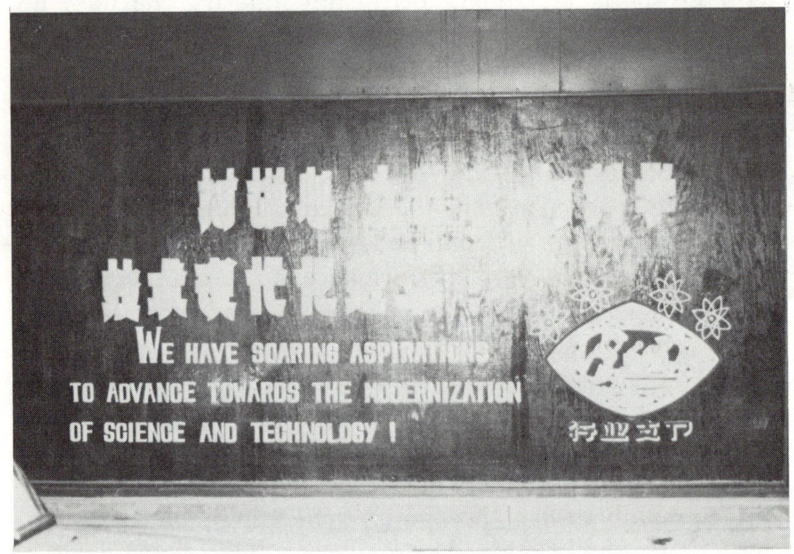

A wall poster on bulletin board at Shanghai Diesel Engine Plant (September 1978).

sion systems to be optimally effective in the short run.

K. P. Wang, in turn, is optimistic about the outlook for modernization of China's coal mining industry. He supports this optimism with the observation that the gap between the P.R.C.'s present mining technology and the optimal technologies of choice for the future is "not nearly so large as it might appear."

In Chapter 9, Jonathan Pollack explores the modernization of China's defense establishment. After noting past Chinese successes and failures in military R & D, he examines a number of constraints currently impeding rapid modernization of the defense sector: deficient and outmoded weaponry; lack of serial production capability for modern, high-technology military hardware; a chronic shortage of skilled scientific and engineering manpower; lack of adequate budgetary support for developing (or purchasing) and rendering operational expensive new weapons systems; the residual legacy of a decade of Chinese technological dependency on the Soviet Union; and the absence of a well-articulated organizational infrastructure of technological R & D in both military and related civilian industrial sectors.

Given these weaknesses and given the relatively low priority accorded to national defense in the current Ten-Year Plan for development, Pollack believes that the P.R.C. will continue to lag several generations behind the United States and the Soviet Union in terms of military capability. And, he believes, limited (or even massive) purchases of advanced foreign weapons prototypes will not fully resolve this time lag problem. In his view, it will take years (perhaps even decades) for the Chinese to absorb, assimilate, adapt, and mass produce advanced foreign weapons systems—by which time the systems in question will in all probability have become obsolete.

Commenting on Pollack's analysis, Almon R. Roth agrees that the P.R.C. will have enormous difficulty catching up with the United States and the Soviet Union in defense technology. Given China's past difficulties in such areas as reverse engineering and the modification, design, and serial production of advanced weaponry obtained abroad (e.g., the MiG-21), the prospects for "leapfrog" military modernization via technology transfers from the West are, in Roth's view, rather dim.

Jeffrey Schultz concludes this volume in Chapter 10, drawing together some of the dominant themes from the preceding essays and commentaries. He summarizes the major technological priorities and policies of the Hua/Teng regime and assesses some of the revolutionary foreign trade practices recently adopted by the P.R.C. to acquire and finance the import of modern industrial plant and equipment—including such politically controversial devices as compensatory trade, joint-stock ventures, and the solicitation of long-term commercial bank loans.

Noting that Peking's desire to emulate certain economic and technological practices of the advanced industrial nations may have a variety of unintended consequences for the underlying ideological and cultural values of the Chinese nation, Schultz asks: "How much Chinese 'essence' can the P.R.C. leadership safely sacrifice" to the technical efficiencies of foreign machinery, organizational forms, commercial practices, and management techniques? To what extent will China's pursuit of rapid modernization give rise to an incipient aping of "decadent" Western ideologies and life styles?

Without providing definitive answers to these elusive questions, Schultz suggests that the process of technological transformation cannot be isolated from its social context, and that it will therefore be extremely difficult for Chinese leaders to contain the burgeoning Western impact to the realm of technology alone. In rendering this speculative judgment, Schultz paradoxically echoes an ominous warning once reportedly issued by the Gang of Four: "When satellites go up to the sky, the Red Flag falls to the ground." Having witnessed the spectacle of Teng Hsiao-p'ing donning silver spurs and a ten-gallon hat during the course of his January 1979 visit to the Houston Space Center, we are inevitably led to wonder whether the Gang might not, in the long run, be proven correct after all?

Notes

1. This phrase (as well as the term Four Modernizations) was coined by China's late Premier Chou En-lai in his speech to the Fourth National People's Congress in January 1975, one year before his death. It was not until 1977, however, that the phrase became a "catchword" for China's modernization drive. See *Peking Review*, no. 4 (January 24, 1975), pp. 21–24.

2. Hua Kuo-feng, "Report on the Work of the Government" (February 26, 1978), *Peking Review*, no. 10 (March 10, 1978), pp. 7–41.

3. See Robert F. Dernberger and David Fasenfest, "China's Post-Mao Economic Future," in U.S., Congress, Joint Economic Committee, *Chinese Economy Post-Mao: A Compendium of Papers*, 95th Cong., 2d sess., 1978, pp. 32–35.

4. *Los Angeles Times*, June 22, 1979.

5. The figure $600 billion for capital investment was reportedly quoted by Deputy Premier Li Hsien-nien in an unpublished interview with a visiting Japanese delegation in September 1978. See Kyodo News Service, September 19, 1978. In Hua Kuo-feng's previously cited speech of February 26, 1978, he stated that China's capital construction budget as a whole over the 1978–1985 period would equal the total for the previous twenty-eight years. See supra note 2.

6. See "Premier Hua Reports on the Work of the Government," *Beijing Review* [hereafter *BR*], no. 25 (June 22, 1979), pp. 10–11. See also, "Vice Chairman Deng Expounds China's Domestic and Foreign Policies," *BR*, no. 16 (April 20, 1979), pp. 13–14.

7. See, for example, "Gang of Four Attempts to Sabotage Foreign Trade," *Hsinhua Weekly*, no. 53 (December 20, 1976), pp. 33–34.

8. *BR*, no. 25 (June 22, 1979), p. 11. See also Foreign Broadcast Information Service, *Daily Report—P.R.C.*, June 1, 1979, pp. D6–7.

9. *BR*, no. 25 (June 22, 1979), p. 11.

10. Ibid.

11. Ibid.

2
The Modernization of Chinese Industry

Chu-yüan Cheng

In the current Four Modernizations program, industry has been the primary focus of attention. In the past, the terms industrialization and modernization were often used synonymously. When Chou En-lai revealed his two-stage modernization scheme in January 1975, the first stage was designed to build an independent and relatively comprehensive industrially oriented economic system before 1980; the second stage was to accomplish the modernization of agriculture, industry, national defense, and science and technology before the end of the century.[1] Apparently, Chou envisaged the establishment of an independent and comprehensive industrial system as a prerequisite for the modernization of other sectors.

The goals to be achieved by modernization of industry in the 1976–1985 time frame were outlined by Chairman Hua Kuo-feng in his report on February 26, 1978, to the Fifth National People's Congress (NPC). During the following year, however, in recognition of the burden that the financing of huge transfusions of foreign equipment and technology would place upon the economy, there was a shift in strategies and priorities. Both investment plans and production targets underwent substantial revision. The purpose of this chapter is to (1) describe the program and its subsequent revisions, (2) identify difficulties already encountered, and (3) assess the probability that the industrial modernization program will achieve its goals.

The Program for Modernization

The program for China's industrial modernization, unfurled by Hua Kuo-feng in 1978, established Herculean goals. During the program's remaining eight-year period (1978–1985), the increase in the output of major industrial products was to exceed that of the previous twenty-eight years (1949–1977), and investments budgeted for capital construction during this period were to equal the total for those years.[2]

The entire program for the modernization of Chinese industry hinges on two factors: (1) the expansion of productive capacity and (2) the reform of industrial management and control systems. While the former aims at enlarging the economic base, the latter seeks to revamp the organizational and administrative superstructure.

Expansion of Productive Capacity

During the 1978–1985 period, the original goals of the modernization plan included the completion of 120 large-scale projects, including 10 iron and steel complexes, 9 nonferrous metal complexes, 8 coal mines, 10 oil and gas fields, 30 power stations, 6 new trunk railways, and 5 key harbors.[3] As a result of these planned expansions, industrial output was expected to grow at more than a 10 percent annual rate for the eight-year period. By the end of this century, Hua said, "the output of major industrial products will approach, equal or outstrip that of the most developed capitalist countries."[4]

The major burden of industrial development was to rest on such basic industries as steel, coal, petroleum, electric power, and nonferrous metals. Although the proportion of investment to be allocated to heavy and light industries was not disclosed, official pronouncements indicated that the relative share for light industry was originally anticipated to be less that 5 percent,[5] compared with the reported 12.5 percent of the First Five-Year Plan (1953–1957). This would imply that approximately 95 percent of the capital investment for industry in the current plan was originally assigned to the development of heavy industry.

The Steel Industry. For years, the steel industry has been identified by Chinese Communist leaders as the "key link" in industrial development. In the first decade of the People's Republic, the steel industry achieved rapid progress. With the help of the Soviet Union, a number of large iron and steel bases were developed in the 1950s. Among them were the expansion of the Anshan Iron and Steel Company in Liaoning and the construction of two steel complexes in Wuhan and Paotow. By 1952, production of crude steel had already surpassed pre-Communist highs. In 1957, output of crude steel was four times the output in 1952, rising from 1.35 million tons to 5.35 million tons.

Despite this marked progress, the Chinese leadership demanded a more rapid growth and in 1958 launched the Great Leap Forward. Small iron and steel plants known as "backyard furnaces" were built by the hundreds of thousands, giving rise to exaggerated claims of huge increases in iron and steel production. By late 1958, it became apparent that these plants were using large amounts of valuable raw materials and labor to produce a nearly useless product. Many of them had to be closed down in 1959.[6]

In the meantime, the large modern sector of the steel industry continued to expand. Installation of new equipment was speeded up, and attempts were made to increase production by using equipment around the clock with practically no shutdown for maintenance and repair. This, together with the introduction of poor grades of iron in the modern steel plants, caused a reduction in quality of output and damage to equipment. Nevertheless, useful production from these plants did increase considerably, though not as much as the government announced. The claimed increase in steel production from modern plants more than doubled from 5.35 million tons in 1957 to 12.45 million tons in 1960. Total steel output from both modern and indigenous plants amounted to 18.67 million tons in 1960.[7]

During the retrenchment period following the Great Leap, almost all of the small iron and steel plants were closed down. Production of steel fell sharply to 8 million tons in 1961 and did not recover to its claimed 1960 level until 1970, when 17.8 million tons were produced. Since 1970, small and medium steel plants have once again begun to play an important role. Steel output reached 25.5 million tons in 1973. In 1974, as intraelite conflict over ideological principles intensified, work stoppages erupted in major steel centers and steel production fell back once again. Output dropped to 21 million tons in 1976. Thus, for sixteen years after 1960, the Chinese steel industry manifested extreme fluctuations, with only small net gains in output.

In the 1976–1985 developmental plan, the Chinese leaders originally placed heavy emphasis on modernizing the steel industry. The planned ten projects involving the steel industry included the construction of five entirely new complexes and renovation and expansion of five existing facilities. Before the recent revision of the plan, China had contracted with Japan for a modern integrated steel complex to be built at Paoshan in the northern suburb of Shanghai at a cost of more than $2 billion. The designed capacity of the plant was 6 million tons of steel per year.[8] The complex included coking, iron-smelting, steelmaking, preliminary rolling, chemical, and other plants. Complete sets of equipment were to be provided by the Shin Nippon Iron and Steel Company (Shinnittetsu).[9]

China also signed a preliminary agreement with West Germany to construct a new giant steel complex in eastern Hopei Province near Shihchiachuang at a reported cost of $14 billion.[10] That agreement, however, may not become final as a result of the recent retrenchment. Other new iron and steel complexes in the original plan included the Panchihua plant to be built in Szechwan Province, the Shicheng plant in Kweichow Province and the Chiayukuan plant in Kansu Province. Expansion and renovation also involved existing major steel mills in Anshan, Wuhan, Paotow, Peking, and Pench'i. The original plan envisioned a steel output of 60 million tons in 1985. Production was expected to reach approximately 180 million tons in 1999 when the twenty-three-year, long-range grand plan was to be completed.[11]

The Petroleum Industry. The large planned outlays for new industrial plants have created an enormous demand for foreign exchange in which the petroleum industry was expected to play a critical role. Originally identified as the weakest link of China's modern industry, China's petroleum industry enjoyed a spectacular growth in the eighteen years after 1960. Before 1957,

China's petroleum industry produced only 1.46 million tons of crude oil per year, which could only meet 45 percent of domestic needs. A dramatic change began in 1965 when the Tach'ing oil field in Heilungkiang Province began to operate on a large-scale basis. Subsequently, the Shengli oil field on the Shantung Peninsula and the Takang oil field in the Tientsin area were opened. China's output of crude oil doubled between 1960 and 1965, doubled again by 1969, and by 1978 had reached 2 million barrels a day (or 100 million tons a year), which was nineteen times China's 1960 output and seventy times its 1957 output.[12]

The rapid growth in Chinese crude oil output in recent decades gave rise to the hope that China soon might become a major oil exporting country. The policy of exporting crude oil in exchange for foreign equipment and technology thus became a central feature of the current modernization plan. In May 1977, Hua Kuo-feng announced that China would build ten new oil fields comparable in size to Tach'ing but did not spell out the details as to their locations. Nor did he announce the output target for crude oil production for 1985. Pro-Peking newspapers published in Hong Kong disclosed that China had target goals calling for the production of 500 million tons of crude oil by 1985, a figure almost five times the actual output of 1978. Recent scattered data from China reveal that major oil fields under construction, or at the stage of exploration, include:

1. Jenchiu oil field, near Changchou in Hopei Province
2. Lisoho Plain in central Liaoning Province in Manchuria
3. Nanchiang oil field in southern Sinkiang Province
4. Sansui oil field in southern Kwangtung Province
5. Nanhai oil field, close to Kwangchow (Canton)
6. Chuchiang oil field, an offshore oil field at the entrance of the Pearl River
7. Peipuwan (Northern Gulf) oil field in the South China Sea
8. Po Hai oil field in Po Hai Bay of the Yellow Sea[13]

The construction of these oil fields requires tremendous outlays to procure the massive drilling rigs and sophisticated equipment necessary to extract large quantities of oil. The oil fields will also need thousands of miles of pipelines to transport crude oil to the export terminals. Between 1953 and 1974, China invested some $9 billion in its petroleum industry, half of which was for the purchase of foreign equipment.[14] Given the capital/output ratio of the past twenty-one years, in order to increase crude oil production from 92 million tons in 1977 to 500 million tons in 1985, China will have to invest $60 billion in the petroleum industry—a figure approximating 10 percent of the total investment for the current Ten-Year Plan of modernization.

The Coal Industry. In contrast to the rapid growth of the petroleum industry, the coal industry, which provides 70 percent of China's primary energy, has experienced an erratic growth rate. This rate, starting at 14 percent per year in 1952–1957, dropped to 7.8 percent per year in 1957–1965, 6.6 percent per year in 1965–1970, and reached only 5.6 percent per year in 1970–1974.[15] Two factors are primarily responsible for the declining rate of increase in coal production.

First, there is a geographic disparity between the regional demand for coal and the location of coal reserves. Although Manchuria ranks highest in regional coal production, the area possesses only small coal reserves. In 1970, Manchuria produced 30 percent of China's total coal although it possessed but 2.7 percent of the estimated coal reserves.[16] Since the rich coal mines near the major metallurgical centers in southern Liaoning Province, such as Pench'i and Fushun, have been extensively mined for more than half a century, the most accessible and best situated coal veins have already been depleted. A rise in coal production in this highly industrialized region would require increased recovery costs, making it difficult to sustain the former high rates of growth.

Second, over the past two decades there has been a relatively small investment in the coal industry, and this inadequate investment in the construction of new coal mines has caused a decline in coal production. Since 1961, the priority for the development of energy industries has apparently shifted from coal to oil. Funds available for the development of the coal industry have been sharply curtailed. Increases in coal production have therefore relied heavily on small locally run mines instead of on the development of large-scale major shafts. In 1973, small mines were said to have produced 28 percent of China's total coal output. The share of small coal mines increased in 1974–1975, accounting for 50 percent in Kwangtung and Yunnan Provinces. Even in China's leading coal-producing province of Shansi, small mines turned out 40 percent of the 1975 output.[17] Although small mines are easily and quickly opened at relatively low capital expense, they are frequently exhausted in a short period of time. By relying on small mines, the Chinese planners opted for a short-term solution to a long-term problem.

In the current modernization program, Peking plans to double coal production between 1978 and 1985 with a targeted output of more than 1 billion tons per year. This implies an average annual growth rate of 7.2 percent compared with the actual 6.3 percent average growth in coal production between 1970 and 1977. To accomplish this goal, the plan calls for the opening of eight new mines and an increase in mechanization at existing mines. In September 1978, Peking concluded an agreement with West Germany to provide the technology and equipment needed to build five new deep coal mines and to modernize an existing one, in addition to constructing two large open-cast lignite mines. This agreement, if implemented, will cost about $4 billion.[18] The open-cast mines—the largest in China—are officially identified as the Haolingho (Hualinhe) coal field, which is located in western Kirin Province in Manchuria, with a designed capacity of 20 million tons per year.[19]

Electric Power. Electric power is another weak link in China's modern industry. Installed capacity on December 31, 1977, was estimated to be 40,500 megawatts. The bulk of this capacity is found in the 192 known thermal and hydro stations of 30 megawatts capacity and over. In 1978, electric power production in China was estimated at 162 billion kilowatt hours, which makes China the ninth largest electric power–producing country in the world. Per capita electricity production is still extremely low, however, and is below that of India and Pakistan.[20]

According to official reports, from 1949 to 1978 China's electricity output increased fifty-seven-fold, with an average annual growth rate of 15 percent.[21] However, in the 1971–1975 period, the average annual growth rate was only 11 percent. Consequently, there exists a widespread shortage of electric power, which has adversely affected the economy. To support a 10 percent rate of industrial growth, the power industry would need to grow at a pace of 13 to 14 percent a year. The current Ten-Year Plan calls for the construction of thirty power stations in the 1978–1985 period, twenty of which will be hydropower stations.

Of the major power projects under construction, the Kochoupa hydropower project on the middle reaches of the Yangtze River is the biggest. The project, which consists of two hydroelectric power plants with a combined capacity of 2.7 million kilowatts, is under construction near Ichang in Hupei Province. When they are completed, these two stations will supply 13,800 million kilowatt hours of electricity a year, approximately 9 percent of the 1978 electricity output.[22]

The second largest hydropower station under construction is the 1.6-million-kilowatt Lungyang Gorge Station on the upper reaches of the Yellow River near Sining, capital of Tsinghai Province.[23] Other major electric power projects under construction include the Manas River hydropower station in northwestern Sinkiang Province, the Yangpaching geothermal power station in Tibet, the Wanan hydropower station in Kiangsi Province, the Peishan hydropower station on the Songhua River in Manchuria, and the Wuchiangtu hydropower station in Kwangsi Province.[24]

Apart from the construction of these hydropower stations, Peking is also seeking the latest power-generating technology from the West. In December 1978, China signed an agreement with the French government to procure two 900,000-kilowatt nuclear-power plants worth an estimated $4.5 billion. Also included in the Sino-French seven-year trade agreement were a hydroelectric power plant and two coal-fired power plants that would generate 600,000 kilowatts of electricity each. In May 1979, a group of major French banks signed an agreement to lend China $7 billion, primarily to finance these procurements.[25]

The thirty new power plants, together with capacity increases at smaller plants and additional expansion of existing facilities, should enable China to expand capacity to 6 to 8 million kilowatts per year, compared with a 5 million kilowatt average annual increase in recent years. Even assuming the successful completion of these planned projects, however, electricity supply will still have difficulty keeping pace with increasing demand. Given the 8.5 percent and 9.8 percent increase in power generating capacity in 1976 and 1977 and the lead time required to install new capacity, it would appear difficult to accelerate development to the required 13 to 14 percent growth rate prior to 1980.[26]

Agricultural Machinery. Besides the steel and energy industries, the supply of agricultural machinery has a great bearing on the Four Modernizations program. The program places heavy demands on agriculture for foodstuffs and industrial raw materials, both for domestic consumption and for exports. Peking's production target of 400 million tons of grains in 1985 implies an average annual growth of 4.3 percent in 1978–1985, compared with the 2 percent growth since 1957. In order to accelerate agricultural growth, current policy emphasizes increased mechanization along with a push for farmland improvements. The original Ten-Year Plan stipulates that 70 percent of all major farm processes will be mechanized in 1980, and by 1985 the degree of mechanization will increase to 85 percent. Other goals for the modernization of agriculture include:

1. A 70-percent increase in large- and medium-sized tractors to reach 1.2 million standard units
2. A 110-percent increase in machine-drawn farm implements to reach 4 million pieces
3. A 32-percent increase in drainage and irrigation machines to reach 40 million horsepower
4. A 59-percent increase in chemical fertilizer production to reach 66 million tons

Since these objectives are ambitious and the agricultural machine industry in China remains very backward, the Chinese government has adopted several measures to accelerate the program. The farm machinery industry was selected as the first industry to be reorganized by the Hua/Teng administration.

Many small, locally managed plants were to be absorbed into local or regional networks featuring large-scale specialized production and assembly factories. In early 1979, the Ministry of Agricultural Machinery was resurrected. Another important measure was the Party's decision to set up machine and tractor stations in the rural areas. Most of these are to be set up by communes and production brigades with their own funds; but if they lack funds, they can seek state loans.[27]

To greatly expand agricultural machinery production, state-supplied steel for the manufacture and repair of farm machines during 1978–1980 will be raised by a total of 50 percent over the previous three-year period. Because the agricultural machinery industry still confronts numerous problems (such as poor machine quality, the lack of standardization, and the limited range of equipment and accessories available), however, the content of the mechanization program has been dramatically cut back and quantitative targets quietly abandoned. In the short run, China will concentrate on the mechanization of agriculture in the Northeast and, at the same time, will experimentally develop one fully mechanized county (*hsien*) per province. The county chosen will be near a major urban or industrial center.[28] In the next few years, China is expected to build a number of highly efficient and productive agro-industrial-commercial complexes in counties where agriculture is mechanized and on state farms in Liaoning, Kirin, and Heilungkiang provinces and in the rural areas surrounding Peking, Tientsin, and Shanghai. These farms are expected to supply the needs of nearby urban populations for grains and nonstaple foodstuffs.[29]

Improvement of Efficiency

The above industrial projects, if completed, would greatly expand China's productive capacity. The construction of new plans and the expansion of existing facilities require long gestation periods, however. Most of these projects will not get under way until sometime after 1981, and the vast majority of them probably will have little impact on economic growth until after 1985. Thus, to accelerate economic growth between 1978 and 1981, the source of growth must be expanded output from existing plants. In his report to the Fifth NPC, Hua Kuo-feng stated, "In the next eight years, and especially in the next three years, our existing enterprises must be the foundation for the growth of production."[30] More recently, Chinese authorities have noted that "this year and next will still be a period of restoration, adjustment, and consolidation."[31]

Thus far, China's economy has been operating considerably below its potential. The initiative and enthusiasm of workers and employees as well as enterprise managers continue to be dampened by eroding income and existing irrationalities built into the system. Vice-Premier K'ang Shih-en, chairman of the State Economic Commission, recently commented:

> Our present economic management system is overcentralized, with overlapping administrative structures and too many procedures. This has restrained initiative and enthusiasm on the part of localities and enterprises. . . . It is essential to set up various specialized companies, to break the barriers among various regions and trades and to reorganize industry in accordance with the principle of specialization and coordination and with rational economic requirements.[32]

Thus, the current emphasis on industrial modernization involves the promotion of worker's incentives and initiatives, the reform of industrial organization, and the strengthening of enterprise management.

Material Incentives. Peking's success in stimulating economic growth during the 1978–1980 period depends heavily on its ability to improve worker incentives and boost labor productivity. The record of the past twenty-eight years discloses a close correlation between wage hikes and labor productivity increases. According to Hu Ch'iao-mu, president of the Chinese Academy of Social Sciences:

> During the First Five-Year Plan period, when workers' wages increased at an average rate of 7.4 percent annually, labor productivity advanced at an average annual rate of 8.7 percent and gross industrial production rose at 18 percent per annum. During that period, rising labor productivity accounted for 59 percent of industrial growth with the remaining 41 percent attributed to the increased size of the labor force. After 1958, as

wages failed to increase, labor productivity stagnated. Consequently, the growth of industrial output largely depended on increasing the number of workers.[33]

During the Cultural Revolution, as bonus systems were abolished and egalitarianism prevailed, workers increasingly resorted to slowdowns and absenteeism. To arouse workers' enthusiasm, the new leadership decided to return to material incentives. In the summer of 1977, 64 percent of the nonagricultural workers in China were granted a pay hike of around 10 percent. Although the raise was the largest in two decades, many Chinese still regarded it as inadequate. As a supplement to the general wage rise, bonus and piece rate systems were restored in 1978. They were defended as a supplementary mechanism for achieving remuneration according to work done (rather than need), making up for inadequacies in the wage-scale system.[34]

Reform of Industrial Organization. One major attempt to streamline the industrial system centers around revamping industrial organization. The machine-building industry was chosen as the initial target for rationalization. Current problems plaguing China's machine-building industry include inefficient management, lack of specialization and standardization, and overlapping authority at the planning level. Consequently, parts and accessories are frequently made at a plant site without regard for compatability with those produced in a different locale. Ministerial directives from different industries frequently require different specifications for products that could have been standardized.[35]

Since July 1978, the agricultural machinery department within the machine-building industry has been reorganized along the lines of specialization and coordination. Farm machinery corporations have been set up in each of the country's six major economic regions to serve as coordinating centers. In each province the tractor manufacturing industry and the power accessory component industry have been rationalized. Each province now has a tractor motor company, an instruments and meter company, a bearing company, and a machinery export company. Existing tractor plants and diesel-

Tool-making shop at Huangtu commune near Shanghai (May 1975).

engine plants, which traditionally have been almost autonomous in producing their own component parts, have narrowed the range of their activities to achieve greater specialization while relying upon other firms to specialize in the production of standardized component parts necessary to produce the final product.[36]

The main idea behind this rationalization is to break down the old boundaries between trades, enterprises, and administration. Each company is expected to be an independent enterprise armed with the power to decide on manpower, finance, materials, production, supply, and marketing of its subordinate enterprises. Such enterprises would be "specialized" rather than "all-inclusive," making it possible to reduce costly duplication in organization, personnel, and fixed assets.

Improvement of Management. Paralleling Peking's attempts to reorganize industry, efforts have also been made to improve enterprise management. During the 1950s, the Chinese management system was based on the director-responsibility system of

Top: *A female worker wearing a gauze mask at Shenyang Machine Tool Plant (September 1978).* Bottom: *A female machinist working at a lathe, Shenyang Machine Tool Plant (September 1978).*

the Soviet Union. In 1960, Mao personally endorsed the more egalitarian "Charter of the Anshan Iron and Steel Company" as the model of management. This model incorporated Mao's basic precepts for successful management, such as putting politics in command, employing mass movements, cadre participation in labor, and worker participation in management. During the Cultural Revolution, revolutionary committees made up of workers, cadres, and soldiers replaced specialized management committees. Many traditional work rules and regulations were discarded, and managerial personnel were downgraded. The consequences bordered on economic debacle.[37] Since 1977, strenuous efforts have been made to reinstitute the old management system. In February 1978, Hua Kuo-feng, in his report to the NPC, set accountability and efficiency as two primary management goals. Hua emphasized that in 1978 Chinese managers would be obligated to equal or better previous production levels. Additionally, those managers who failed to meet planned state targets would be subjected to disciplinary action.[38] In July 1978 the Chinese Communist Party (CCP) Central Committee issued a thirty-point document, "Decisions Concerning Some Problems in Speeding Up the Development of Industry (Draft)," which was to be the "basic guide for socialist enterprises." Although the Chinese have not released the text of this document, official statements reveal that the new guideline was adapted from "several previous documents of similar nature," notably the "twenty-point program" drafted under the aegis of Teng Hsiao-p'ing in 1975.

In essence, the new guideline focused on three recommendations. First, it demanded the restoration of plant-director responsibility in place of the joint responsibility previously assumed by the director and the Party committees. Second, it called for the establishment of eight economic norms to measure the performance of each enterprise with respect to output, variety, quality, cost, profit to the state, resource allocation, and productivity. Third, it recommended the restoration of the "five fixed quotas" and the "five-guarantees" system that had prevailed during the post–Great Leap era. Under this system, the state would designate fixed quotas for each enterprise with respect to output, personnel and organization, raw materials, capital assets, and the amount of liquid capital. In return, the enterprise would submit five guarantees to the state with regard to quality and quantity of product, total wage bill, costs, expected state profit, and the life span of major equipment. Enterprises overfulfilling their five guarantees would be entitled to retain a portion of the planned profit as a bonus fund to improve the well-being of the work force.[39] Thus, the new guidelines were more profit-oriented, using material rewards as incentives to induce greater efficiency and productivity. In essence, they constituted the virtual antithesis of the Anshan Charter.

The Problems

The execution of China's industrial modernization program will not be an easy task. Constraints, barriers, and internal resistance will tend to make implementation a formidable job.

Capital Investment

First, the modernization plan requires enormous amounts of capital. Between 1949 and 1959, to support the first stage of industrialization, China invested 120 billion yuan (1957 prices), or $46.2 billion. In the current plan, investment is officially estimated at one trillion yuan, or $630 billion at the prevailing exchange rate.[40] During the 1949–1959 period, approximately $10 billion of the investment fund came from the confiscation of property from landlords and capitalists; some $3 billion came from Soviet loans and credits; and the remainder came from the agricultural sector through low-price procurement of agricultural products and higher prices for industrial products sold to the agricultural sector. After 1960, private property and Soviet aid were no longer available; and, as agriculture stagnated, most of the new capital formation had to be generated through the earnings of state enterprises. During the past few years, the trauma of political storms and industrial unrest has resulted in heavy losses for most industrial enterprises. As Chairman Hua Kuo-feng indicated, "Between 1974 and 1976, the influence of the Gang of Four had caused losses worth 100 billion yuan [$63 billion] in industrial output and 40 billion yuan [$25 billion] in state revenue."[41] As late as September 1978, fully one-quarter of the state enterprises were still operating at a loss. The average rate of profit for industry dropped to only 16.4 percent in 1978 as compared with 24.3 percent in 1966.[42]

The situation was even worse in locally run enterprises. In Kwangtung Province, for instance, of the eighty-nine small nitrogenous fertilizer plants built in the past six years, the great majority have run at a loss. The loss from 1974 to 1978 amounted to 300 million yuan, 2.5 times the investment in nitrogenous fertilizer capital construction in that province.[43] In Kirin Province, 40 percent of the provincial industrial enterprises have been unable to balance their budgets. Losses totaled 270 million yuan in 1978.[44] In Anhwei Province some 70 percent of the provincial light industrial units reportedly suffered losses.[45] Under these circumstances, the internal accumulation of large amounts of capital becomes extremely difficult. According to Vice-Premier Teng Hsiao-p'ing, China lacks about 300 billion of the planned 600 billion capital requirement necessary to fulfill the current Ten-Year Plan.[46] Although Teng did not elaborate upon his estimates, a simple calculation of GNP and capital investment during the 1949–1959 and the 1978–1985 periods shows that the deficiency of capital may be in the neighborhood of $200 billion if China is to meet its planned goals for 1985.

During the 1949–1959 period, total GNP at 1977 U.S. dollars has been estimated by the U.S. government at $1,150 billion.[47] Capital investment in this ten-year period was officially reported as 120 billion yuan or $46.2 billion in 1957 prices (or about $100 billion in 1977 prices). This would produce an investment rate of 9 percent of GNP.

China's GNP for 1978 was estimated by the U.S. government at $407 billion.[48] Assuming an annual growth rate of 5.5 percent during the twenty years between 1957 and 1977, total GNP for the 1978–1985 period in 1977 prices would be $3,956 billion. If the investment rate is approximately 10 percent, China should be able to raise about $400 billion from domestic savings. This still leaves a shortfall of fully one-third and probably underlies the most recent economic retrenchment.

Absorptive Capacity

Second, since China's modernization program is dependent

upon the acquisition of large amounts of foreign equipment, it necessarily follows that this equipment will require the services of large numbers of technicians, engineers, and managerial personnel. The availability and acquisition of this army of technical and managerial manpower will be an important determinant of China's ability to rapidly absorb modern technology. Between 1949 and 1966, some 1.8 million college students were trained by China's higher education institutions and about half a million of these majored in engineering. Although a substantial number of middle-level factory technicians are available, there is a serious shortage of experienced design and production engineers and other highly trained technicians essential to build and operate a modern factory.

During the turbulent days of the Cultural Revolution, drastic changes took place in China's science and education. Not only was the number of colleges and universities substantially reduced, but the quality of training was lowered. On October 23, 1977, *Jen-min jih-pao* (People's daily) reported that 68 percent of a sample of technical personnel given exams flunked mathematics, 70 percent failed in physics, and 76 percent failed in chemistry. The tests were designed to cover "basic knowledge that high school students should know." Even those technicians and scientists trained before the Cultural Revolution had reportedly failed to keep current in their respective fields after 1966, when China closed itself off from the outside world.

More critical than the shortage of competent engineers and technicians, however, is the lack of managerial expertise suitable for large-scale modern industrial plants. When U.S. Treasury Secretary Michael Blumenthal visited Peking in March 1979, he surmised that Chinese officials lacked an understanding of basic economic fundamentals.[49] This lack of technical and managerial skills will significantly limit China's capacity to absorb foreign technology.

Efficiency and Incentives

Apart from these limitations, the Chinese industrial system is still affected by many deep-seated problems that are not conducive to rapid modernization. Specifically, these include an overstaffed bureaucracy operating with ill-defined boundaries of authority and blindly adhering to formal protocol rather than facing the problems at hand.[50]

Under the existing system, industrial enterprises have several bosses. For example, key steel enterprises are under the joint control of the Ministry of Metallurgical Industry, provincial and municipal CCP committees, provincial and municipal planning and capital construction committees, industrial and communications offices, and provincial and municipal metallurgical bureaus. To initiate an action, all these committees must be consulted. Given this diffusion of leadership, it is not surprising that efficient decision making has reportedly been stifled by lack of consensus.[51]

Within the enterprise, workers' enthusiasm apparently remains rather low. Despite pay raises in 1977 and the restoration of the bonus system in 1978, egalitarianism still tends to dominate the remuneration system. In many enterprises, "everyone gets a share of the bonus regardless of the quality of his work." In some places, bonuses are issued on a rotating basis to each worker.[52]

Since rewards in such cases fail to correspond to individual contributions, workers find little stimulus to take any initiative. Many factories, in order to fulfill their assigned quotas, have had to recruit temporary workers from the countryside. In September 1978, some 10 million of these temporary workers were recruited by departments of industry, transportation, and basic construction. This not only adversely affected agricultural production but also tended to cause labor productivity to decline. Official statistics indicated that labor productivity of nonagricultural labor in 1977 was lower than it had been in 1966.[53]

Apart from low labor productivity, shortages of coal, electricity, and raw materials have also become a severe problem. In Kwangtung and Fukien provinces, deficiencies of power supply have forced many plants to operate only four days a week. In 1978, more than twenty of the eighty-nine small nitrogenous fertilizer plants in Kwangtung totally suspended production due to the lack of coal and electricity. By January 1979, the number had increased to more than thirty and, by February, to more than forty, indicating the increasing severity of electricity deficiencies.[54] In Fukien, where installed capacity and electricity output are below the national average, the shortage of electricity has reportedly "become a striking contradiction in the development of the economy."[55]

The Adjustments

China's limited ability to finance and absorb foreign technology and the appearance of bottlenecks in energy, transportation, and raw material supplies have forced Chinese central planners to reexamine the entire modernization program. Since the beginning of 1979, the evidence derived from official government sources has indicated that a significant reevaluation of the priorities and pace of modernization is under way.

On February 24, 1979, a long editorial in *Jen-min jih-pao*, entitled "Emancipate the Mind for an Overall Balance in Economic Development," enunciated a new strategy recently approved by the Party Central Committee. The editorial primarily reflected a change in attitude with respect to the tempo of development. When in February 1978 Hua Kuo-feng enthusiastically announced the new Ten-Year Plan (1976–1985), it appeared to be dressed in the garb of another Great Leap Forward. After his visit to Yugoslavia in August 1978, Hua went so far as to call for the completion of the Ten-Year Plan in five years.

This boisterous optimism has been subdued since early 1979. Thus, a *Jen-min jih-pao* editorial critically blasted the "big rashness" approach. The editorial contended that, "judging from our experience in the past 30 years, China has suffered more from rashness than from conservatism." The editorial went on to report that some plan figures were not derived from investigation, study, and calculation, but rather from impetuous decision making. The scale of some capital construction projects was said to be too large and well beyond the reach of material and financial resources. "Many projects were started hurriedly without the preparatory work that should have been done prior to construction, thus failing to proceed from the realities. . . . Consequently, a frightful waste of manpower and materials was involved in these projects." Overall, the new tone of the Party's chief media organ signified an awareness of the country's financial limitations and the need to pursue a more cautious modernization program.

The New Priorities

On March 26, 1979, a signed commentary in Peking's *Kuang-ming jih-pao* (Illumination daily) disclosed for the first time that the Party leadership had ordered a fundamental review of the current Ten-Year Plan. With rare frankness, the paper admitted that China's financial resources were still fragile and that its industry faced a series of structural imbalances. Among the imbalances noted were: (1) imbalance within and among industries (such as fuel, power, and raw materials), (2) disequilibrium between light and heavy industries and a lack of coordination between them, (3) the tendency to push new construction projects beyond the country's financial and material resources, (4) imbalance between agriculture and industry, and (5) imbalance between accumulation and consumption. In view of these imbalances, the paper contended, top priority must go to agriculture, followed by light and heavy industries in descending order.[56]

Given these new guidelines, the entire modernization program went through a thorough revision. Agriculture was singled out as the number-one problem to tackle. A State Agricultural Commission was established in March to oversee agricultural development. Capital investment for agriculture was reported to be increased from 40 billion to 90 billion yuan.[57] Light industries and export-oriented industries also received new emphasis. The revised plan called for increased capital investment in light industries, since they generally produce quicker results than heavy industry and therefore warrant greater resource allocation.

Within heavy industry, priority was given to the coal, electrical power, petroleum, and building materials industries, with investment in the steel industry being dramatically curtailed. Many articles and editorials in *Jen-min jih-pao* rebuked the principle of accepting steel as the "key link" in modernization. The target for steel production was lowered from the original plan of 60 million tons in 1985 to only 45 million tons, representing a growth rate of around 5 percent annually.[58]

Curtailment of Construction Projects

In keeping with the new guidelines, capital investment on many fronts was dramatically curtailed. In March, a national Capital Construction Work Conference held in Peking revealed the dimensions of the problem in capital construction and outlined new policies.

An investigation in 1978 showed that tens of thousands of projects were under way throughout the country, with more than a thousand of these being big or medium-sized projects. On the basis of existing material and financial resources, the investigation reportedly concluded that the battlefront was overextended. Lacking material and financial supplies, many projects failed to be completed on schedule. Many nominally completed projects lacked essential features and were thus unable to start production. Because of the prolonged construction period, between 1974 and 1978, less than half of the planned projects were reportedly put into operation on schedule. Statistics show that, of the large and medium-size projects completed in recent years, many were under construction for more than a decade, resulting in extremely high capital/output ratios.[59]

In view of the above problems, the conference formulated the following policies. First, it called for the immediate suspension of those projects in which resources and geological conditions were uncertain, available technology was not up to production requirements, or adequate supplies of fuel, power, and raw materials were not guaranteed. Second, it ordered the assignment of investment priorities to strengthen such weak links in the economy as the coal, oil, power, transportation, communications, and building materials industries and to rapidly develop projects that could be completed in a short time and could earn foreign exchange. Third, the gradual replacement of direct government appropriations with bank loans for future capital investment projects was to be accomplished in order to encourage construction units to conserve capital.[60]

Under the new policies, orders went out to halt thousands of construction projects, including the well-publicized Paoshan steel complex near Shanghai, which had been initiated without the realization that there was neither enough power available for the rolling mills nor a convenient deep-water port for unloading the iron ore that had to be imported from Brazil and Australia.[61]

Freezing of Foreign Orders

In the first half of 1979, tighter constraints were also placed on the procurement of foreign technology. During 1978 China signed or initialed many tentative agreements with foreign countries to purchase equipment for harbors, steel mills, and scores of other factories. Although the total sum of these agreements reportedly reached as high as $30 billion, only about $6 billion consisted of orders considered firm.[62] Given the new emphasis on balanced growth, the Chinese authorities temporarily froze several billions of dollars of tentative agreements with Japan, including the $2 billion order to build China's first fully integrated steel complex at Paoshan.[63] Other agreements facing possible delays are the $14 billion steel complex project with West Germany and the $500 million hotel construction project with the Inter-Continental Hotels Corporation.

The Prospects

These planned readjustments, which are basically in harmony with the realities of the current situation, will obviously have a great impact on industrial output. With less than seven years left to achieve the goals of the original Ten-Year Plan, most of the targets set in February 1978 face further revision. A recent study released by the Japanese Ministry of International Trade suggests that China may have to trim the original investment plan by half, reducing the total investment for the 1978–1985 period from $600 billion to only $300 billion.[64] Although these new projections may prove a bit too pessimistic, a cut of around 30 to 40 percent may not be unrealistic. On the basis of recent economic adjustments and progress revealed by official Chinese sources, the output of electricity and cement may come close to the mark, while the output of steel, coal, and crude oil is likely to be substantially below the originally targeted goals.

On the basis of past average growth rates from 1965 to 1978, the output of steel in 1985 may reach the revised target of 45 million tons, while the output of crude oil would do well to reach 300 million tons in 1985 (as opposed to the planned 500 million tons).[65] Projections for these and other key industrial sectors are given in Table 2.1.

Several implications can be discerned from China's revamped plans. First, there are obvious barriers preventing the economy from attaining a high rate of capital formation. As long as agricultural output continues to grow at a minuscule rate, the country will have to commit a significant portion of its foreign exchange to importing foodgrains and cotton rather than to capital formation. According to a U.S. government estimate,

Table 2.1

Planned and Projected Output of Five Major Industries in 1985

	Actual Output (1965-1978)[a]		Projected Output (1985)	
	1965	1978	Planned	Projected
Steel (million tons)	12.2	31.7	60[b]	45[e]
Coal (million tons)	232	605	900[c]	800[f]
Crude Oil (million tons)	11	100.3	500[d]	300[g]
Electricity (billion KWH)	42	162	230[d]	230
Cement (million tons)	16	67.8	100[d]	100

Sources and Notes:

[a] Central Intelligence Agency, China: Economic Indicators, 1978, p. 1.

[b] Hua Kuo-feng's Report to the Fifth National People's Congress.

[c] Hsiao Han, "Developing Coal Industry at High Speed," Peking Review, No. 8 (1978), p. 6. The original intention was to double output between 1977 and 1987. This figure is derived from annual growth rates set for this period.

[d] From Lin Pin, "Economy of 1978 in Communist China," Chung-Kung Yen-chiu (January 1979), p. 52.

[e] Based on the revised figure reported in the Los Angeles Times, May 10, 1979.

[f] According to Chung Tse-yun, Vice Minister of the PRC Coal Ministry, output for 1985 will be 800-900 million tons. The lower figure is used here. The San Francisco Journal (in Chinese), March 14, 1979.

[g] Based on average annual growth rates between 1970 and 1978.

China will need to import more than 10 million tons of food grains per year during the 1979–1985 period,[66] substantially higher than the 6 million tons per annum imported between 1961 and 1978. The recent reemphasis on agricultural development suggests that the Chinese authorities correctly recognize the importance of this problem.

Second, increasing investment in agriculture will reduce investment funds available for industry. The 1979 Sino-Vietnam border war and continuing tension in the border area have placed additional demands on resources for military use that otherwise might be allocated to industrial modernization. In short, upgrading China's military posture will absorb a substantial number of the best scientists, engineers, and managers from the civilian sector.

Third, since the demise of the Gang of Four, the new leadership has raised the expectations of the population with respect to improved living standards. Thus, a potential conflict exists between rising domestic demand for consumer goods and the need to export more consumer goods to earn the necessary foreign exchange to import the sophisticated capital goods necessary to further industrial modernization.

Finally, China's attempt to finance such an enormous array of contracts through foreign loans and credits may prove to be more difficult than originally expected. In recent years, international financial resources made available to the non-OPEC Third World countries have amounted to around $40 billion per year, with no substantial increase in sight. If China's credit demands were to exceed $10 billion a year, this could impinge upon the credit available to other developing countries. Thus, in the absence of some new aid arrangement by the U.S., Japan, and Western Europe like the Marshall Plan, any industrialization program largely financed through foreign loans and investments could be constrained by the exigencies of a tightening international credit market.

Notes

1. *Peking Review* (hereafter *PR*), no. 4 (January 26, 1975), p. 23.
2. Hua Kuo-feng's Report on the Work of the Government, de-

livered at the first session of the Fifth National People's Congress, February 26, 1978, in *Jen-min jih-pao* [People's daily, hereafter *JMJP*], March 9, 1978, pp.1–5 (hereafter referred to as Hua's Report).

3. Ibid.

4. Ibid.

5. Editorial, "Light Industry Must Develop More Rapidly," *JMJP*, February 20, 1979.

6. Ho Chien-Chang, "The Policy of Adjustment Is Entirely Correct," *JMJP*, April 4, 1979, p. 3.

7. Alfred H. Usack, Jr., and James D. Egan, "China's Iron and Steel Industry," in U.S., Congress, Joint Economic Committee, *China: A Reassessment of the Economy*, 94th Cong., 1st sess., 1975, p. 276.

8. *New York Times*, December 6, 1978.

9. *PR*, no. 12 (March 23, 1979), pp. 14–16.

10. *Chung-kuo hsin-wen* [China news], February 4, 1979.

11. *Hua-ch'iao jih-pao* [China daily news] (New York), February 17, 1979.

12. Chu-yüan Cheng, "China's Energy Resources," *Current History*, 74, no. 435 (March 1978):121–124.

13. *Cheng-ming* [Truth monthly], (Hong Kong), February 1979; also *China Reconstructs*, no. 4 (April 1979), pp. 38–39.

14. Chu-yüan Cheng, *China's Petroleum Industry: Output Growth and Export Potential* (New York: Praeger, 1976), pp. 112–113.

15. Cheng, "China's Energy Resources," p. 124.

16. *People's Republic of China: Atlas* (Washington, D.C.: Central Intelligence Agency, 1971), p. 69.

17. New China News Agency (hereafter NCNA) (Peking), January 26, 1976.

18. *The Economist* (London), September 30, 1978, p. 86.

19. *Chung-kuo hsin-wen*, January 31, 1979.

20. William Clarke, "China's Electric Power Industry," *The China Business Review* 4, no. 5 (September–October, 1977):26.

21. *China Reconstructs*, no. 4 (April 1979), p. 8.

22. NCNA (Peking), January 4, 1979.

23. *PR*, no. 4 (January 26, 1979), p. 5.

24. *PR*, no. 15 (April 13, 1979), p. 5.

25. *New York Times*, May 10, 1979.

26. William Clarke, "China's Electric Power Industry," in U.S., Congress, Joint Economic Committee, *Chinese Economy Post-Mao*, 95th Cong., 2d sess., 1978, p. 424.

27. *PR*, no. 11 (March 16, 1979), pp. 13–14.

28. Thomas Wiens, "Agriculture in the Four Modernizations"

(Paper presented to the Association for Asian Studies, Los Angeles, March 30, 1979), p. 12.

29. Ibid.

30. Hua's Report.

31. *JMJP*, editorial, February 24, 1979.

32. Foreign Broadcast Information Service (hereafter FBIS), January 9, 1979, p. E12–13.

33. Hu Ch'iao-mu, "Act in Accordance with Economic Laws, Step Up the Four Modernizations," *JMJP*, October 6, 1978.

34. Chao Li-kuang, "Refute the Gang of Four's Erroneous Theory Dealing with the Problems Concerning the Form of Labor Payments," *JMJP*, November 22, 1977, p. 2.

35. Changsha, Hunan Provincial Service, January 5, 1979.

36. Yü Ch'iu-li, "Mobilize the Whole Party, Fight a Decisive Battle for Three Years, Strive Hard to Basically Realize Agricultural Mechanization," *JMJP*, January 29, 1978.

37. *PR*, no. 28 (July 14, 1978), p. 3.

38. Hua's Report.

39. This information is based on Chi Ti, "Industrial Modernization," *PR*, no. 26 (June 30, 1978), pp. 7–9; and Wu Ching-lien, Chou Shu-lien, and Wang Hui-pao, "Establish and Improve the System of Retaining Earnings for Enterprise Funds," *JMJP*, September 2, 1978, p. 3.

40. Kyodo, September 19, 1978. The exchange rate used for 1978 is 1.59 yuan per $1.

41. Hua's Report.

42. Chi Hsin, "China Completed Its Sharp Turn," *Ch'i-shih nien-tai* [The seventies] (Hong Kong), no. 109 (February 1979), p. 16.

43. *Nan-fang jih-pao* [Southern daily] (Kwangchow), March 22, 1979, p. 1.

44. FBIS, March 19, 1979, p. S–3.

45. FBIS, March 29, 1979, p. O–12.

46. *New York Times*, February 8, 1979.

47. Arthur G. Ashbrook, Jr., "China: Shift of Economic Gears in Mid-1970s," in U.S., Congress, *Chinese Economy Post-Mao*, p. 208.

48. *China: Economic Indicators* (Washington, D.C.: Central Intelligence Agency, 1978), p. 1.

49. *Chicago Tribune*, March 11, 1979, p. 10.

50. NCNA (Peking), November 28, 1978 (FBIS, November 29, 1978, pp. E1–2).

51. FBIS, December 7, 1978, pp. E15–16.

52. Kung Hsing-hua, "It Is Not Permissible to Have 'Crew Cuts' in Evaluating Bonuses," *JMJP*, December 27, 1978, p. 8.

53. Chi, "China Completed Its Sharp Turn."

54. *Nan-fang jih-pao,* March 22, 1979, p. 1.

55. FBIS, February 26, 1979, p. G-1.

56. FBIS, March 27, 1979, pp. L8-10.

57. Chi, "China Completed Its Sharp Turn."

58. *Los Angeles Times,* May 10, 1979.

59. NCNA reporter's commentary, "Only by Narrowing the Capital Construction Front Can We Advance Faster," NCNA (Peking), March 22, 1979.

60. FBIS, April 3, 1979, p. L14-15.

61. *Los Angeles Times,* May 10, 1979.

62. The $6 billion figure was supplied by Richard Baum.

63. *New York Times,* March 2, 1979.

64. *Hua-ch'iao jih-pao,* May 6, 1979.

65. For details see Chu-yüan Cheng, *China's Petroleum Industry,* Chapter 18.

66. *China: Agriculture in 1978* (Washington, D.C.: Central Intelligence Agency, 1979), p. 4.

Commentaries on Agricultural and Industrial Modernization

K. C. Yeh

First, I would like to address the question of whether agricultural growth will prove to be a severe constraint on China's modernization program. In this connection, the critical issue is whether over the next decade agricultural production will grow faster or slower than the increase in demand for food. If demand grows relatively fast, even a healthy 4 percent growth rate in agricultural production might create difficulties. On the other hand, if demand increases more slowly than it has in the past, a 4 percent growth rate might be more than adequate.

Population growth is certainly one of the most important factors on the demand side, but other factors are also significant. For example, changes in the age structure and degree of urbanization of the population, combined with rising consumer purchasing power, tend to shift the demand for agricultural products toward higher quality foods, such as wheat, meat, and dairy products. Hence, demand conditions must be considered together with growth of output when assessing agricultural constraints on China's modernization program.

Second, although I believe that the acquisition of advanced technology will help to accelerate China's industrial growth, I think that it will not alleviate many of the problems currently facing Chinese planners.

In evaluating the economic impact of China's technology pro-

The commentaries in this section by K. C. Yeh, Thomas Wiens, and William Clarke were originally presented in response to papers that have not been included in this volume. Because each of these commentaries touches directly on important issues raised by Chu-yüan Cheng's chapter, however, they have been edited for inclusion at this point.—*the Editor*

gram, the time horizon becomes extremely important. Are we looking at the impact over the next five years, ten years, or fifteen years? If we were to take a longer-range point of view, say to 1990 or 1995, would our assessment come out differently than if we took a shorter-term view, say to 1985? I believe that it would, and for two reasons. First, most of the complete plants that China has purchased (or is currently ordering) from abroad will not come into full production until the early 1980s; and second, technology acquisition is meaningless until it is integrated into the existing system of production and exchange. This means that it may take rather a long time for China to absorb and make efficient use of the technology currently being imported. In this respect, we might do better to adopt the longer-term view in attempting to assess the economic impact of technology acquisition.

Third, we are told that in the next seven or eight years technology imports into China will amount to more than $50 billion. This implies an enormous domestic investment program, not only because large scale construction will have to accompany the imported equipment, but also because supporting services such as water and power supplies, communications, transportation, and other upstream and downstream facilities will have to be provided. Such support services could conceivably generate a substantial amount of new nonagricultural jobs in the P.R.C., thereby helping to relieve the pressures of rural underemployment.

On the other hand, I believe that the importation of whole plants is likely to have only a marginal direct effect on the employment picture, since the new plants for the most part are highly capital intensive. Indeed, China's nonagricultural sector as a whole currently absorbs only about 3 to 4 million new workers a year, which is less than one-third of those entering working age.

Indirectly, however, the impact of technological imports on employment may be substantially greater. For one thing, China intends to rapidly expand the production of consumer goods (primarily light industrial manufactures) for export purposes so as to earn foreign exchange with which to pay for imported technology. Since light industrial production is relatively labor intensive, this will mean the creation of a substantial number of new jobs. Moreover, the construction industry (which will be called on to build new light industrial facilities) is itself highly labor intensive and will thus generate even more jobs. Assuming that there is not already a great deal of excess slack in these industries, the overall impact of China's technological modernization program on the employment picture could thus be rather favorable.

Thomas B. Wiens

I would like to discuss the role of agricultural mechanization in China's modernization campaign, and I would like to begin with a quote from a background briefing by a P.R.C. official:

> We already have many more machines than we have had previously. Why can't we correspondingly raise our labor productivity in agriculture? An important reason is that our machines do not fit together to form complete sets, [and] cannot play their part.

What is meant by "complete sets" in this context? The phrase is used very frequently in recent discussions of the agricultural machinery industry. First, I think that the above quotation refers to a lack of accessories, particularly multipurpose accessories. In a sense, the same problem arises in agricultural machinery that has arisen in the production of machine tools. The Chinese have done very well with agricultural equipment such as tractors and pumps, just as they have done very well in producing general purpose lathes. But the Chinese have weaknesses on the accessory side of agricultural equipment production, just as they have weaknesses in the area of special purpose machine tools.

The question also refers to the lack of a systems approach to mechanized farming. The machinery, along with the accessories that are now produced, tends to be directed at individual operations in agriculture in a piecemeal fashion. This frequently means that the full productivity increase potential of this machinery is not realized for one of two reasons. First, unforeseen bottlenecks reduce the efficiency of machine use. The Chinese development of a rice transplanter provides an excellent example. I was told at one point while in China that the transplanter did not work very well. Chinese planners believed that the machine was basically sound, but it could transplant seedlings much faster than manual workers could move the seedlings from flats into the machine. In short, the machine had to be stopped frequently while many laborers reloaded it with seedlings. It was therefore unable to reach its rated potential capacity.

Second, the inability of the Chinese to completely mechanize the agricultural process prevents full substitution of machinery for labor and animals. For example, in the Northeast, plowing and harvesting have been basically mechanized, but farm workers lack effective machines for fertilization or field management—cultivation, weeding, and so forth. As a result, less labor and fewer draft animals are released per hectare than would optimally be the case.

One reason for the weakness of accessory production has been the emphasis on small-scale, local production facilities. The problem here is that these factories need simple equipment that can be produced at the local level. Multipurpose equipment of the type that is in demand is complex and requires greater designing facilities than exist at the local level. Engineering talent is spread very thin at this level.

Third, in China, local agricultural machinery production tends to be based on cast iron and steel parts, rather than on sheet steel (rolled steel). The Chinese press has cited the example of a machine invented in a northeastern county. This multifunctional machine loosens soil, removes stubble, banks ridges, packs soil, and seeds all in one process. It cuts 20 to 30 days off of the time required for sowing in the Northeast—a very important advantage. The problem is that there is not enough sheet steel of the type needed to expand production. This may in part be due to a shortage on the supply side, but it is also due to the expense and complexity of the equipment required to process sheet steel at the local level.

All this tends to suggest that China's past extensive development of tractor, power tiller, and irrigation pump production is partly counterbalanced by weaknesses in other areas. The industry is now supposed to begin to overcome these basic weaknesses. The demand now is for more complex and better designed machinery requiring individual attention to the local topography, crops, and cropping system. That is to say, a great deal of engineering talent needs to be directed to regional and local problems. Also, special attention must be paid to seeding (except for wheat, which is already highly mechanized), rice transplanting, cultivation, harvesting, threshing, and drying. In these areas, there are some problems that are special to China. Borrowing foreign technology may therefore be difficult without major changes in the Chinese cropping system.

What can be said about the planned pace of mechanization and its relevance in the Chinese context? I would like to draw from some of the private briefings provided by Chinese planners to U.S. delegations. These briefings are a bit more frank than some of the public information that has come out. First of all, Chinese planners appear to place mechanization as the fourth ranking goal or requirement in Chinese agriculture, following water conservancy, rural electrification, and agricultural chemicals. They say that mechanization is the only one of these four objectives over which there has been substantial controversy concerning where and what.

Second, some of the ambitious targets for farm mechanization that have been stressed in the last couple of years, according to Chinese leaders' own current assessments, will not be achieved on schedule. They have, for example, targeted 70 percent mechanization for 1980. This means that 70 percent of each major operation in agriculture should be done by machine. They actually expect to succeed in mechanized plowing, draining, irrigation, machine sowing for wheat, processing of agricultural products, transportation, and plant protection. Of these, they have already succeeded (passed their 70 percent target) for drainage, irrigation, machine plowing and processing, leaving only machine sowing for wheat, transportation, and plant protection. In these areas, the Chinese are relatively advanced by their own standards of mechanization, though not necessarily by ours. However, the Chinese now expect to fail to achieve their targets for rice cultivation, fertilizer application, threshing and drying of grain, as well as field management. Evidently, this is either a case where the targets were meant to be purely hortatory or where the Chinese have had to revise downward their ambitions as they looked more seriously at the problem of mechanization.

The major sources of controversy over mechanization lie in the two areas of potential problems: (1) the release of labor and (2) doubts as to the yield-increasing benefits of mechanization. Mechanization, the Chinese argue, is supposed to increase labor productivity. But they define labor productivity in an interesting way. For them, the whole idea of raising labor productivity is first to make each laborer farm more land; second, to make each *mou* (one-sixth of an acre) of land produce more products.

The emphasis here is not on releasing labor from the land, but on getting more land farmed per laborer. Also, the goal of increasing yields per acre gets as much emphasis as that of higher acreage per worker. In this connection, it is relevant to note the recent experience of the Sino-American Friendship Farm (developed by John Deere in Heilungkiang Province) in the first year of its operation. Chinese officials point out that the introduction of systematic mechanization on this farm released 280 workers (93 percent of the labor force) to go out to open up new land. Secondly, they point out that yields on this experimental farm were increased by 20 percent through mechanization. The problem, however, was that this highly mechanized and very expensive U.S. farm equipment was being used to replace 280 laborers. The displaced workers presumably picked up their hoes and carrying baskets and went out to open up new land at very low productivity rates—a solution that is not applicable in many parts of China, where virgin land is either nonexistent or nonarable.

In some situations, the benefits of mechanization are clear and we may expect these areas to receive obvious emphasis in the next few years. First of all, the Chinese have defined twelve commercial grain bases, of which four are located in the Northeast or Northwest—essentially in frontier areas. Most of the Northeast is included in the commercial grain bases. The upper Yellow River and the region from Inner Mongolia through the

Kansu corridor are all part of these grain bases. Much of the work involves the opening up of new land, so there is an obvious use for additional labor. Because these areas are relatively underpopulated, the labor release problem is not so serious. Moreover, the cropping season in these areas is very short so that speedy plowing, sowing, harvesting, and drying, which result from mechanized agriculture, are important to the realization of decent yields.

The second area that is important and will see mechanization is that of farmland construction and improvement. One obvious prerequisite for intensified high-yield agriculture is better land. This can best be accomplished with mechanization—bulldozers, ditch diggers, and cranes—to supplement the labor-intensive methods that have been used in the past at low productivity rates.

Third, in mountainous areas and to some extent in the animal husbandry areas, the Chinese intend to stress transportation as the problem. They are opening up new roads and acquiring new vehicles (which may be tractors or trucks) to provide transportation.

Finally, mechanized pig and chicken raising on commercial farms in the suburban areas is apparently needed to provide, on the one hand, a very quick increase in urban supply and, on the other hand, some dependable supply planning in urban areas for meat production. If China is going to launch a major industrial program, then the urban labor force will increase, as will urban wages. This will lead to an increased demand for meat, so that meat production will have to increase rather quickly. That is one side of the problem. Presumably the other side is the need to provide consumer goods in the urban areas commensurate with the increased emphasis on material incentives.

However, one instance where mechanization may be replaced by chemicalization is in intertillage. The main objective of intertillage is to eliminate weeds, and most U.S. and Japanese technologies have incorporated weed killers rather than machines. The Chinese tried weed killers for the first time on a large scale in Heilungkiang Province with apparent success. It looks very likely that they will move in the direction of weed killers in the future, at least in certain areas.

Beyond these examples, the consensus seems to break down. Chinese planners seem to be somewhat at a loss about how best to mechanize and at what pace. I think the concern here is more long term than short term. A decision has been made to experiment in a very sensible way. Each province has been told to devote one county to complete mechanization. This county is to be located near a major city or a major industrial base, for obvious reasons. These urban-industrial areas are a better source of supply for the materials involved; there is better transport; and especially there is potential employment for the released labor.

In conjunction both with this program and with the longer-term program for mechanization, the Chinese are increasingly emphasizing industrial subcontracting as a solution to the labor release problem. Urban industries are supposed to concentrate on producing the main products and to subcontract the manufacture of other parts and supplies to rural communes or even small urban industries. China thus has adopted the "Japanese solution" to the labor absorption problem.

Finally, there is the problem of peasant demand for machinery. Various articles have suggested that a high proportion of the machinery sold to the communes is defective and remains inoperative. It seems true that often in the past guarantees were not honored, or else the terms of the guarantees were so complex that it was too expensive for the peasants to get them honored. A question arises as to why the peasants have been buying this machinery if it does not work. Does it just sit around, being too expensive to maintain or repair? Did they have any choice in the matter? These are questions to which I do not have answers.

Whatever the case, a number of recent articles have suggested that peasants are not willing to purchase more machinery or even chemical fertilizers, given the current price structure. The articles mentioned, for example, that the annual cost of maintaining a tractor, including fuel, is around 10,000 yuan—a figure equivalent to the annual yield of approximately 400 *mou* of land in the Northeast. Hence, a large percentage of the crop output value goes toward maintaining the tractors. Similar cost-efficiency considerations apply to chemical fertilizers. Consequently, the Chinese regime's announcement that it will raise the state purchase price of grain 20 percent beginning with the 1979 harvest is, I think, a critical factor in promoting further mechanization.

William Clarke

Looking at China's steel industry, we can see clearly the tremendous investments that the Chinese are now contemplating. These new investments (in iron ore and coal mining as well as in whole plant purchases of steel mills) suggest a basic attempt to rectify a critical situation that arose as a result of years of neglect.

The iron content of Chinese ore as mined is roughly 25 to 30 percent—well short of the optimal level of 55 to 60 percent. With insufficient beneficiation capacity, this means, in effect, that China's blast furnace capacity is not operating at its optimal level. The current approach to steel industry development is designed, in part, to correct this situation.

The output of pig iron from blast furnaces is extremely important to the steel industry in China, particularly since China is chronically short of iron and steel scrap. The Chinese have to make up for this shortage of scrap with higher charges of pig iron in their steel-making furnaces. In this connection, the technological advance represented by oxygen steel making in converters has much to recommend it. But China's steel industry has not yet widely participated in the worldwide revolution in oxygen converters of the last twenty-five years. They do have a few such converters, but they have not assimilated this technology in the way it has been assimilated in Japan, Western Europe, and the United States. For example, one such facility in Northeast China, completed in 1974, has a designed annual capacity of about 1 million tons of steel. Yet this mill has never produced any steel at all because operators have not been able to get the oxygen plant to supply the oxygen converter. This certainly suggests that they have encountered some substantial technological difficulties.

More interesting, perhaps, is the proposed Paoshan steel mill near Shanghai—a $3 billion plant that is expected to turn out 6 million metric tons of steel per year. The plant is to be created from the ground up in swampy land on the edge of the Yangtze River. It is to be a copy of the Japanese Kimitsu plant. The strategy involved in this project is to use an already existing, highly modern Japanese plant as a prototype, thus saving about one year in the planning and designing process.

In watching the development of this plant, it will be particularly interesting to see how quickly, and with what facility, the Chinese can assimilate Japanese technology. Before the plant can become functional, they will need to drive some hundreds of thousands of tons of steel piling simply to support the structure of the coking plants, the electric power plants, the blast furnaces, and the steel plants, all of which will go to make up the Paoshan complex. They will also need to dredge the Yangtze River in order to be able to bring in Australian ore to charge the blast furnaces. With all these tasks confronting them, they are nevertheless projecting an output of 3 million metric tons of iron from this plant as early as 1980. I do not hesitate to say that this will not be done; simply, it cannot be done.

I would also note in passing that the location of this plant near Shanghai does seem to indicate an end to the old policy of inland dispersion of industry, away from the major urban centers along the East coast. It seems to me that the choice of Paoshan was dictated primarily by economic, rather than demographic or political reasoning.

The Chinese are contemplating construction of another big steel plant, to be located in eastern Hopei Province (Chitung), but they have not yet selected the site for it. It is to be an extremely large, integrated plant—the largest in the world ever built from the ground up in one continuous movement. It is a $14 billion plant with a planned capacity of 10 million metric tons. And although they have not even sited the plant yet, they nevertheless expect it to produce 6 million tons of steel by 1985. This is extremely doubtful. I would further note that the siting of this plant in the earthquake-prone region of eastern Hopei suggests that economic reasoning overrode other considerations concerning its location.

In 1978 the Chinese produced a fairly respectable 31 million metric tons of steel, up from 23 million tons in 1977. This increase is partially misleading, however, since it largely reflects the reactivation of capacity idled earlier for various reasons. It seems clear that there is still a great deal (probably on the order of several million tons) of unused Chinese steel capacity lying idle or not being fully used, due most probably to power shortages.

It will be recalled that China's announced target for steel production is 60 million tons by 1985.* The Chinese would need to add around 30 million metric tons of new capacity to fulfill that target. Paoshan and Chitung together will only contribute 12 million of this 30-million-ton capacity. The balance of 18 million tons would have to come from the revamping of the seven existing major steel plants. It just does not seem realistic for the Chinese to accomplish this in so short a time.

I do think that the Chinese are taking the right approach, however. They are not searching for "quick fixes." They have been so preoccupied with their major new investments in Paoshan and Chitung that they have not yet thought through the question of the role of smaller steel plants. I believe that the so-called mini steel plant would have a very important role to play in China. Such plants bear no relation to the small-scale, county-run steel plants now in operation; rather, I am talking about a modern, Western-type, mini steel plant with the direct reduction of iron ore. I would expect the Chinese to move to this type of technology once the larger, major investments in new steel capacity are well under way.

In sum, I certainly would not agree with the *Jen-min jih-pao* (People's daily) editorial of December 11, 1978, that claimed that the sky above the Ministry of Metallurgical Industry is clear at last. It seems that there are still quite a few clouds overhead.

*This target was revised downward to 45 million tons in the spring of 1979.—*the Editor*

3
Recent Policy Trends in Industrial Science and Technology

Thomas Fingar

To transform China into a "powerful, modern, socialist country by the end of this century" will require far-reaching changes in all sectors and policy areas, but industrial modernization is the sine qua non.[1] Dramatic advances in the range, quantity, and quality of industrial products are imperative if China's agriculture, national defense, and science and technology are to attain advanced world levels and if the quality of life is to improve as promised by the post-Mao leadership. As presented by P.R.C. leaders, the current modernization program is supposed to achieve rapid economic and technical progress without significant individual sacrifice. On the contrary, it is supposed to produce tangible benefits in the short run.[2] This promise complicates the task of development and increases the political risk of failure. Current policies entail relatively high social and ideological as well as economic costs. Achievements must be prompt and tangible if skeptics and critics are to remain silent.[3]

Recognizing that industrial modernization is critical to the attainment of its overall objectives and perhaps to its continued tenure in office, the Hua/Teng leadership has devised a broad array of industry-related policies. Three features of this policy set are particularly noteworthy: (1) it evinces a "maxi-max"

The research for this paper was supported in part by the Stanford University Arms Control and Disarmament Program through a grant from the Ford Foundation.

strategy involving high risks in order to achieve maximum benefits;[4] (2) it stresses the multiplicity of factors shaping industrial science and technology and the need to deal with all of them simultaneously; and (3) it emphasizes personal, enterprise, and local discretion within the framework of comprehensive, centralized planning. Striving for balance between rhetorical generalities and minuscule case studies, this chapter will survey the measures to foster change in China's industrial sector that have been adopted, reiterated, or implemented since 1976.

Problems and Objectives Addressed by Recent Policies

Current industrial science and technology policies exhibit substantial scope and integration. Eschewing the search for a single panacea to cure industrial ills, China's leaders have acknowledged many problems and many causes. Following the December 1976 publication of Mao's 1956 speech, entitled "On the Ten Major Relationships," commentators began to assert the interconnection of seemingly discrete policies and the need to pursue multiple objectives within a framework of clear priorities.[5] In explaining priorities and policy linkages, spokesmen have identified several attitudinal, organizational, technical, manpower, managerial, and financial problems that must be overcome to promote and profit from advances in industrial science and technology. Their assessment of these problems is summarized below. The analysis will then discuss policies aimed at overcoming the problems.

Attitudinal Problems

The current drive for modernization is being pursued on so many fronts and with such a degree of urgency that the Chinese people must make and adjust to changes that may be even more far-reaching than those demanded in the first years after Liberation.[6] Modernizers in Peking recognize that it is not enough to request or compel people to adopt new ways—they must also change the way people think about what they do.[7] For that reason, attitudes and conceptual obstacles to rapid industrial modernization have been matters of great concern to the leadership. Recent commentaries have characterized many cadres and ordinary citizens as unwilling (or unable) to think and act in accord with the dictates of a modern industrial society. The following excerpt is typical.

> Some leading cadres are conservative and backward in their thinking. They feel no qualms about the old equipment, techniques or work processes which they have been using for decades, or about manual labor which has been in force for decades or even centuries, and will not forsake them. They are always suspicious of all new things, always asking "can it really work?" When they hear the word reform, their first response is to say that it is "too much trouble." They are unwilling to learn from the latest science and technology. When they cannot master the skill of operating new machines, they just let the machines stand idle. Some comrades even say that people aspire after new techniques and equipment because they want to "do less work" and are "afraid of toilsome labor." . . . Modernization calls for the constant replacement of the old and the outdated with the new. If we follow the beaten track, refuse to make changes and do not have even the least positive and enterprising spirit, how can we lead the masses in carrying out a great revolution in science and technology and insure that our national economy can catch up with and surpass advanced world levels?
>
> In short, in our thoughts and conceptions, working methods, specific policies and rules and regulations, there are some backward things, some that are even deep-rooted, that are incompatible with the requirements for achieving the four modernizations and that seriously hamper our advance.[8]

One manifestation of attitudinal or "political" difficulties is the reported reluctance of many cadres to implement current policies.[9] Diatribes denounce such behavior as fealty to the Gang of Four, but less inflammatory articles suggest that some cadres—uncertain about the longevity of present policies—are adopting a very cautious stance.[10] Officials and entire organizational units seem to be holding back for fear of retribution should the line shift in the future.[11]

A related attitudinal problem involves cadres who dislike the new program because it threatens their positions. In particular, some activists elevated to cadre status during the Cultural Revolution are understandably uneasy about recalling specialists and veteran officials with skills needed in the drive for rapid modernization. Personal ambition rather than political caution seems to be the primary motivation in such cases, but the result is the same: policies are not effectively carried out.[12]

The third and most difficult attitudinal problem discussed in P.R.C. media derives from ignorance or misunderstanding about modern society. Part of the problem is that many workers simply do not understand the operation and requirements of sophisticated equipment and processes.[13] Another difficulty involves administrators who do not grasp the utility of "scientific" managerial practices, such as operations research and systems analysis.[14] There is an educational component to this problem (discussed below), but commentators have also emphasized the widespread failure to appreciate the need for discipline on the shop floor, for more attention to quality and trial production, and for countless other specific requirements. Apathy and antipathy to elements of the developmental strategy are both described as significant problems.

Organizational Problems

Industrial modernization is also seen to have been inhibited by a number of organizational shortcomings. Perhaps the most serious was the development (through deliberate policies and simple coping mechanisms) of comprehensive or self-reliant enterprises, whether large and complete or small and complete. In the current view, these enterprises prevented specialization, standardization, serialization, and other hallmarks of modern industry.[15]

Another organizational or structural problem was the lack of contact between manufacturer and end user. In the recent past, there seems to have been little systematic tracking of new products to determine how well they performed, what technical or operational modifications were made by engineers and workers in individual enterprises, or what modifications should be incorporated into revised designs and instruction manuals.[16] The latest verdict seems to be that meetings to exchange experiences failed to provide adequate feedback to personnel at design and manufacturing facilities or suitable information for others wrestling with similar technical problems.

Structural and communications shortcomings over the past decade are seen to have impeded research and development. On the one hand, comprehensive enterprises contained small R & D operations, but their small size and the lack of incentives for developing new products and technologies combined with the generally low level of research skills to inhibit the emergence of new techniques. On the other hand, the concentration of design skills in institutes under central ministries and ineffective feedback mechanisms combined to decrease the relevance of much of the R & D work that did occur. The problem, as viewed by the current leadership, is to devise an organizational system that will mitigate these weaknesses.[17]

Technical Problems

Paradoxically, technical impediments seem to be regarded as both the key bottleneck to rapid industrial modernization and the most easily remedied of the many problems facing China. By any reckoning, and as P.R.C. leaders keep reminding us, China's industrial technology lags far behind that of advanced industrial states.[18] Equipment is generally outdated by fifteen to thirty years, levels of automation are extremely low, and total capacity is much too small to produce the quantity and variety of goods needed for the Four Modernizations. The quickest and easiest—albeit very expensive—solution is to import a great many complete plants and individual machines and to purchase advanced technologies from abroad. Since China cannot possibly import all that is required (and would not want to do so even if it were possible), there must also be an effort to upgrade existing equipment and enterprises by giving full play and support to indigenous designers and equipment manufacturers.[19]

The technical problem is, of course, much more serious. At the very least, it will require difficult and informed decisions on the priority to be accorded to various technologies in different industrial branches, reasonably accurate estimates of the time and resources required to develop components that are to be produced domestically, and detailed preparations for absorbing both imported and advanced indigenous techniques and equipment. Thus, the boundary between technical problems and those of manpower and management is an imprecise one.[20] Chinese commentaries suggest that obtaining advanced hardware and expertise will be much easier than deciding what to procure and how to use it most effectively.[21]

Educational and Manpower Problems

Recent addresses by P.R.C. leaders have highlighted the need to train more engineers, technicians, and other specialists, and the need to raise the educational and skill levels of ordinary workers. In part, they are addressing the attitudinal problem, noted above, in the belief that, when people working in all phases of industrial science and technology have a better understanding of what is involved, they will think and act in accordance with the requirements of modern industry. At the same time, they cite the need to upgrade technical skills in order to produce and use advanced technologies.[22]

China has an acute shortage of engineers and industrial scientists. Many of those nominally in this category are, by admission of the P.R.C. leaders, either woefully undertrained (as a consequence of policies and practices over the past decade) or badly out of touch with international developments in their fields. The short-term problem is to retrain and upgrade the skills of the existing pool of technical specialists; the longer-term need is to greatly expand that pool while raising the general level of competence.[23]

Ordinary workers pose a similar dual problem for the leadership. The current industrial workforce (especially those who entered factories after 1965) has what is described as a weak educational background and only relatively low-level technical skills. In other words, the training and experience of today's workers are inadequate even for current technologies; workers must be retrained if the advanced imported equipment and processes are to be used effectively. The problem is not only to provide additional training, but also to persuade workers that it is important for them to upgrade their skills and to abandon many practices of the past decade. While the current workforce is being upgraded, better general education must be provided for the next generation.[24]

Yet another aspect of the manpower and education problem involves the necessity for trade-offs among constituent parts. For example, time spent by engineers to upgrade their skills cuts into time that might otherwise be devoted to designing new machinery or retraining workers. Success requires dealing with all parts of the problem simultaneously, but the current shortage of skilled manpower makes this extremely difficult.

Managerial and Leadership Problems

There is an absolute shortage of skilled and experienced management personnel, and this problem has been discussed more extensively than has any other obstacle to rapid industrial modernization.[25] For more than a decade, rhetorical policies have denigrated the need for managerial specialists.[26] In addition, the long reliance on revolutionary committees rather than traditional managerial organs decreased the effectiveness of people with managerial experience.

As with other problems discussed here, management subsumes a number of distinct but closely related difficulties. In addition to the attitudinal and organizational problems noted above, management has been plagued by obscure lines of responsibility, low levels of expertise, and political constraints on managerial effectiveness. For example, in the recent past no person or organization has had clear responsibility for industrial science and technology, either nationally or in individual enterprises. Hence, no one used bureaucratic position or political capital to press for funds, skilled technicians, time to develop new products and processes, or other requisites of research and development.[27]

Management also has suffered from the shortage of people with both administrative skills and an understanding of science and technology. Forced to focus on profits, quotas, and assuring adequate supplies of essential materials (when not concentrating on political campaigns), managers have had little time and few incentives to promote industrial science and technology (S & T). Even if they had the time, resources, and inclination to improve industrial S & T, they lacked the necessary managerial skills. Without a system of individual responsibility, they could not easily trace the source of low-quality products or the cause of production bottlenecks and equipment failures. Unable to enforce industrial discipline or to provide material inducements to spur innovation and more effective use of existing technologies, they could do little to raise the level of industrial S & T. The severity of these and other problems obviously varies from one enterprise to another, but recent commentaries have elevated them to the status of general systemic defects. The following passages illustrate the current assessment:

> A modern enterprise requires scientific management which cannot exist without a strict system of responsibilities, a clear-cut division of labor and good discipline. Every piece of work and every job must be assigned. The duties of every cadre, worker and technician must be clearly defined. We must resolutely follow the system of responsibility involving factory managers under the leadership of the Party committee. . . . Another problem in management involves learning how to manage. Not knowing how to manage is now a universal problem. A large number of new cadres have assumed leadership roles over the past 10 years. Among the workers, the number of new employees has been steadily increasing. This situation has led to a temporary shortage of technical workers. These new workers, who are unfamiliar with past good experiences, traditions and styles, lack managerial experience. For veteran cadres and workers, there is the problem of inheriting, carrying forward and improving management skills. New developments never cease. We cannot stay in a rut.[28]

Financial Problems

Industrial science and technology in China have been plagued by an absolute shortage of funds and the lack of financial incentives (to both individuals and enterprises) for innovation or research and development. In addition, enterprises have not been able to procure new equipment and techniques without going through complicated and time-consuming procedures that act as powerful disincentives.[29] According to recent articles, excessive centralization and the credit policies of the People's Bank have made it too difficult for enterprises to obtain funding for development of new technologies.[30] Another factor has been the policy governing disposition of any profits retained by the enterprise. All these constraints must be reduced if industrial science and technology are to prosper.

Other finance-related constraints noted by official spokesmen include inappropriate pricing policies that make it difficult for enterprises to recover costs of research and development and insufficient budgetary appropriations for R & D.[31] The bottom line is simply that not enough money was appropriated for industrial science and technology in the past and that more must be made available.

The problems summarized above are neither unique nor surprising. What is unique is the way in which they have been linked together in official assessments. Space does not permit extensive quotation, but the following excerpt is typical:

> The leaders of some units are conservative in their thinking. They stay in a rut, are unaware of the pressing need for mechanization and modernization and pay very little attention to imported technology and equipment. Influenced by the remnant poison of Lin Piao and the "gang of four," they even hold that, because the technology and equipment were imported from capitalist countries, it is not very honorable to use them. In fact, there is nothing amiss in that at all. . . . Without advanced technology and equipment, there will be no high speed development. The question of properly studying, using and managing imported technology and equipment is not only an economic one but also an important question having a bearing on the rapid realization of the four modernizations in our country.
>
> The leaders of some units are vague about the complexities of imported technology and equipment. They believe that once these are acquired, everything will proceed smoothly. They expect the imported equipment to play its role in due course. . . . Without a good knowledge of advanced and complicated technology and equipment, nothing can serve production well. Therefore, if we do not try to understand advanced technology and equipment and know them well and if we do not know how to operate them and make them work, even advanced technology and equipment will be of little use to us. . . . That is why technological training for the workers, particularly those who are using the imported equipment and who are not technologically proficient, must be stepped up. Moreover, those workers who are to use the imported equipment must also be trained so that they will become familiar with their operating principles

and procedures and be able to keep the equipment in serviceable condition under normal or abnormal circumstances. . . . Of course, trained personnel, whether they are workers, technicians or leading cadres, should continue to study hard at their work posts so that they will become professionally proficient in handling the imported technology and equipment. Next, supply work must be undertaken properly. This requires that complete sets of accessories and parts be purchased in order to keep the imported technology and equipment in serviceable condition. Urgently needed parts and accessories in short supply must be imported. This is because the replacement of worn-out parts by imported ones can restore a complete piece of equipment to optimum. . . . [M]any of the units which have imported technical equipment lack proper ways to manage them. Those that have drawn up simple regulations are lax in enforcing them and do not have well defined responsibilities binding on the leading or technological personnel. . . . In addition to organizing the study effort, we must strengthen scientific research related to the imported technology and equipment to meet the requirements of scientific managing of the imported things.[32]

Since the problems are interrelated, the solutions must be also. The next section describes some of the policies adopted to deal with obstacles to industrial modernization. Problem and policy areas are examined individually for ease of presentation, but all are part of a single program.

Recent Policy Developments

Recent policy developments, like the problems faced by the leadership, fall into six categories similar to those discussed in the section above: attitudinal policies, organizational policies, technical policies, educational and manpower policies, managerial and leadership policies, and financial policies.

Attitudinal Policies

To overcome cadre reticence about implementing educational, organizational, and other policy directives, national leaders have stigmatized such behavior as evidence of deliberate or unwitting fealty to the Gang of Four.[33] The (third) campaign to criticize the Gang of Four seemed designed, in large part, to intimidate hesitant cadres into carrying out policy guidelines.[34] By casting this as a mass campaign, officials enhanced the likelihood of compliance. If for no other reason, lower-level cadres are likely to implement directives to avoid charges of loyalty to Chiang Ch'ing and her unhappy cohorts.

A similar but distinct media campaign has decried the persistence of "small-producer mentality" among a number of the country's administrators, managers, and other officials. This campaign combines intimidation and education. On the one hand, it prods officials to act in certain ways by suggesting that contrary behavior is due to ignorance or, worse, to a low level of political consciousness. On the other, it cites numerous instances of acceptable behavior so that reticent or confused officials will have positive role models to emulate.[35] Cadres need not be especially clever to recognize that continued failure to implement policy decisions opens them to charges of stupidity and political backwardness.

Another measure calculated to alter cadre attitudes has been the insistence that all officials deepen their understanding of scientific principles. As officials have stated repeatedly, the objective is not to transform administrative generalists into chemists or applied physicists, but simply to impart a greater appreciation of the difficulties, importance, and requirements of basic and applied research—a better understanding of the magnitide of the modernization effort and the reasonableness of requests from S & T personnel.[36] Toward this end, special seminars have been held for administrative cadres. Seminars given by prominent scientists and attended by leading political figures have been widely reported in the media as an incentive for lower-ranking cadres to follow suit.[37]

Officials also have endeavored to persuade cautious cadres that current policies will not be reversed in the near future, and that there will be no future retribution for obeying current directives. Perhaps the most important measure in this regard was the decision to emphasize stability that was adopted at the Third Plenum in December 1978.[38] The campaign to study the principles of democratic centralism and to return to the traditions of the Party is also part of this effort, as are the frequent upbeat assessments of the political situation. These campaigns obviously have other targets and other purposes as well, but when discussed in reference to science and technology or industrial development, they are clearly intended to reassure "good" but reluctant cadres.[39]

In addition to efforts to deepen cadre understanding of science and technology through seminars and study sessions, China has begun to assign more leadership posts to practicing scientists and engineers. They are assumed to understand the importance of R & D in the drive for industrial modernization and are expected to help educate and advise cadres who lack their technical background. Moreover, at the same time that the CCP has been assigned the primary role in promoting science and technology (including industrial S & T), growing numbers of science professionals are being invited to join the Party.[40] This has the additional objective of reassuring technical personnel that the central elite is serious about the need "to unite with and give full play to the role of scientists and other intellectuals." A great deal of effort has gone into obtaining their support and persuading others that intellectuals can and must play a key role.[41]

It is much too early to pronounce judgment on the efficacy of these measures, but at least one thing is clear. The leadership has come to realize that changing attitudes will be a long and difficult process. Old attitudes and political memories die hard, but the central leadership is sparing no effort to bring about desired changes.

Organizational Policies

Organizational change can be nearly as difficult as attitudinal change, but P.R.C. leaders have acted with equal determination to alleviate structural impediments to industrial science and technology. To combat inefficiencies arising from duplication of effort and inadequate specialization, officials have called for dissolving comprehensive enterprises and for establishing more rational forms of industrial organization. Rather than produce every component of a few products, enterprises are now enjoined to manufacture a limited number of parts that can be used in several different pieces of equipment. This effort has at least four objectives: specialization, standardization, serialization, and superior quality.[42]

Enterprise specialization has numerous advantages from the viewpoint of improving industrial S & T. For example, specialized factories need fewer different machines than do comprehensive plants, and once those machines have been set up to produce certain parts, they can operate for longer periods without readjustment to make different components. Each piece of equipment can be used for longer periods; operators can become more familiar with machine operation; and components can be standardized more easily. In short, specialization facilitates serial production of high quality, standardized components. Among other consequences, this makes it easier to trace the cause of product defects and to improve the quality of individual components.[43] Test facilities and R & D requirements can also be simplified because fewer specialists using less equipment can concentrate their efforts on a small range of products.

For specialization and the breakup of comprehensive enterprises to work effectively, it has been argued, national planning and coordination within and among industrial branches must be strengthened. P.R.C. officials have devoted considerable attention to this problem, and several specific measures have been announced.[44] One example is the re-creation of supraprovincial economic regions.[45] To plan for the entire country is a formidable task; reestablishment of the economic regions effectively subdivides this task into a number of less complicated chores. So, too does establishment of specialized plants organized into large combines or "corporations."[46] The hope is that, by disaggregating the planning task, more control and greater feedback and flexibility can be built into the process. Provincial plans for industrial S & T are supposed to be coordinated with provincial and regional economic (investment and production) plans to insure that attention is focused on the most important problems, and that individual R & D units obtain the proper mix of equipment, skilled technicians, and reagents needed in their work.[47]

Below the provincial level, similar coordinating functions are to be performed by newly forming administrative bodies that cut across ministerial and administrative boundaries. Some commentaries imply that the present bureaucratic structure inhibits interaction between units that need to be in close contact and causes inefficiencies in industrial S & T, but officials have been very cautious about dismantling the total system. What we see instead is a rather conservative attempt to make marginal adjustments that increase efficiency but do not jeopardize the system as a whole or tread on too many bureaucratic interests. It remains to be seen whether this kind of tinkering will be effective.

Well aware of the impossibility of doing everything at once, P.R.C. officials have revived the practice of designating key points for investment, research, development, or other forms of resource-demanding attention. In the industrial sector, this entails the designation of both key industries and key enterprises. For example, steel, basic chemicals, fuel, and electric power have been designated as key industries with a priority claim on funds, imported technologies, administrative and technical manpower, and everything else needed to guarantee rapid development.[48] In addition to the designation of key industries, certain enterprises in both these and other industrial branches have been selected as key points. This means that the selected enterprises will be favored with greater funding, more and better equipment and technical personnel, and relatively more assistance in overcoming organizational, administrative, scientific, and other problems. The key points for these enterprises are to serve as both pacesetters for the national economy and sources of rapid and, it is hoped, dramatic achievements furthering the cause of national modernization. The expectation is that, by concentrating scarce resources and carefully studying the results, technical advances will be made and the country will gain experience to facilitate even more rapid progress in enterprises that do not have key point status.

Another change affecting individual enterprises is the way in which center-local relationships have been defined. For more than a decade after 1966, enterprises enjoyed a high degree of substantive, if not always formal, autonomy. Autonomy resulted primarily from the inability of the center to exercise effective control, but it also reflected awareness on the part of central officials that, given the exigencies of the situation, the overall level of production and technological progress was likely to be higher if enterprises were left pretty much to themselves. Even though the system was not optimally efficient, it did produce tolerable levels of achievement, and it was thought best not to tamper with the arrangement for fear of destroying what was in place without being able to construct a viable replacement. For some time, proponents of rapid modernization have believed that they knew what had to be done to reorganize the system and make it more efficient, but it was not until the removal of the Gang of Four in late 1976 that it became possible to do so.[49]

In addition to the other organizational changes mentioned here, the restructuring process has involved an interesting combination of tighter centralization and greater enterprise autonomy. This seeming paradox may be explained as follows. For purposes of planning and to accomplish the kind of specialization discussed above, it has been thought necessary to tighten central control through better lines of communication and the appointment of cadres who owed their primary loyalty to the center rather than to individual enterprises or regions of the country, and to tighten Party leadership in all enterprises and organizations. At the same time, it was recognized that rapid progress, including progress in industrial S & T, would be impossible if enterprise managers (and Party committees) had to work exclusively through the cumbersome red tape of a centralized bureaucracy.[50] Decisions on this matter seem to have been influenced by both the negative example of the Soviet Union and perceptions of what had enabled corporations in the United States, Japan, and Western Europe to innovate and expand as rapidly as they have. Current P.R.C. policies permit enterprise managers to make a number of key decisions without involved consultation with higher levels. For example, they apparently can decide which foreign equipment or process should be imported, what proportion of the enterprise budget should be earmarked for R & D, and, within limits, how to motivate ordinary workers.[51] The degree of autonomy presumably varies with the type of enterprise, quantity and cost of equipment to be purchased, the political reliability of the manager, and myriad other factors. The crucial point, however, is that greater autonomy is clearly sanctioned by current policies.

Numerous examples of ministerial, industrial, and enterprise reorganization have appeared in P.R.C. media since mid-1978 but it is still too early to judge the effectiveness of these changes. Organizational policies differ from attitudinal ones in that they seem to evince somewhat more caution about offending entrenched interests and raising bureaucratic hackles. What is clear is that important structural changes are to be made over the next few years.

Technical Policies

Technical problems identified by P.R.C. commentaries divide into two broad categories: acquisition of equipment and know-how, and use of both domestic and imported technologies. To state the general policies adopted to deal with these problems is a relatively easy matter. Unfortunately, we know very little about the details or about how they are supposed to work in specific circumstances. The Chinese have said almost nothing about the precise mechanisms of technology acquisition or use, but in time we should be able to infer guidelines and procedures by looking at a number of concrete examples involving foreign sales and consulting services.[52]

Probably the most visible change in industrial S & T policy in recent months is the dramatic upsurge in foreign purchases. After months of comparative shopping and (presumably) discussions of the political and economic implications of purchases from particular firms and countries, China has entered the high technology market with a vengeance: steel-making equipment and techniques, nuclear power plants, petrochemical and communications technologies—the list goes on and on.[53] Credits and medium-term loans have joined deferred payment and barter arrangements as respectable means for financing imported goods. And it is not only hardware and processes that the Chinese are buying. In recent months they have engaged foreign consulting firms for advice on what equipment, processes, infrastructural requirements, and so forth are needed to establish or update specific industries and enterprises. There are still many unknowns (e.g., if or at what stage consultants will be drawn into Chinese planning processes, whether purchases are being made by individual enterprises or as part of a larger plan allocating sales to several different countries or companies, and how well imported technologies will mesh with existing infrastructures), but the point is that China has again begun to use imports to help close the technology gap.[54] The net result seems to be that if a technology is seen as necessary for rapid industrial modernization and is not available domestically, every effort will be made to acquire that technology abroad.

P.R.C. leaders are well aware that imports can never satisfy more than a small percentage of the country's need for industrial technology, and they are not neglecting indigenous R & D. As the above discussion indicates, a number of measures to strengthen industrial science and technology have been announced in the media and certain steps have been taken to upgrade and expand the nation's capacity to develop new products and processes as well as to copy foreign-made prototypes. Specific steps include the reassignment of people with technical training to positions that will enable them to use their training and experience,[55] the authorization of enterprise managers to channel more funds into R & D, the endorsement of trial production of components or complete machinery with sufficient allowances for failures and necessary modification prior to going into serial production,[56] and the instruction of Party committees at all levels to pay more attention to (i.e., to insure success in) industrial research.[57]

Perhaps the most novel suggestion yet advanced by a P.R.C. official calls for the institution of a royalty system whereby research institutes (the context implies that they would be engaged primarily in industrial science and technology) would be funded primarily through royalty payments on devices or processes that they had developed.[58] A variant of this proposal was adopted a few months later when it was announced that design institutes would henceforth be treated as profit-making enterprises.[59]

Numerous articles have noted the importance of studying the examples provided by successful enterprises in capitalist countries. Although they do not advocate blind duplication of R & D establishments and inducements found in the West or Japan, they do point out the need to distinguish between what is "evil

A Chinese-built computer at Shenyang Computer Research Institute (September 1978).

and capitalist" and what is "modern and scientific" in foreign examples.[60] The implication seems to be that China can adopt extensively without fear of becoming capitalist or bourgeois because it is a socialist country and because cadres would not have the same motives as capitalist businessmen.

Invention is obviously an important aspect of industrial S & T, but it has been relatively neglected in the general P.R.C. media. Bonuses will be offered for successful innovations, and all are encouraged to think about ways to improve efficiency, quality, and other aspects of production.[61] However, we still know virtually nothing about the procedures used to submit or evaluate inventions and technical proposals.[62] Rightly or wrongly, the impressions conveyed by recent articles and speeches is that central leaders expect relatively little of significance to come from worker innovation.[63] At best, such innovation is seen as making a marginal contribution to existing technologies; what is desired is a qualitative leap to new tech-

Two workers lean against an automated control console for programming a precision lathe, Shanghai Turbine Plant (May 1975).

nologies or sophisticated adaptation of advanced technologies from abroad.

Recent P.R.C. industrial science and technology policies have emphasized utilization as well as the acquisition of equipment and technical know-how. Several commentators have lamented the underutilization of existing plant capacity and have pleaded for measures to insure that more advanced technologies, whether indigenous or imported, will be used efficiently.[64] Specialization, standardization, and serialization will help, but more is needed. For starters, Chinese industry must begin to use the tools of industrial engineering and operations research. Chinese factories are notoriously inefficient. Machines sit idle, finished products accumulate in large inventories, and production lines move slowly and stop frequently because of shortages in parts. Much remains to be done if industrial technologies are to reach advanced world levels; recent policies indicate that steps are underway to rationalize the productive process and make better use of equipment. The Chinese are clearly aware of the problem, but they have barely begun to do anything about it.

Factories in China are automated only in the most rudimentary sense of the word. Most equipment is semiautomated at best, and no facilities are computer-regulated from start to finish. This is seen as a major problem by P.R.C. officials, and the drive to develop computer networks announced at the National Science Conference in March 1978 should be regarded as an initial step toward more advanced production facilities.[65] However, computers are still little more than handcrafted toys in the P.R.C., and it will be a long time before more than a tiny percentage of industrial capacity is modernized to the degree found in the West or Japan. Nevertheless, China has made a beginning. Besides the program of hardware and software development announced at the National Science Conference, China has begun to develop programs in systems engineering and operations research to train future managers and industrial designers. This effort involves foreign consultants and the collection of materials from leading foreign business and engineering schools. Initially, at least, this program is being managed by the First Ministry of Machine Building, which has also been assigned the principal role in effecting industrial reorganization.[66]

With the partial exception of the "quick fix" afforded by purchases of foreign technologies, policies to overcome technical obstacles will require a long time to produce hoped-for results. Indigenous R & D capacity is being strengthened, but there are too few skilled technicians and too few well-equipped facilities. Although technical problems are viewed as "simple" in one sense, they are also recognized as requiring a long time for solution. Again, concrete steps are being taken to solve the problems, but it will be some time before the results begin to show up.

Educational and Manpower Policies

According to Chinese commentators, other parts of the current program to strengthen industrial science and technology are certain to falter unless there are significant increases in both the number and the quality of engineers, technicians, and enterprise managers and unless the skills of ordinary workers can be upgraded without delay.[67] In addition to this short-term problem, China must train even larger numbers of more highly skilled personnel (professionals and specialized workers) to fill positions in the expanding and increasingly sophisticated industrial sector. Responding to this challenge, P.R.C. officials have launched a multipart program to train and retrain personnel.

Two, and possibly three, measures have been adopted to meet the large and growing demand for skilled professionals. The first is essentially a one-shot measure intended to quickly boost the number of industrial scientists, engineers and professional technicians. A national survey was conducted in the fall of 1978 to identify all persons trained for careers in science and technology. The survey revealed that many S & T personnel were working in positions that did not use their specialized training.[68] Armed with this information, the central government reiterated earlier instructions that all those trained for (or experienced in) careers in industrial S & T should promptly be reassigned to positions requiring their specialized skills.[69] Press reports from China indicate that there has been some difficulty securing compliance (partly because of the attitudinal problems discussed above), but it is clear that the ranks of nominal S & T professionals have grown considerably in the past several months.

Even though the number of S & T professionals working in industrial research and development has increased dramatically, many of those added to the rolls lack familiarity with developments in their fields over the past decade or more. In short, the number has increased, but serious problems of quality remain.[70] Official policies specify that these personnel should spend most of their time on professional work, including reading journals and papers in their fields so that they can be brought up to date.[71] By itself, this policy is likely to prove inadequate. I suspect, therefore, that China will send industrial S & T professionals abroad for crash courses much as the Academy of Sciences is doing with research scientists. Whether it is realistic or not remains to be seen, but the expectation seems to be that six to eighteen months working with colleagues in advanced industrial countries will enable veteran scientists and engineers to close the knowledge gap and to master the intricacies of high technology.

Future generations of engineers and scientists are to be trained in colleges and research institutes funded and administered by industrial ministries. Each relevant ministry is supposed to establish or adapt colleges to train engineers and other professionals in disciplines germane to the work of that ministry.[72] Some of these colleges have been designated as key institutions and have been endowed with better equipment and instructors than regular institutions. All of these institutions will apparently participate in the national entrance examination and placement procedures administered by the Ministry of Education.[73] Relatively few engineers will move into industrial positions after graduating from comprehensive or scientific universities such as Peking University (Peita) or Tsinghua University; most will be trained at specialized colleges for careers in research institutes and enterprises under the jurisdiction of the same ministry. This approach resembles the Soviet system.[74] Elsewhere, it has the advantage of training large numbers of relatively low-level specialists and the disadvantage of impeding cross-fertilization of disciplines and research fields. Graduate instruction will take place in ministry-run research institutes.

In addition to training and retraining S & T professionals, China must quickly upgrade the skills of ordinary workers and lower-level technicians. As might be expected, a number of different and compatible means of carrying out this task are being employed simultaneously. One method has involved the upgrading of "July 21 Universities" to make them more effective centers for training technical personnel. These are now full-time institutions staffed by full-time instructors, and graduates are no longer expected to return to their original jobs with merely a smattering of Marxism and little additional technical knowledge. On the contrary, they are expected to fill the growing number of semiprofessional positions opening in Chinese industry.[75]

Ordinary workers are expected to acquire new skills and brush up on techniques and procedures in spare-time classes and in full-time courses offered for several weeks or months at a time on a rotating basis. The form of these classes resembles those introduced during the Cultural Revolution, but the content has changed dramatically. Curricula now emphasize technical subjects and worker discipline as well as materials designed to change worker attitudes about modern industry.[76]

The training of younger workers will begin in the primary schools where curricula will devote more time and attention than heretofore to basic science and mathematics. One objective of this new emphasis is, as Hua announced at the Fifth National People's Congress, "To raise the scientific and cultural level of the entire Chinese nation." Hua and other leaders have repeatedly stressed that for China to become a modern industrial state, all citizens, not just the professionals, must appreciate and understand the leading role of science and technology. Only then, it is said, can workers grasp the complexities of the modern factory.

The next generation of workers will come, in large part, from the technical middle schools that are currently being revived or newly established. These are essentially vocational high schools and, like the specialized colleges, many will be administered and funded by industrial ministries. In other words, the training and channeling of people into industrial S & T careers will begin in the middle school and continue through college or even graduate-level training in facilities run by a single specialized ministry. This system contrasts sharply with the kind of training, recruitment, and career patterns found in the United States. The contrast is noteworthy because, as will be seen in the discussion of management-related policies, there is much in the current program for industrial modernization that borrows heavily from the American experience.

Managerial and Leadership Policies

Almost without exception, recent measures to strengthen industrial science and technology have assumed or assigned critical roles to managerial personnel and enterprise Party committees. People in these positions must break up the comprehensive enterprises and consolidate functions in specialized facilities. They must oversee the retraining of workers and insure adequate support for research and development. They must also adopt more efficient ways to use existing equipment and select more advanced technologies from the international market. In short, they are the key to both short-term and long-term success; without effective management, gains and successes in other policy areas will not produce the desired results.[77] To insure that managers and enterprise Party committees are able to play the role demanded of them, central officials have announced a number of potentially important policy changes.

One set of changes has involved the strengthening of Party committees and managerial authority and the abolition of enterprise "revolutionary committees"—those once ubiquitous offspring of the Cultural Revolution. Several reasons seem to have underlain the decision to abolish revolutionary committees in virtually all industrial facilities. Besides the rather formalistic reason that such enterprises are not "organs of government," central leaders appear to have considered these cumbersome and unspecialized bodies to be serious obstacles to industrial modernization.[78] To unfetter the hands of managerial personnel and clear the way for other changes, these bodies were simply abolished. Another reason is that enterprise revolutionary committees were perceived to be too parochial or "departmentalist." Given the desire to tighten central control, break up comprehensive enterprises, and achieve new forms of cooperation within the industrial sector, bodies with a narrow perspective and a potentially self-centered approach to policy implementation were seen as obstacles to progress.

Strengthening Party committees has been described as a way to insure that enterprises will be responsive to the will of the center (through Party discipline exercised by and on individual members and the committees as a whole), that enterprises will not adopt a departmentalist attitude, and that adequate political and logistical support for industrial R & D will be provided.[79] The Party committees, especially the secretaries, are clearly responsible for providing managers and technical personnel with whatever they need to carry out the mandate to catch up with advanced world standards.[80] If other enterprises balk at providing needed equipment or releasing inappropriately placed personnel, for example, it is up to the Party committees to find a solution.

Another way in which enterprise Party committees are to contribute to the modernization effort is through their authority and capacity to change worker attitudes and practices. There are Party groups in each shift of each workshop, and shop/shift foremen are frequently CCP members. This means that Party authority can be invoked to enforce worker discipline on such matters as proper maintenance of equipment and absenteeism. By combining "education" and intimidation, the Party hopes to overcome some of the attitudinal problems discussed above. At the same time, it is to serve as an important channel (with the newly revived trade unions) for monitoring worker sentiment and responding to the concerns of people who are bound to be somewhat confused and possibly alienated by the drive to automate, modernize, and be more efficient.[81]

Day-to-day supervision of industrial enterprises is the responsibility of specifically designated managers. There is to be a general manager responsible for overall operations, and, depending on the type and size of the facility, assistant managers for each of the subspecialties.[82] Research and development is presumably one such subspecialty. The general principle underlying the entire system is that of individual responsibility.[83] Career prospects and even take-home pay of every individual in the enterprise, including management personnel, are supposed to be dependent upon performance.[84] This contrasts sharply with the situation in 1976 when responsibility was diffuse and performance of little consequence.

Personal responsibility is not merely a slogan; measures have been implemented to enable management to act more effectively. For example, daily records are kept for all personnel. These records are prominently displayed and show how many hours were worked, how many components were produced, how much raw material was used, and various other data.[85] Quality controls are used to determine which machines or workers are producing inferior parts, and records are kept to show that proper maintenance has been performed on all equipment. Shop foremen and fellow workers can tell at a glance if individual workers are absent frequently, abusing equipment, or otherwise failing to perform as required. Data acquired in this fashion also are used to reward superior performance through bonuses, conferral of "model worker" status, and other incentives.[86]

Individual responsibility and managerial authority are seen as important elements in industrial modernization, but the key to advancement via science and technology is through employment of "scientific management techniques."[87] Managers have been enjoined to study foreign management techniques, including those of capitalist countries.[88] Inventory control, flexibility in scheduling, ability to grant bonuses and impose sanctions, and authority to make a wide range of discretionary decisions without first consulting higher-level bodies have all been cited as examples of modern management.[89] The Academy of Social Sciences has established an Institute of Industrial Economics to study problems of management, and the first gray-suited M.B.A. candidates from China have already enrolled in U.S. business schools. The determination to strengthen management techniques seems real, but this will be another long and difficult process.

Managers will apparently have greater authority to reassign or even dismiss workers and technicians who fail to perform adequately. In addition to the daily performance data mentioned above, managers will soon have the results of annual skill and knowledge tests administered to all workers.[90] These tests are supposed to encompass both skill in the workshop and technical knowledge relative to on-the-job performance. The fact that people must pass these tests in order to retain their positions is a strong inducement to attend and take seriously the spare-time classes designed to raise skill levels and understanding of more advanced techniques and equipment.

Other incentives and sanctions are available to both managers and higher-level authorities. For example, if enterprises consistently fail to produce high quality products or to attain planned targets, large portions of managers' salaries may be retained by the state until the situation improves.[91] Unprofitable or badly run enterprises may be temporarily or permanently closed down.[92] It is not clear what would happen to workers, technical personnel, or management in such enterprises, but presumably fear of losing jobs and being reassigned to less convenient and possibly less satisfactory posts will induce all employees to do their utmost to avoid such a possibility.

Individual incentives in the form of bonuses and wages based on piecework have been reinstated, but we do not yet know the details of how they are to work in practice.[93] It appears, however, that a sizeable percentage of the workforce will receive bonuses of some kind.[94] Not all incentives take the form of cash awards; symbolic rewards such as model worker status and red banners for particular workshops or shifts are still an important part of the Chinese industrial scene.

Management remains a very formidable problem in the P.R.C., but the present leadership seems determined to strengthen this "key link" as quickly as possible. Several concrete steps have been taken toward this end, and most entail substantial copying of foreign practices. In no other area have the calls to emulate and learn from the experiences of advanced foreign firms been as explicit as on the question of management science. The starting point seems to be that capitalist enterprises are nothing if not concerned with maximizing speed and efficiency. Since the record indicates that these enterprises have done far better than any of the experiments attempted in China, leaders seem to have concluded that it is prudent to study their experiences. In this case, "study" seems to mean adopting their techniques.

Financial Policies

Three measures have been announced to help solve the problem of providing adequate funding for industrial S & T. One is the granting of loans and investment funds to individual enterprises.[95] Foreign exchange has been turned over to some enterprises so that they can purchase technologies abroad.[96] Central ministries have allocated money for the purchase of domestically produced equipment and upgrading of facilities. In addition, it appears that more central funds are earmarked for research and development and that much of that money will be used for industrial R & D.

A second measure has been to modify requirements governing the use of profits retained by individual enterprises. In at least some industries, up to 10 percent of retained funds are to be used for product improvement.[97] Although policies are still not clear, at least not to this observer, it appears that profitable enterprises may be permitted to retain an increasingly large share of the profits if they demonstrate effective use of these funds. If this is correct, it should serve as an important incentive and facilitator for advances in industrial S & T.

The final policy affecting the amount of money available for industrial S & T involves changing the pricing system to insure that enterprises are able to recover the costs of new product development in a reasonable amount of time. Discussions of the labor theory of value have devoted considerable attention to allowing research institutes and industrial laboratories to pass the cost of R & D on to those who benefit from their work.[98] In the past, enterprises have often had little incentive to develop new products because to do so made it more, rather than less, difficult to earn profits for the state, the enterprise, and for distribution in the form of bonuses. This is supposed to change, but it is not yet clear precisely what the change will entail.

Summary and Prognosis

Beginning in late 1977, China's leaders launched a broad and multipart program to upgrade the country's industrial science and technology. Each of the parts has been formulated with at least two objectives in mind, namely, to facilitate rapid and sustained industrial modernization and to enhance the political appeal of current policies. The first of these objectives provides both the starting point and the integrating theme for all of the policies discussed above. Rapid modernization has been accorded overriding importance, and industrial modernization is seen as crucial to the success of that effort. To achieve industrial modernization, advances must be made in science and technology, and it is toward that objective that specific policies have been adopted in areas ranging from ideological education to the training and placement of skilled personnel. Each of the policy areas summarized in this chapter (attitudinal, organizational, technical, manpower, managerial, and financial) reflects conscious decisions on the part of central leaders to do all that is necessary to insure both short-term and long-term advances in industrial S & T.

The second objective entails considerations that are almost

without precedent in the P.R.C. In addition to the various mass campaigns to shape cadre and mass attitudes toward the current program through combinations of education and intimidation, the leadership has taken a number of concrete steps to increase support for its policies. For example, by moving cautiously on the organizational front, officials appear to have considered the danger of opposition from entrenched interests in the bureaucracy. By strengthening curricula at all levels of the school system and increasing the number of mobility paths, they have attempted to make policies that are inherently elitist somewhat more palatable to the general public. By promising higher incomes and more consumer goods, they have attempted to sweeten the demand for tighter worker discipline and the need to adjust to new technologies. The list could be extended, but the point is simply that modernizing leaders have drawn lessons from the past and have attempted to head off immediate criticism of the current program. In doing so, they have promised a great deal to each of several interests or constituencies. They must deliver on those promises in fairly short order if they are to retain the support of skeptics and those who legitimately feel disadvantaged by the program.

This combination of maximum effort to achieve rapid modernization and high risk of political (if not economic) failure gives the current program the first of the characteristics noted in the introduction. Policy failure is often a matter of perception, and it is possible (perhaps even probable) that the benefits of current programs will not accrue quickly or visibly enough to satisfy doubters or political rivals.[99] If that happens, present leaders may be blamed for failure even though the program as a whole demonstrates substantial viability. Such an eventuality would probably produce changes of personnel without major shifts of policy. There may well be a kind of technological imperative driving China down a road similar to that traversed by other modernized and modernizing states. If so, leadership changes will become increasingly less significant to the policy-making process.

The second general characteristic noted in the introduction (i.e., awareness of the myriad interconnected factors that impinge on industrial science and technology) is reflected in essentially all of the articles and speeches on modernization that have appeared in recent months. This chapter could have included long quotations to demonstrate the linkages among policy areas and the integrating theme of the Four Modernizations, but I believe that the discussions of specific policies and their objectives make the point sufficiently clear. Hua, Teng, and others in the elite seem to have a relatively clear sense of the total situation. If they fail, it will not be for failure to appreciate that what one does (or does not do) in ancillary policy areas is often more important than steps taken on central questions.

For more than twenty years P.R.C. leaders have attempted to strike a proper balance between centralization and decentralization, tight planning and market socialism, and other factors shaping industrial development. The current program combines elements from both aspects of these dialectical pairs and argues the need for avoiding one-sided solutions. This is a familiar refrain to students of the P.R.C., and it is still too soon to determine whether the present version will be substantially different from or more successful than those of earlier periods. To begin to ascertain differences and similarities, we need to examine each of the policy elements outlined here in much greater detail.

Notes

1. On the importance of industrial modernization to the realization of "Chairman Mao's . . . grand plan for building a powerful, modern socialist country," see Yü Ch'iu-li, "Mobilize the Whole Party and the Nation's Working Class and Strive to Build Tach'ing-Type Enterprises Throughout the Country" (Report at the National Conference, Learn from Tach'ing in Industry, May 4, 1977), *Jen-min jih-pao* [People's daily] (hereafter *JMJP*), May 8, 1977, especially section 4, pp. 2–3. This speech is translated in Foreign Broadcast Information Service (hereafter FBIS), *Daily Report: People's Republic of China*, May 9, 1977, pp. E5–26. Also see editorial, "Conscientiously Study and Resolutely Implement the 'Thirty-Point [Decision] on Industry,'" *JMJP*, July 4, 1978.

2. For a comprehensive overview of the current program, see Hua Kuo-feng, "Unite and Strive to Build a Modern, Powerful, Socialist Country" (Report on the Work of the Government delivered at the

First Session of the Fifth National People's Congress, February 26, 1978), *JMJP*, March 7, 1978, especially pp. 2–4. This speech is translated in *Peking Review* (hereafter *PR*), no. 10 (March 10, 1978), pp. 7–40.

3. This point is developed further in Thomas Fingar, "Domestic Policies and the Quest for Independence," in Thomas Fingar and the Stanford Journal of International Studies, eds., *China's Quest for Independence: Policy Evolution in the 1970s* (Boulder, Colorado: Westview Press, 1980). For more general treatment of the risks of rising expectations and politically induced change, see Chalmers Johnson, *Revolutionary Change* (Boston: Little, Brown, 1966); and Chandler Morse et al., *Modernization by Design* (Ithaca: Cornell University Press, 1969).

4. The literal definition of "maxi-max" strategies is: those strategies that accept maximum risks in order to achieve maximum results. In practice, few leaders are willing to take such high risks and must scale down their expectations accordingly. For a general discussion of the strategy and its advantages to leaders in developing states, see Yehezkel Dror, *Public Policymaking Reexamined* (San Francisco: Chandler, 1968).

5. Although the broad outlines of the speech were discussed by Liu Shao-ch'i at the Second Session of the Eighth National Congress of the Communist Party of China in 1958, and an unofficial version of the address was published during the Cultural Revolution, the first official publication was in *JMJP*, December 26, 1976 (translated in *PR*, no. 1 [January 1, 1977], pp. 10–25). The need to set clear priorities in the pursuit of multiple objectives was affirmed in commentaries on "On the Ten Major Relationsips" broadcast by Peking Radio (sixteen broadcasts) and Shanghai Radio (eleven broadcasts) in January–March 1977. Translations of these commentaries are available in copies of FBIS published between February 7 and March 14, 1977.

6. The sense of urgency underlying pronouncements on the need for industrial modernization is apparent in Yü Ch'iu-li's speech at the 1977 Tach'ing conference.

> Only when industry develops faster will it be possible to push the entire nation forward rapidly and strengthen the material basis for consolidating the dictatorship of the proletariat. And only when industry develops faster will it be possible to better carry out the strategic policy "Be prepared against war, be prepared against natural disasters, and do everything for the people," strengthen our national defense capabilities, and be well prepared against a war of aggression. The question of speed in industry concerns the victory of the proletariat over the bourgeoisie and of socialism over capitalism, and concerns the future and destiny of

> our country. . . . We must fully understand this and never waste time which is so precious to us. We must seize every minute and second, work with tremendous exertion to make up for the losses caused by the "gang of four" and exert every ounce of energy to accelerate the rate of industrial growth.

Yü Ch'iu-li, supra note 1 (translated in *PR*, no. 22 [May 27, 1977], pp. 17–18). Also see Ku Mu, "Talk to Young Comrades on the Four Modernizations," *Chung-kuo ch'ing-nien pao* [China youth news], January 4, 1979, as broadcast by Peking Radio on January 27, 1979 (translated in FBIS, February 5, 1979, pp. E10–11).

7. The importance of changing the way people think (through education, indoctrination, and implementation of the "mass line") is fundamental to the style of leadership practiced in the P.R.C. See, for example, Martin King Whyte, *Small Groups and Political Rituals in China* (Berkeley: University of California Press, 1974), especially Chapter 2; James R. Townsend, *Political Participation in Communist China* (Berkeley: University of California Press, 1969), especially Chapter 4; and John Wilson Lewis, *Leadership in Communist China* (Ithaca: Cornell University Press, 1963), especially Chapter 3.

8. Commentator, "Adapt Our Thinking to the Requirements of Modernization," *JMJP*, August 29, 1978 (translated in FBIS, September 8, 1978, pp. E13–15).

9. Examples include Commentator, "Can Implementation of Policy Be Called Deviation to the 'Right'?" *Kuang-ming jih-pao* [Illumination daily] (hereafter *KMJP*), July 9, 1978; and editorial, "One Cannot Be Indifferent About Not Using What One Has Learned," *KMJP*, July 13, 1978.

10. Commentary, "Pay Attention to Teaching Cadres about Policy," *JMJP*, July 13, 1978; and Hsieh Tien-pin and Chang Lei-k'o, "Do Not Become a 'Man in a Straitjacket,'" *JMJP*, November 1, 1978.

11. The need to reassure cadres and the populace as a whole that policies would not change dramatically in the near future seems to have been one of the reasons underlying the decision of the Third Plenum to shift the emphasis in Party work from criticism of the Gang of Four to the pursuit of socialist modernization. See, for example, editorial, "Shift the Emphasis of the Whole Party's Work to Modernization," *JMJP*, December 25, 1978.

12. This is implied in Commentator, "Commenting on the So-called 'Expert Line,'" *KMJP*, October 20, 1978.

13. See "Adapt Our Thinking to the Requirements of Modernization," supra note 8; and Ni Chih-fu, "The Great New Historic Mission

of the Chinese Working Class" (report delivered at the Ninth National Trade Union Congress, October 12, 1978), *JMJP*, October 16, 1978, especially p. 3.

14. Examples include Commentator, "Quickly Raise the Level of Enterprise Management," *JMJP*, July 13, 1978; "It Is Necessary to Let the Entire Party Be Aware of the Immense Importance of Managerial Skills," Liaoning Radio, August 7, 1978 (translated in FBIS, August 11, 1978, pp. L2–6); and Li Chih-sheng, "Use Management Methods to Achieve Victory," *KMJP*, November 4, 1978.

15. See, for example, Li Hsien-nien, "Speech at the Opening Session of the National Conference on Learning from Tach'ing and Tachai in Finance and Trade Work" (June 20, 1978), *JMJP*, June 27, 1978, especially section 1; and Hu Ch'iao-mu, "Act in Accordance with Economic Laws, Speed-up Realization of the Four Modernizations," *JMJP*, October 6, 1978.

16. See "Continue the Battle to Improve Product Quality" (State Economic Commission Circular), *JMJP*, October 10, 1978; and Hsi Cheng-yung, "Introduction to Quality Control in Foreign Countries," *KMJP*, October 21, 1978. Inadequate feedback mechanisms and the failure of manufacturers to benefit from design modifications made by end-users have been noted by several technical visitors to the P.R.C. See, for example, Genevieve C. Dean and Fred Chernow, *The Choice of Technology in the Electronics Industry of the People's Republic of China: The Fabrication of Semiconductors* (Palo Alto, Calif: Stanford University, United States–China Relations Program, 1978), pp. 61–65.

17. See, for example, Fang Yi, "The Working Class Must Strive to Master Modern Science and Technology," *KMJP*, November 14, 1978.

18. This point is made in virtually all articles and reports on the Four Modernizations. See, for example, editorial, "Study and Apply Advanced Foreign Experience," *JMJP*, November 3, 1978.

19. Prohibitive cost is only one of the factors limiting China's capacity to import advanced equipment and technologies; the inability to absorb massive imports of technology is a more serious constraint. Advanced technologies require skilled managers, engineers, technicians, and workmen as well as guaranteed supplies of raw materials, power, and other inputs. Experience around the world has shown that it is far from easy to absorb or "digest" technologies. Knowledge of this fact will have a restraining influence; as difficulties develop, imports will be limited even further.

20. See, for example, Commentator, "Study, Use, and Manage Imported Technology and Equipment," *JMJP*, October 19, 1978.

21. Ching Wen, "Importing Technology Must Not Follow A Single Pattern,'" *KMJP*, December 2, 1978.

22. Examples include Ni Chih-fu, supra note 13; and Yüan Pao-hua (vice-minister of the State Economic Commission), "Raising the Technical Level of Staff Members and Workers Is a Pressing Task," *JMJP*, August 12, 1978.

23. Ni Chih-fu, supra note 13; and Yüan Pao-hua, supra note 22.

24. See Hua Kuo-feng, supra note 2, especially p. 4; "Actively Develop '21 July' Universities for Training More Qualified and Capable People," *KMJP*, April 5, 1978; and Lu Lin, "Raise the Scientific and Cultural Level of the Entire Nation," *JMJP*, June 23, 1978.

25. See "It is Necessary," supra note 14; Commentator, "Management and Technology Should Be Imported Simultaneously," *KMJP*, February 10, 1979; and the State Council Circular of April 26, 1978, on strengthening management, increasing profits, and reducing losses. The April 26 Circular is discussed in "Enterprise Management, the Virtue of Profits, and the Irrationality of Losses," *JMJP*, April 29, 1979.

26. As used here, the term "rhetorical policies" refers to statements about policy carried in P.R.C. media during the period when it was under the control of the Gang of Four. Rhetorical policies can differ from both the formal measures adopted by authoritative bodies and from the actual policies implemented by subordinate officials. Rhetorical policies, like campaign rhetoric, are often exaggerated statements designed to mislead the reader. For a more detailed discussion, see Fingar, supra note 3.

27. To correct this shortcoming, officials reestablished the State Scientific and Technological Commission in early 1977 and directed the first secretaries of Party committees to assume responsibility for scientific and technical matters. See the "Central Committee Circular on Holding a National Science Conference" (September 18, 1977), *JMJP*, September 23, 1977. An English translation of the circular can be found in *PR*, no. 40 (September 30, 1977), pp. 6–11.

28. "Quickly Raise the Level," supra note 14 (translated in FBIS, July 21, 1978, pp. 11–13).

29. See, for example, "Design Institutes Should Be Enterprises, Not Establishments," New China News Agency (hereafter NCNA) Domestic Broadcast, January 22, 1979 (translated in FBIS, January 26, 1979, p. E25); and editorial, "It Is Necessary to Increase Enterprise Authority," *JMJP*, February 19, 1979.

30. Hu Ch'iao-mu, supra note 15, section 3.

31. For example, Commentator, "Hasten the Popularization and Application of Scientific Research Achievements," *KMJP*, November 1, 1978.

32. "Study, Use, and Manage," supra note 20 (translated in FBIS, October 27, 1978, pp. E25–26).

33. See, for example, "Can Implementation of Policy," supra note 9.

34. The three stages of the campaign to expose and criticize Lin Piao and the Gang of Four are summarized in "Mass Criticism of Lin Biao [Lin Piao] and the 'Gang of Four' Winds Up," *Beijing Review*,no. 3 (January 19, 1979), pp. 4–5.

35. See, for example, "Adapt Our Thinking," supra note 8.

36. See, for example, Hsieh Ying-lei, "Leading Cadres Must Learn Science and Technology," *JMJP*, April 27, 1978.

37. Examples include Chao Tzu-yang (first secretary, Szechwan CCP Committee), who attended a series of lectures on science and technology (Peking Radio, May 3, 1978 [translated in FBIS, May 8, 1978, p. J1]); and Wu Nan-sheng (secretary, Kwangtung CCP Committee), who presided at a science meeting for provincial officials (Kwangtung Radio, May 13, 1978 [translated in FBIS, May 17, 1978, pp. H5–6]).

38. See "Communiqué of the Third Plenum of the Eleventh Central Committee of the Chinese Communist Party," *JMJP*, December 24, 1978 (translated in *PR*, no. 52 [December 29, 1978], pp. 6–16), and "Shift the Emphasis," supra note 11.

39. Editorial, "Let the Whole Party Struggle with One Heart and the Country Struggle with a Single Will to Realize Socialist Modernization," *Hung-ch'i* [Red flag] (hereafter *HC*), no. 1 (January 1979), pp. 22–26. Much of the discussion of "democratic centralism" has centered on Mao's 1962 address at an enlarged working conference convened by the CCP Central Committee. The speech was published officially for the first time on June 30, 1978, in *HC*, no. 7 (July 1978) and republished the next day in all major Chinese newspapers. An English translation is in *PR*, no. 27 (July 7, 1978), pp. 6–22. For a typical commentary on the speech, see Ma Wen-jui, "Restore and Carry Forward the Fine Tradition of Democratic Centralism," *HC*, no. 7 (July 1978), pp. 43–50.

40. On the key role of the Party, see for example "Party Committees Must Be Good at Leading Scientific and Technical Work," *HC*, no. 4 (April 1978), pp. 48–53; and the Liaoning Radio Broadcast of September 26, 1977 (translated in FBIS, September 30, 1977, p. L3). On the need to recruit more scientists and technical personnel into the Party, see "Pay Great Attention to the Work of Recruiting Party Members From Among Scientists and Technicians," *JMJP*, July 3, 1978.

41. Efforts to end mistreatment of intellectuals and to enroll them in the drive for modernization began almost immediately after the ar-

rest of the Gang of Four. Typical expositions of current policy include Shen K'o-ting, "Refuting the 'Gang of Four's' Theory of the 'Stinking Ninth Category,'" *HC*, no. 7 (July 1977), pp. 55–62; and Teng Hsiao-p'ing, "Speech at the Opening Ceremony of the National Science Conference," *JMJP*, March 22, 1978 (translated in *PR*, no. 12 [March 24, 1978], pp. 9–18).

42. See Li Hsien-nien, supra note 15; NCNA broadcasts on the re-organization of the First Ministry of Machine Building excerpted in FBIS, June 21, 1978, pp. E5–7, and FBIS, August 29, 1978, pp. E1–2; and Chi Ti, "Bring About Industrial Modernization," *JMJP*, May 23, 1978.

43. On standardization and quality control, see for example Hsi Cheng-yung, supra note 16.

44. See Li Chih-sheng, supra note 14; and Commentator, "Strive for Rapid Development of the National Economy," *HC*, no. 1 (January 1978), pp. 11–15.

45. Re-creation of the large economic regions was first announced at the 1977 National Conference, Learn from Tach'ing in Industry. See Yü Ch'iu-li, supra note 1, section 4. Regional planning forums were reported by NCNA in a domestic broadcast of May 21, 1978 (translated in FBIS, May 24, 1978, pp. E1–2).

46. Ch'ien Min, "The Rate of Industrial Development in Old Industrial Cities Can Be Stepped-up Considerably," *JMJP*, February 18, 1978; and the NCNA broadcast of August 27, 1978, excerpted in FBIS, August 29, 1978, pp. E1–2.

47. See the Hunan Radio report of preparations for the National Science Conference summarized in FBIS, October 17, 1977, pp. H1–2; and Genevieve Dean and Thomas Fingar, *Developments in PRC Science and Technology Policy, October–December 1977* (Palo Alto, Calif: United States–China Relations Program, 1978), pp. 21–23, and the references cited therein.

48. See "Begin to Implement the 'Thirty-Point [Decision] on Industry' Throughout the Country," *JMJP*, July 4, 1978; and "Strive for Rapid Development," supra note 44.

49. For a discussion of the factors that delayed implementation of this strategy, see Fingar, "Domestic Policies," supra note 3.

50. See "It is Necessary to Increase," supra note 29.

51. Ibid.

52. For general discussions invoking the authority of Sun Yat-sen and Lenin, see Lo Yao-chiu, "Sun Yat-sen's Views on Accelerating Development of the National Economy," *KMJP*, December 31, 1978;

and T'ung Chih-min, "How Did Lenin View the Introduction of Advanced Technology and the Admission of Foreign Capital?," *KMJP*, August 18, 1978. Also see Ching Wen, supra note 21, and the Hong Kong report of a speech purportedly delivered by Li Hsien-nien in September 1978 in Liang Yüan, "The Nine Principles of Importing Technology and Equipment into the PRC," *Ch'i-shih nien-tai* [The seventies], no. 109 (February 1979), p. 20 (translated in FBIS, February 27, 1979, pp. N5–6).

53. Programmatic statements and announced plans indicate a desire to enter the world market in a big way, but difficulties have already begun to force officials to slow the pace of technology imports. See, for example, Tracy Dahlby, "Peking's Delay Worries Japan," *Far Eastern Economic Review* 103, no. 11 (March 16, 1979):108–109.

54. Importing technology to meet developmental objectives is not a new policy in the P.R.C. See Robert F. Dernberger, "Economic Development and Modernization in Contemporary China: The Attempt to Limit Dependence on the Transfer of Modern Industrial Technology from Abroad and to Control its Corruption of the Maoist Social Revolution," in Frederic J. Fleron, Jr., ed., *Technology and Communist Culture* (New York: Praeger, 1977), pp. 224–264. For a recent Chinese statement on this point, see Ching Wen, supra note 21.

55. Commentator, "Redouble Our Efforts to Solve the Problem of Scientists and Technicians in Unrelated Jobs," *JMJP*, May 6, 1978; and "Grasp and Resolve the Problem of People Working in the Wrong Jobs," *KMJP*, October 19, 1978.

56. See "Hasten the Popularization," supra note 31; and "Continue the Battle," supra note 16.

57. See, for example, "Implement a Strict System of Technical Responsibility," *KMJP*, July 7, 1978.

58. Royalties for research units were proposed by Minister of Commerce Yao I-lin in an interview with reporters that was broadcast by NCNA on November 8, 1978 (translated in FBIS, November 13, 1978, pp. E11–14).

59. See "Design Institutes," supra note 29.

60. See Hsi Cheng-yung, supra note 16; "Study and Apply," supra note 18; and the report of an interview with Sung Chi-wen (vice-minister of Light Industry), broadcast by Shanghai Radio on January 21, 1979 (translated in FBIS, January 22, 1979, pp. E15–16).

61. See "State Council Circular on the Revised 'Regulations on Rewards for Inventions,'" *JMJP*, January 17, 1979.

62. For a comparison of Soviet and Chinese procedures for rewarding technical innovations and comments on how little was known about Chinese practice in earlier periods, see Rensselaer W. Lee, III, "Mass Innovation and Communist Culture: The Soviet and Chinese Cases," in Fleron, *Technology and Communist Culture*, pp. 265–311.

63. "Innovation," as used by the Chinese, suggests modification of existing practice to produce greater efficiency or production of a new product using different techniques. This chapter follows Chinese usage rather than the more specialized definition of an innovation as the successful development of a new product or process through stages beginning with discovery and continuing through serial production or adoption of the new process as standard procedure.

64. See, for example, "Management and Technology," supra note 25; and "Study and Apply," supra note 18.

65. The importance of developing computers and software was affirmed by Fang Yi in his report at the National Science Conference (delivered on March 18, 1978). An abridged version of the report was published in *JMJP* on March 29, 1978 (translated in FBIS, March 29, 1978, pp. 1–22). See also the interview with Sung Chi-wen, supra note 60.

66. Information on the First Ministry of Machine Building's effort to develop a program in systems engineering was provided by a Canadian citizen hired by the ministry to help design the program.

67. At the National Science Conference in March 1978, Fang Yi announced the goal of raising the number of professional research personnel (including engineers and industrial R & D personnel) to 800,000 by 1985. See Fang Yi, supra note 65. On the general situation, see Scientific and Technological Committee of Shashih Municipality, "Actively Develop Scientific and Technological Work According to the Characteristics of Small Cities," *KMJP*, March 24, 1978; and "Intensify Technical Training," *JMJP*, October 4, 1978.

68. "Relevant Department Answers *Jen-min jih-pao* Reporter's Questions About the Survey of Scientific and Technical Personnel," *JMJP*, September 3, 1978; and the NCNA English release of October 29, 1978, reprinted in FBIS, November 2, 1978, p. E17.

69. See, for example, "Redouble Our Efforts," supra note 55; and "Grasp and Resolve," supra note 55.

70. Officials of the Chinese Academy of Sciences provided this assessment during my October 1978 visit to Peking. Their analysis confirmed the assessment given by several members of technical delegations from China who visited the United States in 1977–1979.

71. The policy of allowing technical personnel to spend five-sixths

of their time on professional work was announced in the Central Committee Circular on Holding a National Science Conference, supra note 27. See also editorial, "On Five-Sixths of the Time," *KMJP*, July 16, 1978.

72. See for example, Theoretical Group of the Ministry of Education, "It Is Imperative to Run a Group of Key Schools Well," *KMJP*, January 13, 1978. The role of ministries in running middle schools and colleges was discussed at length with officials of the Ministry of Education and the Chinese Academy of sciences during my October 1978 trip to Peking.

73. The national entrance examination is discussed in the NCNA domestic broadcast of June 13, 1978 (translated in FBIS, June 19, 1978, pp. E16–19).

74. This information was obtained in discussions with officials of the Chinese Academy of Sciences in Peking.

75. See, for example, "Grasp Well the Running of Different Types of Schools," *KMJP*, December 18, 1977; and "Actively Develop," supra note 24.

76. See Kwangtung Provincial Education Bureau, "Run Spare-Time Education Even Better," *Kwang-tung jih-pao* [Kwangtung daily], April 24, 1978 (translated in FBIS, May 8, 1978, pp. E19–20); and "Intensify Technical Training," supra note 67.

77. See, for example, Li Chih-sheng, supra note 14; and "It Is Necessary," supra note 14.

78. Plans to abolish most revolutionary committees were first reported by Kyodo News Service on November 15, 1977 (reproduced in FBIS, November 15, 1977, pp. E1–2). Formal confirmation was provided by Hua Kuo-feng in his address to the First Session of the Fifth National People's Congress. He affirmed that,

> With the exception of those factories, mines or other enterprises where government administration is integrated with management, factories, production brigades, schools and colleges, shops, Party and government organizations and other enterprises and establishments will no longer set up revolutionary committees inasmuch as they do not form a level of government. In lieu of revolutionary committees, a system of division of responsibilities should be adopted with factory directors, production brigade leaders, school principals, college presidents, and managers taking charge under the leadership of Party committees.

See Hua Kuo-feng, supra note 2 (the translation is from *PR*, no. 10 [March 10, 1978] p. 32). Discussions with factory managers in various Chinese cities confirmed that revolutionary committees either had been or would be dismantled within weeks after Hua had delivered his report to the Fifth NPC.

79. See, for example, Teng Hsiao-p'ing, supra note 41; "Party Committees Must," supra note 40; and the report of Pai Ju-ping's speech to the Shantung Provincial Science Conference broadcast by Shantung Radio on May 15, 1978 (excerpted in FBIS, May 19, 1978, pp. G5–10, especially p. G9).

80. At the National Science Conference, Teng Hsiao-p'ing announced that he would take principal responsibility for logistical work in support of science and technology at the same time that he reaffirmed the leading role of Party committees. See Teng, supra note 41; and Hsü Chia-tun's report to the Kiangsu Provincial Science Conference as broadcast by Kiangsu Radio on May 19, 1978 (excerpted in FBIS, May 25, 1978, pp. G1–8, especially p. G7).

81. On the role of the trade unions, see Ni Chih-fu, supra note 13, especially p. 4. Information on Party groups for each shift and workshop was obtained on visits to factories in Harbin, Shenyang, and Shanghai in March 1978.

82. See "It Is Necessary," supra note 14; and "Quickly Raise," supra note 14.

83. See the speech by K'ang Shih-en to a Peking rally on "Quality Month" activities in industry broadcast by Peking Radio on August 31, 1978 (excerpted in FBIS, September 1, 1978, pp. E2–4); "Quickly Raise," supra note 14; and "Continue the Battle," supra note 16.

84. See Hsiao Liang and Chang Wen-min, "Improve the Bonus System, Give Full Play to the Role of Bonuses," *KMJP*, November 11, 1978; Ma P'iao, "Conscientiously Implement the Principle of Material Benefits," *KMJP*, October 21, 1978; and "Continue the Battle," supra note 16.

85. Data on individual worker performance were obtained during visits to factories in March 1978. Also see, K'ang Shih-en, supra note 83.

86. Information obtained during my March 1978 trip to China.

87. See Wu Chia-p'ei, "Economic Results and Economic Management," *KMJP*, August 12, 1978; and Li Chih-sheng, supra note 14.

88. Chiang Hsüeh-mo, "Talk on Learning From Enterprise Management in Capitalist Countries," *KMJP*, September 23, 1978; Li Chih-sheng, supra note 14; and Sung Chi-wen, supra note 60.

89. See, for example, "It Is Necessary to Increase," supra note 29.

90. See Yüan Pao-hua, supra note 22.

91. See, for example, "Continue the Battle," supra note 16.

92. See, for example, the NCNA English report of K'ang Shih-en's

comments at a meeting of the State Economic Commission as reproduced in FBIS, September 25, 1978, pp. E2–3.

93. See the Tientsin Radio broadcast of September 2, 1978, excerpted in FBIS, September 8, 1978, pp. K3–4; and Hsiao Liang and Chang Wen-min, supra note 84.

94. Commentator, "The Practice of Rashly Giving Bonuses Must Be Corrected," *JMJP*, January 25, 1979.

95. See, for example, the editor's note, entitled "Make Credit Loans Selectively," *JMJP*, January 25, 1979.

96. See the NCNA English release of September 15, 1978, reproduced in FBIS, September 19, 1978, p. E9.

97. For a report of 10 percent of retained profits being applied to research and development, see *Report of a Visit to the People's Republic of China by the Stanford International Security and Arms Control Group* (Palo Alto, Calif: United States–China Relations Program, 1978), p. 5.

98. For example, Ma P'iao, supra note 84.

99. The February 13, 1979, editorial in *JMJP* cautioned that living standards would have to be raised gradually. It is possible that people have already begun to demand concrete benefits from the modernization program, but it is also possible that the editorial was designed to blunt such demands before they could develop very far. See "Workers' Living Standards Must Be Improved Gradually on the Basis of Production Growth," *JMJP*, February 13, 1979.

4
A Note on Recent Policy Changes

Genevieve C. Dean

China's strategy for technological modernization is to "concentrate all forces to fight a battle of annihilation." Since 1977, the country's economic planners have made a series of decisions to implement this strategy. Having identified energy, raw materials, communications, and transport as "weak links" restricting industrial growth,[1] a high priority is given to the equipping of these sectors with more efficient technologies. The reason for focusing initial efforts on these critical sectors is to enable China's industry to attain advanced world levels of productivity as quickly as possible and to catch up with technological advances made elsewhere during the past ten years. Accordingly, the State Planning Commission has catalogued some sixty "new techniques" for dissemination to "key points throughout the country" by 1980.[2]

These new techniques will have to be imported because events since 1966 have left few new technologies in China's R & D pipeline and the lead time from research to usable technology is too long to meet urgent industrial needs. After the initial "battle of annihilation," however, a policy of import substitution will come into effect. From then on, the 120 "large-scale basic industrial projects" scheduled for construction in the Ten-Year Plan (1976–1985) for economic development will be the "key to developing the national economy."[3] Further growth and technological advance will then depend primarily on these key industries.

The decision to import industrial technology on a vastly increased scale is among the more sensational policy changes

China's new leaders have made. But this is basically a crash program for catching up with an earlier timetable, not a new approach to technological development—the dramatic contrast with previous policy notwithstanding. With allowances for differences in the sources of imported technologies and adjustment for different rates of investment, basic elements of current policy are similar to those in China's First Five-Year Plan (1953–1957): initial concentration of highly efficient, imported technologies in a "key" industrial sector, with minimal investment outside this sector until domestic industry can supply capital goods embodying new technologies. Nor has the ultimate goal of development plans changed. China apparently still intends to build a "complete" modern industrial system, though the time horizon may be longer now than first envisioned.

Technology policy includes more than the acquisition of technology, however. Ultimately it concerns *innovation:* inducing and then sustaining an ongoing process of technical and technological change that, in industrially advanced countries, is the basis of economic growth. Only part of such change is realized by adopting totally new technology. Economic growth also results from a flow of rather prosaic improvements in technologies already in use; these innovations are economically significant, though they may be technologically unspectacular. Technology policy extends to the ways in which policymakers try to influence the flow of such incremental improvements.[4]

So broad is the scope of technology policy that one author has recently sidestepped the problem of definition by identifying, instead, topics of science and technology policy research. These topics have a broad range, including weighing the costs and benefits of acquiring known technology against the risks involved in trying to develop new technology, discovering what determines the "innovativeness" of industrial enterprises and their readiness to develop new inventions or research results into usable technologies, and assessing the economic and social consequences of alternative technologies.[5] Coincidentally, the chairman of China's State Planning Commission has also referred to "technical policy" in terms of innovation-related problems needing study and solution: "the questions of encouraging inventions and adopting new techniques . . . and of introducing necessary advanced technical equipment and patented techniques from abroad more economically and effectively."[6]

Technology Policy in China

The lack of a systematic Chinese approach to the problem of technological innovation is one theme of this chapter. Given the underdeveloped condition of social science generally in China, it is no surprise that recent P.R.C. policy seems based on a premise now largely rejected in Western technology policy studies: innovation—"innovativeness"—is inherent in modern technology and transferable in machines bought from advanced countries. In line with this rather simplistic premise, China's current policymakers seem to maintain a belief in the cultural and social neutrality of institutional structures for scientific research and management. In their view, technology and the dynamics of technological change are "classless" and operate in the same way in all societies, regardless of institutional structure.

Despite recent Chinese professions of faith in the inherent transferability of technological innovativeness,[7] massive import of advanced technology in the 1950s did not automatically make Chinese industry innovative. On the contrary, twenty years later, industrial labor productivity "remains at the levels of the 1940s and 1950s," with the biggest gap between Chinese and the best (foreign) practice ironically occurring in "newer," more advanced industries.[8]

China's industrial growth during the Great Leap Forward resulted "entirely or for the most part" from investment in additional means of production rather than from increasingly efficient use of existing facilities.[9] This critical neglect of productivity-raising measures resulted in the virtual stagnation of technical innovation in many industries. In order to remedy this historical defect, China's newly rehabilitated social scientists have recently begun to focus their attention on industrial management and organization as major issues in technology policy, viewing these factors as prime variables in the generation of productivity-raising innovation.

However, the empirical evidence apparently has not yet led

the Chinese to reexamine their premise that innovativeness is inherently transferable in modern technology and related institutions. Indeed, in comments published in October 1978, the head of the new Chinese Academy of Social Sciences, Hu Ch'iao-mu, seemingly endorsed this premise in recommending that China import management techniques from countries with high levels of productivity—i.e., from capitalist countries, where "highly efficient" systems have evolved to manage production in accordance with "objective economic laws," which, it is said, also apply to enterprises in China's socialist economy. Hu further asserted that the experience of "developed capitalist countries" shows that industrial specialization is "an inevitable law governing modern mass production" and an "inevitable trend in modern industrial development."[10]

Two Approaches to Technological Planning

In taking this position, Hu Ch'iao-mu restated the arguments on one side of a policy debate that was in full swing some fifteen years earlier. That debate stemmed from China's disillusionment with Soviet institutional patterns following the P.R.C.'s First Five-Year Plan, the abortive attempt during the Great Leap Forward to compensate for shortcomings in the Soviet model, and the political and ideological rift between the two countries after 1960. On one side were those who still advocated a centrally planned and coordinated industrial policy. But China by the early 1960s had entered an era in which, by comparison with the expansive 1950s, investment had to be stringently limited. Therefore, the other side in the debate argued for allocating modern capital goods (now in short supply) chiefly where they would be used more efficiently. In other words, they were for adopting planning methods that based technological decisions on current economic performance.

The latter approach implied selectively concentrating state investment and technological advance on those enterprises that were already most productive—i.e., "building on the best." The opposite view was that a state "technical policy" should comprehensively promote "the entire development of social production" across the spectrum. This, however, assumed a higher rate of capital investment than China could sustain after 1960 (as well as at least temporarily subsidizing unprofitable ventures), and hence the comprehensive approach had lost currency even before the Cultural Revolution began. Ironically, this approach could have generated the kind of systematic policy studies that might have challenged some of the premises on which present technological decisions in China seemingly are based.

According to its proponents, a comprehensive national technology policy would be based on "integrated technical economics."[11] Technical economics represented the socialist equivalent of engineering economics in capitalist systems. Unlike engineering economics, however, which were described as confined to "one enterprise or one group of monopoly capital," technical economics would "integrate" and interrelate the economic effects of technological choice in different sectors of the economy. Using such analyses (and taking advantage of socialized ownership of the means of production), state planners could allocate investment and technological change according to development priorities. Thus, it was argued, investment could be maximized in "key sectors" considered vital to long-range industrial development, but where a long period was necessary to recover investment costs and where current rates of capital formation were low.

However, integrated technical economics remained only a potential tool for investment planning. Though individual "departmental" studies of technical economics—i.e., studies conducted by various production departments, such as metallurgy, power, and machine building—had reportedly "spread very widely" by 1964, integrated technical economics required much more sophisticated methods of analysis and, in any case, was not pursued—given the immediate economic exigencies of the early 1960s. Had it been pursued, it might have become an important first step toward a concept of technology as part of a *system* and eventually toward some notion of *modern* technology—i.e., a total package of technologies, as a variable, to be adapted to specific economic and social parameters.

Instead, China's economists set out in the opposite direction, tailoring institutions to available technology. Hence they sought to identify and modify structures restricting innovation in Chinese industry. Under Sun Yeh-fang, then head of the Economics Research Institute (and later castigated as "China's Liberman"), the trend in economic thinking in the early 1960s was toward using some measure of current productivity—specifically, enterprise profit—as the criterion for investment. Introducing competition on such a basis into the allocation of new technology, it was expected, would provide an incentive for enterprise managers to maximize the productivity of their existing equipment, thus increasing output even before the state invested additional capital. One spin-off of the proposed system, therefore, would be a flow of "prosaic," minor, relatively inexpensive technical improvements upgrading current technology, initiated by individual enterprises as appropriate to the unique conditions in each. This kind of innovation, which by its nature cannot be centrally planned, would be particularly "economically significant" under the circumstances in China in the 1960s. (There had been some innovation of this sort, but it would seem that much of the incremental production capacity thus created was never registered with state planners, instead being kept by enterprise managers for more profitable production outside the economic plan. Consequently, to some extent inefficiency referred to underutilization of capacity for *planned* production, not to completely unexploited capacity.)

At this time, the economists began thrashing through the problems of adapting mechanisms of a centrally planned economy to the requirements of a new system that allowed enterprise managers greater scope in technical decision making. For example, there is a voluminous literature from this period on such questions as when renovation becomes innovation. Discussion concerned what degree of technical change could be financed out of maintenance and repair funds at the disposal of the enterprise manager, and what constituted capital investment requiring approval by state economic authorities; and how depreciation funds should properly be used to replace worn-out equipment with equipment embodying technical improvements, as opposed to investment in new technology. Essential to the proposed new planning system was a method of strict economic accounting, partly as a device to bring actual capacity (original designed capacity plus increments resulting from subsequent technical innovations made by the enterprise) into the scope of state economic plans. Understandably, enterprise managers tried to evade such measures.

Critics of this trend in economic policy charged that management responded to profit-maximizing pressures with demands for additional allocations of new plants and equipment and by diverting funds to unauthorized purchase of capital goods and not, as intended, by using their current technology more efficiently. Some of the later polemics accusing "bourgeois revisionist" enterprise managers of suppressing "worker innovation"—minor technical improvements—provide evidence of quite rational management behavior, given profit-maximizing incentives on the one hand and opportunities to manipulate the capital allocation system on the other. Thus, the lack of suitable administrative mechanisms (and, specifically, of a "strict system of accounting") meant that, though these measures accelerated technological advance and modernization they failed to confine such investment to the planners' development priorities and thus intensified China's capital shortage.

1978: Revival of an Earlier Approach

It is not clear how widely these proposals were ever adopted in practice nor how many of the problems headed off by the Cultural Revolution were real or anticipated. Now, fifteen years later, Hu Ch'iao-mu has restated virtually the same arguments in favor of economic rather than administrative mechanisms to manage industrial production, acknowledging shortcomings in the first experience but ignoring other consequences once condemned as incompatible with socialism. For Hu, the question is how to absorb modern technology: how to operate it with maximum efficiency and then make technical changes that increase its capacity still further. His answer is to adopt the institutions he sees as engendering innovativeness in technologically advanced economies—in capitalist systems, the profit-maximizing behavior of enterprises. Where advocates of a centralized technology policy once scorned engineering economics because it was limited to analyzing the economic costs and benefits of technology to a single monopoly, Hu Ch'iao-mu now endorses capitalist management techniques that optimize the plan of the individual enterprise.

The gist of the policy that has been emerging since the spring of 1978 is that productivity is a function of management as much as of technology and that enterprise profit is a measure of management efficiency. Thus a State Council circular announcing a "national conference of enterprises to strengthen management, stop losses, and increase profits" (April 26, 1978) asserted that:

> Our construction funds come mainly from increasing production and practicing economy and from accumulation within socialist enterprises. To a great extent the profit level of an enterprise depends on the success of its management.
>
> If an enterprise is not properly managed, it may . . . cause serious production loss and waste even though it possesses modern technical equipment.[12]

These are far from being proposals to replace economic planning with a market economy. Technology, production levels, production costs, and the kind and quantity of output are negotiated betweeen enterprise management and state planners and contractually fixed in annual economic plans.[13] Capital investment and allocation of new technology remain functions of state planning. Specific production or market conditions influence these decisions indirectly.[14] The scope of managerial discretion is limited to the operation of existing plant and equipment and to technical and other changes that make it more efficient and hence more profitable. Thus, according to Hu Ch'iao-mu, enterprise profit results from maintaining a steady pace of production—that is, coordinating different stages of production and eliminating bottlenecks in the supply of materials, parts, equipment, and labor—and from generally striving to reduce production costs. The latter requires enterprise managers to use both labor and capital more efficiently and especially to increase labor productivity as they adopt more capital-intensive technologies ("continuously achieve the optimum ratio between the costs of labor and materials . . . and the economic effect").[15]

Hu considers the experiments of the 1960s incomplete and insists they were terminated by political interference, not because of any inherent shortcomings, ideological or otherwise. He makes this explicit in connection with another reform revived in the Central Committee's "Thirty-Point Decision on Industrial Development" in April 1978: industrial reorganization along lines of specialization.

> In the early 1960s we made some attempts in this respect. We set up on a trial basis 13 specialized companies under the industrial and communications departments of the central government and also ran some others in certain provinces and municipalities. . . . Except those set up in Shanghai, all the other specialized companies operated for a short time.
>
> Despite interference by Liu Shao-chi and Chen Po-ta, coupled with inexperience as well as shortcomings and mistakes in work, these companies still played a certain role in promoting the development of production.[16]

Though Hu presents the case for specialization primarily in terms of its administrative advantages (specialization facilities "switching . . . the maximum volume of economic work" from the government bureaucracy to enterprises), he also cites both Marxist-Leninist canon and "the experience of developed capitalist countries" to show its implications for technology. According to Hu, "purely administrative methods" tend to put "administrative convenience" above economic rationality and require "mechanical" adaptation of "economic activities" to administrative structures. The result is duplication, red tape, and general inefficiency, giving rise to practices that circumvent the official economic system and planning controls.[17] "Specialization and coordination," Hu states, will "raise production technology and labor efficiency," improve product quality, and cut production costs and are "inevitable in modern mass production."[18]

Fifteen-year-old arguments spell out the technical superiority of specialized production over vertical integration in more concrete detail:

> 1. Less investment, more construction;
> 2. Higher productive efficiency;
> 3. Higher product quality;
> 4. Lower costs;
> 5. Ease in realization of product standardization, generalization, and systematization, facilitating . . . the development of a (variety of product) types;
> 6. The cadres and workers have an easier grasp of the techniques, rapid elevation in the level of technology, ease in development of new techniques; and
> 7. Mutual coordination between the small-, medium-, and large-sized factories . . . becomes possible.
>
> For instance, in certain machine factories, the desire to have a comprehensive factory, without reliance on others, led to too much spreading out, resulting in larger investment, slow construction, too much human labor, too few type of products, high costs, compounded by difficulty in improving and adding products. The Shanghai Agricultural Machinery Works [producing cars, tractors, spare parts, and farm equipment] is composed of specialized medium- and small-sized factories. Due to their proceeding along the path of specialization and cooperation, they required only a small amount of investment to produce cars and tractors in batches. Between 1957 and 1963 the State only invested 36,880,000 yuan in this company. Its fixed assets had a net worth of only a little over 78 million yuan. In the same period, the amount of profit turned over to the State was over 600 million yuan. The quality of product, cost, and labor productivity of many specialized factories in this company are among the most progressive in the country.[19]

The tendency for enterprises to produce most of their own intermediate inputs, parts, and components had led to underutilized capacity in these subsidiary operations. Well-equipped workshops, particularly in the priority enterprises, had more capacity than required to meet the needs of a single parent enterprise but were a hedge against supply bottlenecks, and their surplus output could be used for trade outside state economic plans. To change such structures entailed dividing "all-around" enterprises into several units, each specializing in a particular process or in production of a limited variety of parts and components, and its complement, "rationally reorganizing" and combining the scattered operations of small plants and workshops. Then, the argument ran, economies of scale could be realized in larger, specialized factories, production could be mechanized and automated, and product quality would improve accordingly. Management, and specifically management of technical change, it was claimed, would be easier in specialized enterprises.

The State Council circular of April 26, 1978, directed profit-making enterprises to "eliminate products and workshops that cause losses."[20] If mid-1960s policy is any precedent, these presumably will be combined into larger, specialized, and, it is hoped, more efficient operations.

Previous experience, however, has revealed the reluctance of enterprises to surrender any degree of self-reliance while supply remained uncertain and inefficient and while there were opportunities for profitable production outside state plans. To deal with this problem, Hu Ch'iao-mu would expand the "contract system" between enterprises. Such a system is "conducive to the development of specialization and cooperation in production," facilitating the flow of goods and services between enterprises and absorbing excess capacity in this trade.[21]

Missing from current discussions of specialization is any mention of enterprise scale, which was a consideration in the earlier debate. In that experience, specialization shaded into a tendency to set up small-scale operations, either collectively owned or owned at local levels of government that escaped regulation by state economic plans. Specialization is now discussed with reference to the thirteen experimental companies established in the 1960s (one of which may have been the Shanghai Agricultural Machinery Works described in the quotation above). Following this model, specialized factories would be units of large companies or combines, not independent contractors offering goods and services to a number of enterprises.

Design Reform: An Alternative Approach

Design reform was a final element in the complex of technical policies in China in the mid-1960s. Like industrial reorganization and reform of management structures, it aimed at modifying the behavior of institutions to accord with new priorities in technology policy. But like technical economics, design reform might have led to a concept of technology as something to be shaped to China's particular conditions and goals rather than imposed to conform with some external model of a technologically advanced society.

The Party Central Committee launched the "design reform campaign" at the end of 1964. This was an attempt to change procedures that had originally been devised to make engineering design a conduit channeling imported technologies into Chinese industry. These were no longer appropriate after 1960, when political and economic circumstances restricted new industrial construction in China and even more stringently limited its import of technology to levels well below those of the 1950s. To reduce the costs of new construction, the new policy called for making maximum use of existing facilities in new designs. Similarly, designers were to devote more attention to improving current plant and equipment: making minor changes that would raise productivity at relatively little cost. In the case of product design, designers were to conduct some form of market research, including surveying the manufacturers as well as the users, and to redesign machines incorporating improvements suggested in these surveys. In other words, the goal was to redirect part of China's design industry away from exclusive concern with advanced (therefore, by definition, imported) technologies, toward technically "unspectacular" but, under the circumstances, "economically significant" innovations.

The new procedures were sloganized as "on-the-spot," or onsite designing. One purpose of the design reform campaign was to correct certain obvious shortcomings, such as procedures that failed to make the designer responsible beyond the blueprint stage. But it also would have opened, for the first time in Chinese industry, a "feedback loop" through which current production needs (as opposed to state planners' visions of modern technology) could be communicated to the R & D system. The campaign also produced the first—and still the only—clear statement of innovation as a process consisting of a number of separate stages. Under a system described in 1965 as "stringing together seven things," the design engineer would have been responsible for integrating and coordinating research, experimental development, design, trial-manufacture, testing, installation, and preparation for full production.[22]

The design reform campaign enjoyed a different political patronage from that of the movement to reorganize industry and change industrial management, and it survived into the Cultural Revolution, somewhat belatedly receiving Mao's imprimatur. It might have established innnovation and technical change as autonomous processes responsive to internal factors, opened up the possibility of alternatives to foreign models, and made China's own R & D system a more immediate contributor to the country's technological development. Instead, the Cultural Revolution aborted these possibilities. The seven stages, to be "strung together" in the innovation process in 1965, were understood to be specialized functions. After 1966, research and all technical activities had to be demonstrably related to production. In effect, all possibility of technical change was limited to the technologically unspectacular when research scientists were turned into technicians working on minor technical improvements rather than on development of new technologies.[23]

Presumably because of its association with the Cultural Revolution, design reform is seldom mentioned as part of current policy. A November 1977 article in *Jen-min jih-pao* (People's daily), which is about the only recent discussion of design, is clearly a holding action reflecting the lack of a new policy direction. It endorses reforms that extend the designer's responsibility into the construction and operation of his other blueprints—a notorious shortcoming of the original system—but the notion of design as a "link" from research to production and back is missing.

China's Need for Technology Policy Studies

Peking's ultimate goal has always been to catch up with and surpass advanced world levels of industrial technology. "Walking on two legs" has, at some stages, been a means to this end but never the end in itself. It was a way for part of the economy to bootstrap itself toward higher levels of productivity while state policy focused on modern industry—the key to eventual modernization of the whole economy. Until very recently, however, this concept has been conspicuously absent from public discussions of technology policy in post-Mao China.

In China as elsewhere, "technology policy" is generally coterminous with policies for acquiring new technologies: trade and import policy, foreign policy as it affects acceptance of foreign assistance (and its availability), science and education policies. As a result of political change since 1976 and on the evidence of recent industrial performance, the overriding immediate concern in China's policy has become acquisition of advanced technology for the key sectors. Notably missing, at least until very recently, has been any visible concern for how the necessary investment will be financed.

But technology is a dynamic, changing entity. Technological change is as important to economic growth as acquisition of technology in the first place. With the goal of reaching world levels of productivity within a specified length of time, China's policymakers essentially have a very limited choice of technology—i.e., few alternatives to rapidly acquiring the best technologies of the industrially advanced countries. There are, however, alternative ways to *manage* subsequent technical and technological changes. A number of these have been tried in China at different times as, for example, when previously centralized planning and management functions were delegated to enterprise managers in the 1960s. Moreover, alternatives for differential technological growth curves exist simultaneously within China. Innovation occurs variably in different sectors of Chinese industry, with some sectors appearing to be more radically innovative than others.[24]

Without technology policy studies, China's leaders find it difficult to trace out the full implications of various alternatives and to assess the innovativeness of some sectors compared to others. At the moment, they are searching for external models of "dynamic" technology and finding that these, more than machines or complete plants, are constrained by social, cultural, economic, and political factors. The consequences of adopting any such foreign model would be profound. If China's policymakers seem prepared to accept these consequences, it may be because they do not yet realize their full potential impact.

Notes

1. Yü Ch'iu-li, speech to the Fourth Session of the Standing Committee of the Fourth National People's Congress, October 23, 1977; *Peking Review* [hereafter *PR*], no. 45, (November 4, 1977), p. 9. CCP Central Committee, "Resolution (Draft) on Some Problems of Accelerating Industrial Development" ("Thirty-Point Decision on Industrial Development"), April 1978; *PR*, no. 28 (July 14, 1978), p. 3.

2. Hsinhua Bulletin datelined Tsinan, January 27, 1978; NCNA broadcast from Peking, January 27, 1978; FBIS, January 30, 1978, p. E10. The "new techniques" specifically mentioned are "utilization of industrial surplus heat, mining mechanization, digital treatment in petroleum seismic prospecting, latest developments in heat treatment technique, ultrasonic fault detection, large integrated circuits, application of electronic computers, simplified programme control, electronic digital control, and lasers." The "key points" are unspecified.

3. *Jen-min jih-pao* [People's daily, hereafter *JMJP*], editorial, "In Capital Construction, It Is Necessary to Concentrate Our Forces and Fight a Battle of Annihilation," May 9, 1978; FBIS, May 10, 1978, p. E2.

4. For present purposes, I accept the proposition that there is little significant difference in the economic impact of a *technical change* involving factor substitution along a given production function, and *technological change*, which advances the production function to a higher level of efficiency. See Nathan Rosenberg, *Perspectives on Technology* (Cambridge, England: Cambridge University Press, 1976), pp. 61ff. See also Nathan Rosenberg, "Thinking About Technology Policy for the Coming Decade," in U.S., Congress, Joint Economic Committee, *U.S. Economic Growth Patterns from 1976 to 1986: Prospects, Problems, and Patterns*, Vol. 9, *Technological Change*, 94th Cong., 2d sess., January 3, 1977, pp. 18ff.

5. C.H.G. Oldham, *An Introductory Note to the STPI Dissemination Meetings* (Ottawa: IDRC, October 1978), pp. 4–11.

6. Yü Ch'iu-li, supra note 1.

7. "Why China Imports Technology and Equipment," *PR*, no. 41 (October 13, 1978), p. 13.

8. Ibid., p. 11.

9. Hu Ch'iao-mu, "Act in Accordance with Economic Laws, Step Up the Four Modernizations," *JMJP*, October 6, 1978; FBIS, October 11, 1978, p. E11. Hu was speaking here specifically about the failure of labor productivity to improve in the absence of wage increases.

10. Ibid., pp. E3–4, E6–7, E14–15.

11. Chao Chun-shan and Huang Chih-chieh, "On Technical Economics," *Kuang-ming jih-pao* [Illumination daily], August 10, 1964; Joint Publications Research Service [hereafter JPRS], no. 26, 327, September 9, 1964, pp. 28–35.

12. NCNA Domestic Service—Peking, April 28, 1978; FBIS, May 1, 1978, pp. E9, E10.

13. In April 1978, the Party Central Committee issued "Thirty-Point Decision on Industrial Development" listing eight "economic and technological targets for all-round checkup of enterprises' production and management." The thirty points also incorporate contractual obligations between the state and state-owned enterprises, which were originally in the "Seventy-Point Regulations" issued in 1961. The latter further directed that all unprofitable enterprises be closed down: in the first instance, those small-scale operations resulting from mass mobilization in the Great Leap Forward.

14. According to Hu Ch'iao-mu, state plans must accord with "objective economic laws." The function of state plans is to establish national investment priorities ("obey the law of proportionate development in a planned way") and to regulate production through the price mechanism ("obey the law of value," value representing the time required to produce a good and, therefore, the technique used in its production). These two "laws," says Hu, are "inseparable." Thus state investment should be economically rational and directed where it will realize maximum returns. However, "our level in doing things according to economic laws is still very low. . . Therefore, technical progress is very slow, labor productivity is very low and costs are very high." (Hu Ch'iao-mu, supra note 9, pp. E3, E5, E7, E9, E10).

15. Hu Ch'iao-mu, supra note 9, p. E7.

16. Ibid., pp. E14–E15.

17. Ibid., pp. E12–E13.

18. Ibid., p. E6.

19. Li Ch'ung-wei, "Several Views on 'More Work Done for Less Money,'" *Ta-kung pao* [Great harmony daily], September 25, 1964; JPRS, no. 27, 033, October, 22, 1964.

20. NCNA Domestic Service—Peking, April 28, 1978; FBIS, May 1, 1978, p. E11.

21. Hu Ch'iao-mu, supra note 9, p. E14.

22. Lin Tsung-t'ang, "Some Understanding in Respect of the 'System of Stringing Together Seven Things,'" *JMJP*, December 1, 1965; *Selections from China Mainland Press* 3598, pp. 2–6.

23. The immediate economic impact of such improvements could be substantial, however. Note also that, in reality, some research on new technologies continued despite the Cultural Revolution, though without the possibility of developing the results into usable technology. See, for example, Genevieve C. Dean and Fred Chernow, *The Choice of Technology in the Electronics Industry of the People's Republic of China: The Fabrication of Semiconductors* (Palo Alto, Calif.: Stanford University, United States–China Relations Program, 1978), reporting on the U.S. Ion Implantation Delegation to China (September–October 1976).

24. Hans Heymann, Jr., *China's Approach to Technology Acquisition* (Santa Monica, Calif.: Rand Corporation, 1975).

Commentary on Science and Technology Policy

C.H.G. Oldham

Fingar did well to identify the six types of problems—attitudinal, organizational, technical, manpower, managerial, and financial—that must be overcome in order for the Chinese to promote and profit from advances in industrial technology. Now the question must be asked: what are the specific implications of these factors for technological decision making?

Fingar treated two types of Chinese S & T policies: those involving technology transfer from abroad and those involving domestic technological innovation. With regard to the former, the paper stops short of detailed information on what the specific mechanisms of monitoring and control are. Genevieve Dean seemed to imply that the State Planning Commission plays the key role here. Fingar gives the impression that individual enterprises may be paramount. Who, for example, bargains on contracts involving technology transfer from abroad? And what of the *implementation* of these policies? Is transfer limited to key sectors or is it to take place across the board?

Regarding the generation of domestic technological innovation, Dean makes a fundamental distinction between incremental innovation (achieved through engineering work) and radical innovation (achieved via the R & D structure). She perceives, moreover, the potential conflict inherent in the current emphasis on profit making. The question of whether profit is an incentive or a disincentive to radical innovation remains moot.

How much continuity and how much change are exhibited by current policies? In answer to this question, Dean comes down firmly on the side of considerable continuity between current

S & T policies and those of the First Five Year Plan and the early 1960s, these later two having been nipped in the bud by the Great Leap Forward and the Cultural Revolution, respectively. Clearly, the difference between these earlier sets of policies and current policies lies in their implementation.

How do current policies differ from those being pursued by other developing countries? In comparing the Chinese approach to S & T with that of other countries undergoing rapid industrialization, it is useful to cite the results of a recent comparative study. This study analyzed the policy instruments used by ten developing countries (including Brazil, Argentina, Mexico, and India) in achieving desired S & T goals. Its major conclusion was that explicit S & T policies have little effect on technological development. Rather, other policies (fiscal, credit, economic, and social policies) have proven crucial. The Chinese seem to be aware of this, witness the broad range of problems perceived by the Chinese as mentioned in Fingar's chapter. One must not underestimate the implication of this central fact for the functioning of the State Scientific and Technological Commission in China, particularly regarding its ability to coordinate closely with other state planning agencies.

A second conclusion of this study of ten developing countries was the central importance, from a policymaking point of view, of the need to achieve S & T self-reliance. China may seem to have strayed from this goal; yet in practice it never fully espoused it. China has never advocated total autarchy; rather policy shifts have altered the *scale* on which China has imported technology from abroad. At bottom, the question of self-reliance is really a semantic one. The capability of making autonomous decisions exists as strongly in China today as it ever has. I do not believe that the Chinese have totally abandoned their policy of self-reliance, as some have argued.

In their discussion of the implications of Chinese S & T policies for the future, both Fingar and Dean touch on the question of whether or not technology is culturally neutral. Apparently the Chinese think it is. Dean, on the other hand, raises the possibility of the "Coca Cola-ization" of China under the indomitable weight of the imperatives of modernization.

Neither author mentions the implications of S & T policy for rural industry, an area formerly the object of much attention. Other questions deserving of further discussion concern the future impact of Chinese scholars and students currently being sent abroad. Will they form the bulwark of a future pro-Western elite? Certainly not, if they follow the precedent set by the Chinese students sent to the Soviet Union in the 1950s. Also important are the implications of the massive debt that China is currently building up; and the relationship between employment-creation and imported technology. With respect to the latter question, labor-saving techniques imported from abroad can only undercut Chinese efforts to keep employment up.

Discussion

William Clarke began by discussing the problems that the Chinese will encounter in the absorption of technology. He suggested that a need exists to clarify what is meant by technology transfer. Very little technology has actually been *transferred* to China thus far, although products and some know-how have been *imported*. For a concrete example, *Clarke* turned to petrochemicals: The Chinese have been taught how to operate petrochemical units, but they have not yet developed the ability to scale them up or down. The Bucy Report (commissioned by the Department of Defense) addresses this issue of transfer of technology in a direct manner, making explicit the distinction between technology and product transfers.[1]

Robert Dernberger added that the Chinese have largely recognized their mistakes of the 1950s with regard to the importation of machines without importing the technology and know-how needed to produce and adapt them. Thus today they are much more attuned to genuine technology transfer.

Hans Heymann agreed that the key factor in Chinese S & T development, far from being Western input—or even fiscal constraints—will be China's ability to create a society that is capable of absorbing technology. It is through the absorption and mastery of technology management that the Chinese will progress in this area, as the Japanese did in the 1950s and 1960s.

Rudi Volti qualified the remarks of *Heymann* and *Clarke*, suggesting that it is necessary to disaggregate industries when talking about the potential roles that can be played by imported technology. Basic machine tools, for example, are relatively easy to copy, once the hardware has been obtained; semiconductors, on the other hand, involve much more subtle—hence less easily copied—techniques. Specific techniques demand different approaches to absorption, and offer different degrees of innovative potential.

C.H.G. Oldham directed further discussion around the twin issues of who makes factory-level S & T decisions and who holds the balance of power in factory-level decision making.

Richard Baum suggested that factory managers are in a position to make recommendations, but final decisions on important matters are made either by enterprise Party committees or at a higher level, often in the ministries.

J. Ray Pace noted that he has encountered some cases where ministry initiative was imperative (and much slower), as well as some cases where initiative from the field was acceptable.

Stanley Lubman made the point that Chinese end-users are becoming much more evident in negotiations for foreign technology. He also observed that end-user corporations are proliferating and are beginning to bypass the previously dominant foreign-trade corporations. The most recent example of this fractionalization of responsibility is the rumor of the imminent formation of a new corporation dealing in precision instruments. Finally, *Lubman* noted that in recent months there has been less state mediation than previously in the negotiation and signing of contracts with foreign firms.

The discussion then moved on to the types of broad structural changes the Chinese system may be undergoing and the barriers that exist to such change.

Doak Barnett asserted that the changes that China is undergoing now go far beyond anything seen in the patterns of the 1950s and 1960s. In fact, Hu Ch'iao-mu is talking in terms of moving toward a "new kind of market socialism," while maintaining centralized planning. The question is how to reconcile these two concepts and how to deal with incipient elitism and corruption within this new system.

Kan Chen pointed out that the forcing of change "from the top down" will inevitably run into problems of Party inertia and cadre cynicism: older Party members will be extremely cautious in the implementation of a new program of reform, the longevity of which has yet to be demonstrated.

John Hardt drew analogies to systemic change undergone by the Communist regimes of Eastern Europe, in particular the reorganization of the Polish Party to make it more compatible with effective industrial managerial practices. Noting that the Eastern Europeans have largely jettisoned the idea of self-reliance, *Hardt* asked if this might not also be occurring in China?

Notes

1. *An Analysis of Export Control of U.S. Technology—A Department of Defense Prospectus: Report of the Defense Science Board Task Force on the Export of U.S. Technology* (Washington, D.C.: Office of the Director of Defense Research and Engineering, February, 1976).

5
The Institutional Structure for Industrial Research and Development in China

Richard P. Suttmeier

To understand the institutional structure for research and development in China, it is important to look beyond R & D institutions per se and examine the whole process of technological innovation. This is necessary because, over the longer run, political support for R & D efforts in China will require the successful development of technological innovation processes. When the Chinese talk about science and technology as the key to the modernization of agriculture, industry, and national defense, they ultimately are talking about technological innovation in the interests of increased economic productivity and sophistication of military technology. But, as a report of the Organization for Economic Cooperation and Development (OECD) put it some years ago, "Technological innovation is more than R & D."[1] Thus, a discussion of the institutional setting for industrial R & D must first ask how technological innovation occurs and will continue to occur in the People's Republic of China.

This chapter draws on my observations and conversations with scientists and administrators in China in May and June 1978 as a member of the Committee on Scholarly Communication with the P.R.C.'s Pure and Applied Chemistry Delegation. I am grateful for the scientists' perspectives that my chemist colleagues shared with me. Subsequent conversations with Alan Schriescheim, a member of the delegation, and with Fumio Kodama of the Institute for Policy Sciences, Saitama University, a Fulbright Visiting Professor at Hamilton College in 1978–1979, have helped my thinking about this topic.

The very question of innovation suggests an image of an interacting network of organizations—in R & D, as well as in education, production, commerce, and finance. R & D institutions operate in a larger matrix of organizations concerned with technological innovation. The image, in short, is one of systemic interaction among relevant organizations.

Unfortunately, however, we lack any clear conception about how innovation occurs in China. Much of our understanding of technological innovation is drawn from studies of market economies, and there are no unambiguous findings to suggest that these models, derived from market economies, apply to China as well. Nevertheless, as we begin a new era in the study of contemporary Chinese society, it is important to identify the study of innovation in China as a high priority topic with considerable implications for economic and political development generally, and the Four Modernizations in particular. Before pursuing the question of innovation and the systemic interaction of innovation-related organizations, it will be useful to review what we know about Chinese R & D organizations.

Historical Background

Although the process of establishing modern scientific research institutes began in China as early as the 1920s, and although the pre-Liberation legacy of scientific research and education is perhaps more important than we sometimes recognize, the major disruptions in Chinese society caused by the war against Japan and the Civil War precluded any serious development of R & D activities or any national R & D system. It was only after 1950 that the new regime could turn its attention to national science policy and the establishment of a national administration for research and development. At first, this national administration drew upon existing scientific institutions and manpower but it was also largely inspired by the Soviet approach to R & D organization. Indeed, the influence of the Soviet model grew throughout most of the 1950s. It has left a permanent imprint on the organization of R & D in China and a philosophical legacy in the persisting Chinese belief that discovery and innovation can be rationalized and promoted through centralized planning and administration.

The centerpiece of the pre-Liberation organization for science was the Academia Sinica. Renamed the Chinese Academy of Sciences (CAS) after Liberation, it resumed its role as the focal point for research organization, and, in the early 1950s for policymaking as well. The development of a strong central academy was, of course, also consistent with the Soviet model.

By the mid-1950s, other aspects of the Soviet model also were coming into place. These included, in particular, research institutes and/or academies under the jurisdiction of production and other ministries. These organizations had, in comparison with the CAS, more of an applied research function in support of the missions of the ministries. During this period as well, one began to see some growth of research in institutions of higher education. Again, however, Chinese experience with research in institutions of higher education tended to follow the Soviet pattern, which deemphasized the research role of institutions of higher education in comparison with the academy and ministerial sectors. This pattern was, however, contrary to the best judgment of China's senior scientists, most of whom had been trained at the great research universities of the West and were strongly committed to the idea of a linkage between research and advanced training.

Until 1956 much of the direction of the national R & D effort was centered in the Academy of Sciences that, again following the Soviet example, had instituted a powerful administrative secretariat in Peking as well as a number of academic "departments" to provide policy advice. However, with the growth of R & D activities in non-CAS sectors, with the introduction of national research planning in 1956, and with the growing concern that scientific research must serve the needs of the economy came an awareness of the need for a national coordinating and policymaking body. Thus, in 1956, the Chinese set up a State Technological Commission and a Science Planning Commission, which merged into the State Scientific and Technological Commission (SSTC) in 1958.

As a result, the main outlines of the R & D system in the pre–Cultural Revolution period included three vertically differentiated sections of research and development activities: the Academy of Sciences, the production ministries, and higher educational institutions. The three sectors were coordinated at the national level by the SSTC. In addition, the Chinese encouraged the growth of professional societies throughout the pre–Cultural Revolution period. After 1958, these were subsumed under the general direction of the Science and Technology Association (STA). It is also important to note the development of subnational institutions concerned with science and technology, particularly those resulting from the decentralization measures of the Great Leap Forward. These included the establishment of science and technology committees to provide leadership in science administration at the provincial and subprovincial levels, provincial and subprovincial branches of the STA, and, in many provinces, branches of the CAS. In addition, efforts were made during this period to bring applied research and extension services to the basic levels of production. Although these decentralization measures were modified somewhat in the early 1960s, the foundation for a nationwide system nevertheless had been laid. The two major building blocks were national research institutes on the one hand and local level experimental groups on the other. Let us consider certain aspects of the national system in greater detail.

The Chinese Academy of Sciences

The history of the CAS in the 1950–1965 period is one of considerable growth and internal differentiation. The academy grew from some 20 institutes in 1950 to more than 120 in 1965. It was led by a president and several vice-presidents and by an administrative secretariat, headed by a secretary-general. The numerous institutes under the academy's jurisdiction were organized under five main departments: mathematics, physics, and chemistry; biological sciences; earth sciences; technical sciences; and social sciences. In addition to research activities, the academy also conducted programs in advanced training and had responsibility for some scientific information services and the development of scientific instruments. Although some alterations were made in the organization of academy institutes during the Great Leap Forward period, the leadership structure before the Cultural Revolution generally included a director who typically was a scientist, several deputy directors, some of whom were not scientists, and an advisory committee on academic affairs.

The Ministerial Sector

Research and development in the ministerial sector before the Cultural Revolution consumed the greatest share of the national R & D budget and absorbed the greatest number of R & D personnel.[2] Research in this sector was quite diversified. For example, the Ministry of Agriculture had its own Academy of Agricultural Sciences with research institutes and a network of extension services. Similarly, the Ministry of Public Health had its own academy and research institutes, which were linked to major hospitals. Within the ministerial sector, I also include defense-related R & D, which was organized nationally around the Science and Technology Commission for National Defense (STCND), which was directly under the Military Affairs Commission of the Party. Reportedly, the STCND had directly under its jurisdiction a number of research institutes that were solely involved with defense.[3] It is likely, however, that the STCND also drew upon and was coordinated with R & D activities in other sectors, particularly the CAS.

In the production ministries, the organizational pattern for R & D was characterized by a series of research and design institutes, which were under the jurisdiction of individual ministries and supported ministerial missions. The institutional setting for R & D in this ministerial sector, however, also included training instititues, which were under the formal jurisdiction of the Ministry of Education but were closely linked with production ministries. These were institutions of higher education, but they specialized in a particular technology following the Soviet pattern. Since many of the graduates of these institutes typically went on to various organizations under the ministry, close coordination was maintained. In addition, a number of professional societies were closely affiliated with the ministerial sector. Chinese professional societies are organized around a given academic discipline or around an area of technology. The latter have had close functional ties with the ministries, with the headquarters of the society sometimes located in the ministry, and with society officers serving concurrently as high ministerial officials.[4]

Institutions of Higher Education

Research in these institutions was not strongly emphasized until 1958. Thereafter it was encouraged, but the emphasis was on applied research, and the objective was to create new cohorts of professional manpower who would be strongly oriented toward application. The applied research orientation seemed to hold not only for the highly specialized single-technology institutes and such polytechnical institutions as Tsinghua, but also for the so-called comprehensive universities.

Two central problems with the national R & D system in the pre–Cultural Revolution period concerned intersectoral collaboration and communication, and the connection of research and development with production. The creation of the SSTC (which was the nation's science policy and administration leader) and the provincial science and technology committees was intended to solve the first problem. The SSTC—which also had responsibilities for national planning, technical standards, and the rationalization of equipment utilization—used a number of means to achieve national intersectoral coordination, including its convening of special conferences and the encouragement of professional societies as forums for intersectoral communication.

Establishing workable linkages between research and production continued to be a problem, at least in the eyes of some, until the beginning of the Cultural Revolution. Complaints in the public media about the divorce of research workers from production activities, which became widespread in the late 1950s, reappeared with a vengeance after the mid-1960s. Although much of the blame for the separation was placed upon the bourgeois orientation of the technical community, the entire structure of R & D and its leaders were attacked during the Cultural Revolution for acquiescing in this separation.

The Cultural Revolution

An adequate account of the impact of the Cultural Revolution (1966–1969) on science and technology has yet to be written. The events of this period unquestionably produced major disruptions in some areas of scientific research. Particularly hard hit was the educational system, where the training of scientists and engineers was severely disrupted. The political objectives of the Cultural Revolution as they affected science and technology were to overcome elitism and to achieve a more direct linkage between production and research. These objectives were approached (1) by disrupting established research routines and moving technical research personnel into production settings; (2) by decentralizing much of the national R & D system and placing a large number of previously centrally controlled institutes under provincial or subprovincial control; (3) by changing the administrative arrangements within research institutes and replacing scientist-directors with revolutionary committees; and (4) by trying to overcome conventional divisions of labor among institutions of higher education, production units, and research institutes. Universities and research institutes were encouraged to start factories, and production units were encouraged to start their own schools and research activities. These attempts to break down organizational barriers in the division of labor were aimed at the creation of a tradition referred to at the time as "open door research."

The Cultural Revolution's impact was unquestionably greatest in institutions of higher education. Not only did these institutions have their educational activities disrupted, but, when classes resumed under a series of Cultural Revolution–inspired reforms in 1968–1969, the applied research orientation that was expected of institutions of higher education was further reinforced. Moreover, university research budgets in the early 1970s were reportedly rather low in comparison with those of the CAS institutes, with the assumption that universities would receive additional funds for contract research.[5] This approach to funding presumably was intended to keep research activities in institutions of higher education closely oriented to practical problems in the society. It is also true that, in most fields of science, the Cultural Revolution and its aftermath eclipsed whatever basic research had been going on. Thus, when the redirection of Chinese science policy began in 1977, following the demise of the Gang of Four, China had no strong tradition of basic research. This has resulted in the current "Edisonian" approach to research. Production problems are referred to research units for study, but, in the absence of a basic research tradition that might contribute to a scientific understanding of the problem at hand, a solution is sought through trial and error, using existing scientific knowledge and technology. This point will be addressed below.

In spite of the serious consequences that the Cultural Revolution had for higher education, research in universities, and basic research, it is not clear that the Cultural Revolution was an unqualified disaster for Chinese technological development. Western scientific visitors, who bemoan the serious problems in basic research, nevertheless have often noted with some admiration the close articulation between production, technical services, development, and some applied research. What is not clear is whether this close articulation is a result of the Cultural Revolution or whether it was already beginning to occur in the pre-Cultural Revolution period. The resolution of this question is beyond the scope of this chapter. But a preliminary analysis of the institutional structure of industrial R & D in China since 1976 indicates that linkages between applied research and production, at least in some areas of technology and industry, are reasonably well established. The existence of such linkages is a matter of no small importance for China's Four Modernizations program and for establishing the necessary "chains of innovation."

The Contemporary Situation

The dramatic changes that began to affect Chinese science and technology in 1977 are in the direction of reestablishing pre-Cultural Revolution patterns. The research system continues to be divided into three main vertical sectors, and there seems to be a growing recentralization of much research and development administration. As a result of the Cultural Revolution, for instance, the number of institutes under CAS jurisdiction was reduced to thirty-six, whereas it now seems that the number is again approaching one hundred. The State Scientific and Technological Commission, which had been abolished during the Cultural Revolution, has been reestablished and is again playing an important role. Similarly, professional societies, which were disbanded during the Cultural Revolution, are again functioning. Also, the revolutionary-committee form of leadership in research institutes during the Cultural Revolution and its aftermath has reverted to the earlier pattern of a single scientific director.

One significant change from the pre–Cultural Revolution period, however, may be the increased institutionalization of the grass-roots innovation, experimentation, and training activities that make up the "mass scientific network." However, whereas the mass scientific network appeared to take the lead in the national research and innovation effort during the Cultural Revolution, the lead has now passed to more conventional R & D organizations and to people with professional training in science and technology. Finally, major national research planning has been reinstituted in a form reminiscent of the First Twelve-Year Plan for Science and Technology, advanced in 1956. Furthermore, the latter is now to be emulated as a model approach to scientific planning. The current national organization of R & D activities is represented in Figure 5.1.

Some sense of the internal workings of the R & D system emerges from a closer examination of the organization of the Academy of Sciences (Figure 5.2). The central academy offices have again been internally differentiated on the basis of broad disciplinary activities. Within the secretariat there are now five central bureaus, which have jurisdiction over research institutes in different fields. These bureaus include one for physics, mathematics, and astronomy; one for chemistry; one for biological sciences; one for earth sciences; and one for new technology. These bureaus seem to be the forums for decisions affecting major allocations of resources to the various institutes in different fields. They appear to be staffed by both technical people and nonscientist administrators. At the same time, the academy is reportedly organizing academic committees composed of leading scientists to serve as advisory bodies to the bureaus.

Figure 5.1

Organization of China's Science and Technology System

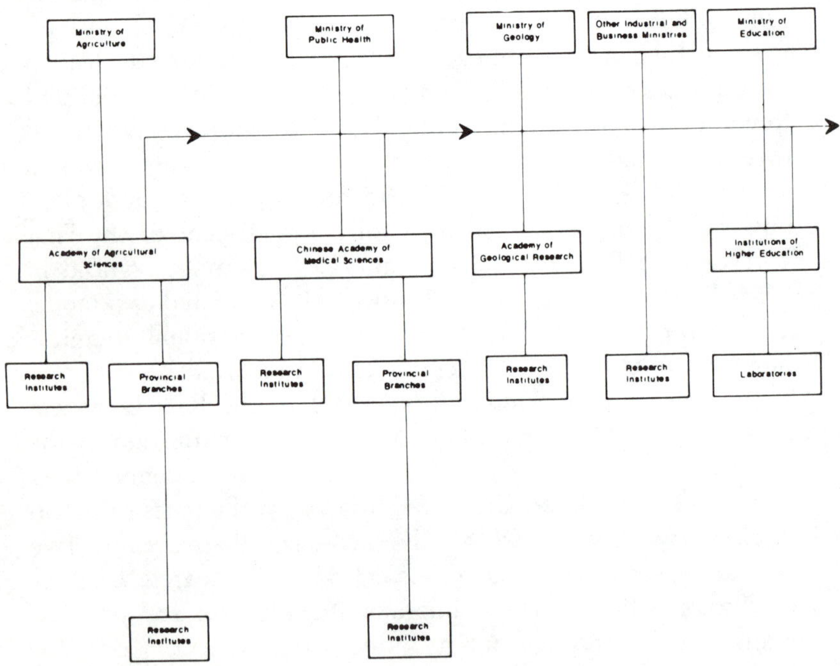

Source: OECD. *Science & Technology in the People's Republic of China*. Paris. Organization for Economic Cooperation and Development. 1977. pp. 72-73.

Figure 5.1 (continued)

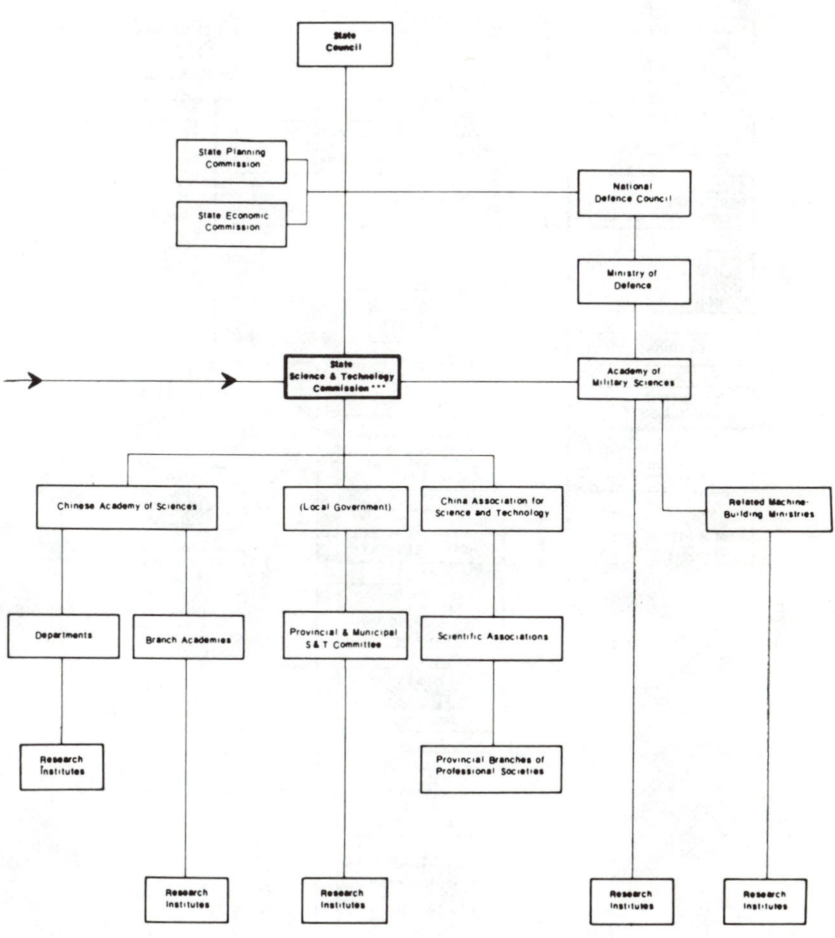

Figure 5.2

ORGANIZATION OF THE CHINESE ACADEMY OF SCIENCES - FOCUS ON CHEMISTRY

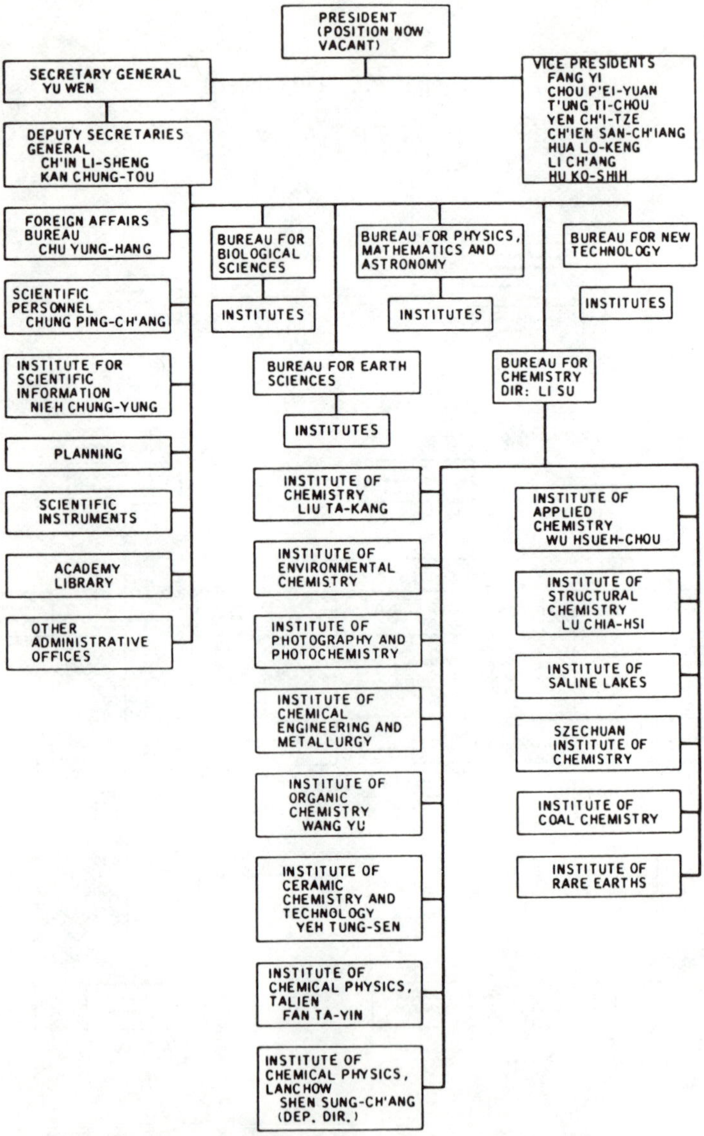

- PRESIDENT (POSITION NOW VACANT)
  - SECRETARY GENERAL YU WEN
    - DEPUTY SECRETARIES GENERAL CH'IN LI-SHENG, KAN CHUNG-TOU
      - FOREIGN AFFAIRS BUREAU CHU YUNG-HANG
      - SCIENTIFIC PERSONNEL CHUNG PING-CH'ANG
      - INSTITUTE FOR SCIENTIFIC INFORMATION NIEH CHUNG-YUNG
      - PLANNING
      - SCIENTIFIC INSTRUMENTS
      - ACADEMY LIBRARY
      - OTHER ADMINISTRATIVE OFFICES
      - BUREAU FOR BIOLOGICAL SCIENCES
        - INSTITUTES
      - BUREAU FOR EARTH SCIENCES
        - INSTITUTES
      - BUREAU FOR PHYSICS, MATHEMATICS AND ASTRONOMY
        - INSTITUTES
      - BUREAU FOR CHEMISTRY DIR: LI SU
        - INSTITUTE OF CHEMISTRY LIU TA-KANG
        - INSTITUTE OF ENVIRONMENTAL CHEMISTRY
        - INSTITUTE OF PHOTOGRAPHY AND PHOTOCHEMISTRY
        - INSTITUTE OF CHEMICAL ENGINEERING AND METALLURGY
        - INSTITUTE OF ORGANIC CHEMISTRY WANG YU
        - INSTITUTE OF CERAMIC CHEMISTRY AND TECHNOLOGY YEH TUNG-SEN
        - INSTITUTE OF CHEMICAL PHYSICS, TALIEN FAN TA-YIN
        - INSTITUTE OF CHEMICAL PHYSICS, LANCHOW SHEN SUNG-CH'ANG (DEP. DIR.)
        - INSTITUTE OF APPLIED CHEMISTRY WU HSUEH-CHOU
        - INSTITUTE OF STRUCTURAL CHEMISTRY LU CHIA-HSI
        - INSTITUTE OF SALINE LAKES
        - SZECHUAN INSTITUTE OF CHEMISTRY
        - INSTITUTE OF COAL CHEMISTRY
        - INSTITUTE OF RARE EARTHS
      - BUREAU FOR NEW TECHNOLOGY
        - INSTITUTES
  - VICE PRESIDENTS FANG YI, CHOU P'EI-YUAN, T'UNG TI-CHOU, YEN CH'I-TZE, CH'IEN SAN-CH'IANG, HUA LO-KENG, LI CH'ANG, HU KO-SHIH

Source: John D. Baldeschwieler (ed.) <u>Chemistry and Chemical Engineering in the People's Republic of China</u>. Washington. American Chemical Society, 1979. p. 171.

At the level of the institute, authority for nonpolitical affairs has been placed in the hands of an institute director, but the Party committee continues to be an important source of overall authority. However, Teng Hsiao-p'ing, speaking at the National Science Conference in early 1978, made it very clear that the main purpose of Party committees in research institutes is to facilitate research and to see that national policies are implemented. Academy institutes typically also include one or more deputy directors, and academic committees have been reestablished at the institute level to review the research of the institutes and to provide advice to the institute leadership.

Institutes typically have important administrative staff offices as well, including one for research planning and personnel training, one for equipment and general technical support, and one for providing general services (housing, kindergarten, health, and so on for the employees of the institute). It appears that the administrative staff at the institute level and at the central bureau level play major roles in research planning, budgeting, staff development, and coordination with other units. The high status now enjoyed by experienced professional scientists, however, insures that the voice of the professional researcher is probably greater now than it has been for at least fifteen years.

CAS planning and budgeting processes remain somewhat obscure to outside observers. At the institute level, there are three budgets. One is a reportedly ample general purpose budget, which appears to offer considerable discretion to the institute leadership. Institutes also have a foreign exchange budget and a manpower budget. Research projects come to the institute as part of a plan, but working scientists have opportunities to propose projects as well. Depending on the scope of the project, decisions can be made at the level of the institute, the bureau, the national academy, or an even higher level. Major projects that cannot be accommodated at the bureau level would presumably be incorporated into the academy or national plan.

The organization of research in the ministerial and higher education sectors is less clear and more varied. It appears that both production ministries and the Ministry of Education have offices for science and technology. These, in turn, seem to be linked to the Scientific and Technological Commission. Centrally controlled institutes in the ministerial sector are linked to the central ministries, although I observed one case—that of the Peking Petrochemical Research Institute—in which the institute reported directly to the manager of the Peking Petrochemical Plant as well as to the ministry. A number of institutes in the ministerial sector continue to be under the jurisdiction of local authorities, which have reestablished provincial and subprovincial science and technology committees. Such locally controlled institutes may receive some funding from the central ministries, but they also appear to receive funding from provincial and some subprovincial governments as well, or from various production units in the province. Coordination of activities at the province level is the responsibility of the science and technology committees, which are closely linked with the provincial Party committees.

The central government will probably dramatically increase its financial support of the higher education sector. This is true not only for the expansion of facilities to meet anticipated growth in enrollment, but for research support as well, since the principle of sponsoring research (including basic research) in institutions of higher education has been strongly affirmed. Nevertheless, local governments continue to make some contribution to the support of research in universities. At Kirin University, for instance, research projects reportedly are funded out of a central Ministry of Education research budget, out of discretionary funds available to the university, and out of funds provided by the local science and technology committee and education bureau, which in turn may come from local production units desiring R & D services.

At the center of the system is the newly reestablished SSTC led by Politburo member Fang Yi. Although not too much is known about the SSTC, it appears to be the locus of national R & D planning and coordination. As such, it facilitates planning and administrative interaction among the three R & D sectors and serves as the link between these and such centers of economic decision making as the State Planning Commission, the State Council, and the Politburo.

The staff of the SSTC numbers approximately 200 at present, but it may grow to its pre–Cultural Revolution complement of

500. The commission is organized into approximately ten interdisciplinary functional bureaus, including a planning bureau (led by a person with training in economics), a bureau for energy and petrochemical research (No. 2 Bureau, led by a chemical engineer), and a bureau for machinery and information technology (No. 3 Bureau, led by a mechanical engineer). These are the only bureaus that I know of, although reportedly there is also a bureau for basic research. On the basis of what is known about the SSTC organization, it would appear that the functions of the bureaus parallel the priority areas of the national science plan.

The national R & D system in China is an administratively complex one. Figure 5.3 conveys a sense of its complexity in showing administrative arrangements affecting research and

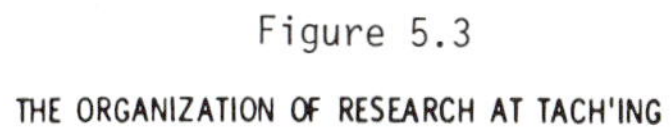

Figure 5.3

THE ORGANIZATION OF RESEARCH AT TACH'ING

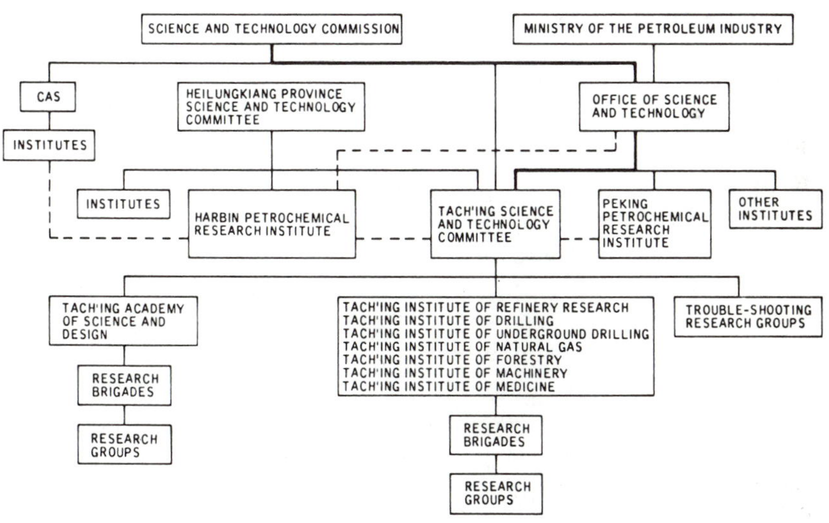

Source: John D. Baldeschwieler (ed.) Chemistry and Chemical Engineering in the People's Republic of China. Washington. American Chemical Society, 1979. p. 171.

development at the Tach'ing oilfield. Although Tach'ing's research is primarily under central government administration, its research organizations maintain some liaison with the Heilungkiang Provincial Science and Technology Committee. In contrast, the Harbin Petrochemical Research Institute is largely under the direction of the same committee and serves mainly the R & D needs of provincial industry. This institute, interestingly, was part of the Academy of Sciences before the Cultural Revolution.

It is not clear at this point whether administrative complexity results in bureaucratic inflexibility or in reasonably effective lines of communication and coordination. If the latter, China may have an effective network of organizations and the articulation of organizations necessary for a viable system of indigenous technological innovation. The reestablishment of professional societies would be an additional indicator that effective sectoral coordination is a real possibility. Reports of meetings held by professional societies beginning in 1977 indicate that they have begun to compensate for the barriers to communication—particularly among more highly skilled and educated technical personnel—that had developed since the beginning of the Cultural Revolution. Nevertheless, the very existence of such a highly bureaucratized, vertically oriented R & D system does raise questions about effective communication and organizational flexibility, two characteristics that are presumably important for technological innovation in China.

Some Broader Considerations

If the past is any guide to the future, China's scientific and technological development will be linked to the continuation of a reasonably stable political environment. The prospects for such stability are in part linked to the success of the Four Modernizations program. The Four Modernizations, in turn, are in part dependent upon the performance of scientific and technological institutions in the short run. It will therefore be useful to look at the problems and prospects of these institutions in a somewhat broader context.

A fundamental issue affecting R & D performance is the

availability of trained manpower. China seems to have a serious shortage of trained manpower that will affect its programs in two ways. First, the immediate shortage of trained manpower—particularly of seasoned senior people capable of leadership—will be a constraint in the short run on the achievement of China's ambitious R & D goals. Second, the shortage of trained manpower will place very large demands on the educational system—demands that may in the short run keep institutions of higher education from developing into important centers for research and development due to pressing demands for educational and training services. Although the questions of education and manpower require broad independent analysis, they are two of the most important factors affecting China's ability to use science and technology to achieve the Four Modernizations.

A second concern is whether China's investment in R & D will produce the practical payoffs in the form of technological innovations that the leadership expects. I have suggested that certain features of China's R & D institutions seem to be supportive of a broad national program of technological innovation. The value of other features, however, appears to be problematic, and our experience with Western models of innovation would lead us to raise some general questions about the innovative potential of China's social institutions.

Although our knowledge of the processes of innovation is still far from complete, it does seem that the articulation of demand for innovation is an important component. In Western economies, this demand articulation is expressed through market signals, or through carefully designed administrative mechanisms. It is still not clear how the articulation of demand occurs in China, nor is it clear how recent economic reforms might affect it. In all but the most simple technologies, however, some degree of technical expertise is usually necessary, not only at the supply end of the equation, as is commonly assumed, but also at the demand end as well. That is, the ability to frame a technological need properly is an important step in the innovative process and requires trained manpower. Thus, the uncertain performance of market signals and the shortage of manpower mean that most enterprises are seriously "under-engineered" and suggest that the Chinese face institutional problems affecting innovation that are not directly problems of R & D.

Problems with demand articulation, therefore, may be a kind of "missing link" in the innovation chain such that R & D institutes are unable to respond effectively to the needs of enterprises. The kinds of reforms designed to remove organizational barriers between research and development institutions and enterprises discussed above may have partly alleviated this problem by exposing R & D personnel directly to the technical problems of production. The current movement away from these reforms, back toward a more differentiated structure in the interest of R & D development, may have serious short-term consequences for the integrity of the innovation chain.

Nevertheless, it seems that greater structural differentiation and division of labor are necessary at this stage of Chinese development. In some industries, at least, it appears that the linkage between production units and R & D units is fairly strong, but the disruption of R & D—and in particular of basic research during the last twelve years—has resulted in a different kind of problem affecting another link in the innovation chain. This problem, which appears to affect large, reasonably well-developed industries and the process technologies they employ, might be described as overcoming "scientific sticking points" and moving beyond an "Edisonian" research strategy. Some examples drawn from observations of the petrochemical industry in May and June 1978 by our Pure and Applied Chemistry Delegation will illustrate the problem. One example is the Chinese approach to the problem of the high paraffin content of Tach'ing's crude oil. The Chinese have been devoting R & D resources to the problems of waxy crude, but in the absence of a strong basic research tradition, the R & D has tended to be more of a trial-and-error ("Edisonian") strategy, characterized by experiments with various kinds of wax crystal modifiers. The Chinese have not moved beyond a relatively gross technological definition of the problem derived from production problems of crude extraction and processing; they have no strict scientific definition aimed at understanding the underlying chemical characteristics. Similarly, work in catalysis seemed to be excessively characterized by trial and error, with insufficient attention being given to the underlying chemical and physical properties of different catalytic agents.

Thus, in certain industries, or perhaps in all industries at a certain level of technological development, the availability of strong basic research activities is an essential link in the innovative chain. Basic research in China is largely the province of the CAS, although reports during the last year indicate that institutions of higher education will have an expanded role in basic research. In industries like petrochemicals, however, a case can be made for carrying out some basic research in the ministerial sector as well. If only one sector of a bureaucratized and vertically differentiated science system is engaged primarily in basic research, administrative barriers can readily arise that will divorce basic research from problems of production. To be sure, a degree of insulation from the demands of practical problems is also necessary. At this point, however, it is not clear whether the Chinese have decided on the proper degree of insulation. One can conclude, however, that the Chinese at present are very sensitive both to the importance of basic research and to the dangers of divorcing research from practical problems. In attempting to deal with the latter problem, particularly with Cultural Revolution–inspired reforms, the Chinese probably did institutionalize mechanisms to link research and production. But these came at a terrible price in terms of basic research. The danger now is that the Chinese might adopt an approach to innovation that focuses excessively on R & D while ignoring the problems of demand. The nature of China's institutions guarantees the presence of such a danger.

Western literature on innovation also calls attention to the distinction between product and process innovation. The above discussion suggests the rough shape of China's system for process innovation, but some of the conditions that are often associated with product innovation are less obvious in China. Specifically, product innovation has been identified in the West with small entrepreneurial firms. Typically, it involves very fluid technologies, where the initial appeal does not lie in cost reduction (as with process technologies) but in some sort of new performance characteristics.[6] It is thought that small firms, operated in an entrepreneurial manner, have the flexibility to manage the technical and economic contingencies that are characteristic of product innovation. Again, just how product innovation is managed in China is not clear, although there are hints in some institutional arrangements (called laboratory factories or laboratory industries), again apparently deriving from the Cultural Revolution.[7] These laboratory factories tend to produce new products on the basis of ideas suggested by research workers. However, while such laboratory factories can produce prototypes, they are not usually the appropriate organizations to develop a new product to the point of commercialization, which is what we normally mean by innovation.

In the absence of private entrepreneurship, the key institutional question is whether or not there are enterprises in the environment of the laboratory that are sufficiently flexible and properly motivated to develop new products. It is at present impossible to answer this. The Chinese, however, do seem to have had experience in transferring the technology for new products out of the laboratory industries. At Kirin University, for instance, members of our Pure and Applied Chemistry Delegation saw an impressive semiconductor plant, which was making semiconductors for commercial use but was also training personnel in the Changchun area in the principles of semiconductor technology and production.

The above discussion illustrates the point that technological innovation is indeed more than R & D and, thus, that the institutional setting for innovation may pose problems that are somewhat independent of R & D institutions. It follows that the Chinese would be making a serious mistake if they were to place all of their hopes for technological modernization on R & D institutions. Instead, they should give serious thought to how they want R & D institutions to operate in the larger setting of institutions concerned with production, finance, trade, etc., as well as R & D.

Although the formal organization of industrial research and development around three centrally directed vertical sectors still seems inconsistent with our image of demand-created innovation as a fluid and decentralized process, Chinese practice in informal operations does come closer to our understanding of the innovation process than formal organization suggests. In the years to come, however, any return to a more bureaucratic and inflexible set of institutions could endanger China's capacity for innovation, even if there are no changes in the formal organization of R & D.

The R & D System and Foreign Technology

The issue of China's ability to import and absorb foreign technology is peripheral to the main topic of this paper. In successful cases of technology transfer, however, the existence of a reasonably vigorous R & D system in a recipient country has been an important factor in avoiding excessive dependency on foreign technology. There appear to be two reasons for this. The first goes back to the notion of the articulation of demand. An effective technology import strategy requires that technical needs be stated with precision, sophistication, and a professional awareness of what the international market for technology has to offer. Although China does not have the technical intelligence capabilities at present that Japan had with its trading companies in the 1950s and 1960s, the Chinese do show an awareness of the importance of international research activities coupled with careful specifications of technical needs, and they appear to recognize the importance of technical personnel for this task. In evaluating foreign technology, China seems to be relying strongly on members of professional societies—particularly those organized around certain areas of industrial technology with very close ties to production ministries.[8] The existence of an ongoing and active R & D system, however, provides the necessary backup for the work of the professional societies.

The second important role of R & D institutions in foreign technology importation is in assimilating and improving upon the technology. Japan's experience in supporting adaptive engineering or improvement engineering, particularly during the 1960s, is important but also suggests a longer-term problem for the R & D system of a country that is pursuing a vigorous technology import strategy. This is the problem of the standing of the R & D sector in the eyes of economic decision makers as the country approaches technological parity with the technologically advanced nations. As the decision makers become more enamored with foreign technology, they may view the R & D sector mainly as a support sector for rationalizing the importation and improvement of technology and overlook its creative potential. The result may be a research tradition that tends to be—or at least appears to be—more derivative than original. In spite of the fact that R & D expenditure increased dramatically in Japan during the 1960s and early 1970s, there is evidence from at least some areas of research and technology that Japanese economic decision makers have not yet given Japanese scientists and technologists the recognition they deserve for their work. Indeed, in some cases, the achievement of Japanese scientists has only been recognized in Japan after it had been recognized by foreign scientists.

At first glance, the Chinese case would seem to be quite different from the Japanese in this regard. Yet, if anything, China has had greater difficulty in dealing with foreign knowledge and technology than has Japan. China has consistently had difficulty steering between the complete rejection of things foreign and excessive awe and deference toward them, a deference that has been derided as thinking that "even the moon over the U.S. and Europe is brighter than it is over China." Although such sarcasm has usually emanated from China's nativists and has been directed toward the cosmopolitan proclivity of China's intellectuals, it does indicate unease with things foreign. It would be quite possible for today's "quasi-nativist" economic decision makers, exposed for the first time to the products of the great world technology supermarket, to become increasingly enthralled by Western technology, to assume the historically problematic role of the cosmopolitan, and then ignore China's own scientific and technological talent.

Conclusion

China is embarking upon the Four Modernizations with a reasonably well-developed system of R & D institutions. The system is characterized by centralized planning and policy-making capabilities, by numerous research institutes, by reasonable geographic distribution of R & D efforts, by certain traditions of close relationships between R & D and production, and by the existence of many ancillary supporting activities, such as professional societies, information services, national standards, and the beginnings of a scientific instruments industry. It seems to be a generously funded system and one that at present enjoys considerable support. It is not without its problems, nevertheless, the most important of which is the shortage of senior manpower capable of exercising leadership.

The longer-term issue, however, is one that can only be touched upon in this paper. It is the issue of continuing political support for the kinds of R & D policies China has been pursuing since 1977. The continuation of this support will be contingent upon payoffs from the R & D system, in the form of technological innovations, within a reasonably short period of time. This need for early results prompts questions about the R & D system, nonetheless. The organization of the system still shows the strong influence of the Soviet model. The underlying assumptions behind that model are that research can be rationalized through planning, and that innovation is also a planned activity. These assumptions are reflected in the design of the system, characterized as it is by centralization and a strong vertical structure. Still, this approach to innovation is somewhat at variance with the views of innovation derived from studies of market economies.

The Chinese, of course, have deviated significantly from the Soviet model. In particular, the Cultural Revolution and post–Cultural Revolution reforms were intended to thrust the needs of production into the consciousness of R & D workers and onto the agenda of R & D institutions. These reforms, however, retarded the basic research that China will increasingly need in order to deal autonomously with the "scientific sticking points" of more technologically advanced industries. In swinging back toward policies and institutional structures more characteristic of the pre–Cultural Revolution period, China seems intent on strengthening basic research. The question is, is this also a shift back toward a system that by design is at variance with our best estimates of what the innovation process is all about?

Notes

1. *The Conditions for Success in Technological Innovations* (Paris: Organization for Economic Cooperation and Development, 1970), p. 56.

2. Unfortunately, hard data on China's R & D effort continue to be quite scarce. See Leo A. Orleans "Research and Development in Communist China: Mood, Management, and Measurement," in U.S., Congress, Joint Economic Committee, *An Economic Profile of Mainland China*, 90th Cong., 1st sess., 1967, pp. 573, 575. Based upon Orleans' analysis, the distribution of effort by sector is as follows:

R & D manpower (scientists and engineers only)

CAS	3,500	(6.6%)
Higher education	4,500	(8.5%)
Ministries	45,000	(84.9%)

Percent distribution of R & D expenditures (based on estimated wage bill per sector of senior scientists and engineers)

CAS	(10%)
Higher education	(12%)
Ministries	(78%)

3. Harvey W. Nelson, *The Chinese Military System* (Boulder, Colo.: Westview, 1977), pp. 60ff.

4. For a discussion of professional societies in China, see Richard P. Suttmeier, "Chinese Scientific Societies and Chinese Scientific Development," *The Developing Economies* 11, no. 2 (June 1973):146–65; and Robert O. Boorstin, "Communication in Science and Technology: Professional Societies in the People's Republic of China" (Washington, D.C.: National Council for U.S.-China Trade, August 1978). I am indebted to Mr. Boorstin and the National Council for sharing this manuscript with me.

5. Based on a discussion with a Chinese scientist-administrator in Peking, May 1978.

6. See, Nicholas A. Ashford, "Summary," in *National Support for Science and Technology: An Examination of Foreign Experience* (Cambridge: Massachusetts Institute of Technology, Center for Policy

Alternatives, May 1976).

7. See Hans Heymann, Jr., "Acquisition and Diffusion of Technology in China," in U.S., Congress, Joint Economic Committee, *China: A Reassessment of the Economy*, 94th Cong., 1st sess., 1975.

8. See Boorstin, "Communication in Science and Technology."

Commentary on the Institutional Structure for R & D

David M. Lampton

A basic continuity exists both in the on-going Chinese commitment to central planning and in the division of R & D into three sectors—the Chinese Academy of Sciences, the ministries, and the institutes of higher education. A number of questions can be asked regarding the institutional structure with its three vertically separated sectors. Is it maximally conducive to innovation? Will there not be many problems arising within such a structure through the duplication of both facilities and research efforts?

Further questions arise as to how central planning can be rendered compatible with increased autonomy at the bottom. More importantly, will central planning and the vertical control structure described above be conducive to the acceleration of industrial growth as called for by the planners?

One final category of questions has to do with the potential losers in the current developmental policy debates. A parallel can be drawn with the early and middle 1960s, when policies emphasizing urban industrial growth succeeded in alienating politically important segments of the population, with rather dramatic results. Similarly, current moves to eliminate inefficient small producers in the rationalization of the economy, purges of nontechnical cadres who rose rapidly during the Cultural Revolution, and a restructuring of regional priorities are bound to create a number of disgruntled constituencies. How to deal with these constituencies should be at the top of the agenda of today's Chinese leadership.

Discussion

Robert Chollar warned against overgeneralizing the conflict between basic research and technology, emphasizing the change in the style of research being conducted in the P.R.C. Some basic research areas can be highly profitable. He suggested that attention should be focused on those areas where basic research can be correlated to productivity, such as the biochemical sciences. Chollar defended the now waning revolutionary committees as significant organs of empiricism, which provided effective feedback loops between laboratory and field.

Betsy Ancker-Johnson questioned the ability of the State Science and Technology Commission to effectively coordinate Chinese S & T. She claimed that the SSTC is uninfluential and, in contrast to the situation in the Soviet Union, has no control over the S & T budget. While admitting that the commission's power may increase with time, she argued that it has few consolidating tools with which to pull together the myriad R & D projects being carried out by the localities and the policymakers at the top.

Several discussants were concerned that the pendulum may be swinging too far away from the excessively practical approach to research of the Cultural Revolution toward what is perhaps an equally excessive tilt to theoretical research, particularly under the newly revised CAS. *C. L. Tien* countered this notion with the observation that most recent CAS expansion has been on the side of the technical sciences. *Richard Baum* added that the "open-door research" program of the early 1970s will have to be redefined in order to make it relevant under the new S & T regime.

Ralph Miller emphasized the crucial importance of the adaptation of new technologies to Chinese conditions. He described the time lag needed to make research laboratories productive. He also suggested that these laboratories now operate primarily as bases of engineering development, which then can be geared up to do research as the need arises.

6
China's Program of Technology Acquisition

Shannon R. Brown

The Celestial Court has pacified and possessed the territory within the four seas. . . . Consequently there is nothing we lack, as your principal envoy and others themselves observed. We have never set much store on strange or ingenious objects, nor do we need any more of your country's manufactures.

—The Ch'ien-lung Emperor, 1793

On the other hand, articles coming from the outside to China can only be used as toys. We can take them or get along without them. Since they are not needed by China, what difficulty would there be if we closed the frontier and stopped the trade?

—Lin Tse-hsü, 1839

From ancient down to modern times, your slave has never heard of anyone who could use mathematics to raise the nation from a state of decline or to strengthen it in a time of weakness.

—Wo-jen, 1867

My purpose in citing these remarks is not to revive old stereotypes of a conservative and obscurantist China, but rather to emphasize the magnitude of emotional and intellectual change that was required for Chinese intellectuals and officials to accept Western science and technology. In the course of the nineteenth century, a gradually increasing minority of Chinese officials, perhaps beginning with the forcible conversion of Commissioner Lin Tse-hsü, slowly developed an appreciation of foreign technology. Among the leaders of this self-strengthening movement were Tseng Kuo-fan, Li Hung-chang, and Chang Chih-tung. Chang's slogan, "Chinese learning for essence [*t'i*], Western learning for use [*yung*]," probably provides a fair summary of the basically conservative objectives of this minority who, despite being labeled "progressives," advocated only a limited introduction of foreign technology. Significantly, with the possible exception of Li, it appears that none of these leaders perceived any contradiction in attempting to mix Chinese learning for "essence" with Western learning for "use."[1]

One of the first Chinese intellectuals who did perceive a contradiction, and who thereby gained insight into the degree of cultural change that the mere use of Western technology would require, was Wang T'ao. Wang, a collaborator of James Legge in translating the Chinese Classics into English, was also an early advocate of Western technology. In the late 1860s he travelled to Britain with Legge and, while visiting an exhibition of military equipment in Edinburgh, "discovered to his horror that the manual on firearms he had coauthored only a few years before [1863] was already out of date."[2] Foreign technology, he began to realize, was not simply a set of "strange or ingenious objects," but rather an ongoing process of change with far-reaching implications for Chinese "essence."

Before 1895, however, few Chinese intellectuals and officials were interested in promoting technological change and the continued strength of the old regime also prevented Chinese and foreign entrepreneurs from becoming significant agents of innovation.[3] But after China's humiliating defeat by Japan in 1895, ethnocentric supporters of Chinese "essence" were rapidly replaced by patriotic advocates of national salvation. And, by 1919, many of these patriots spoke of "Mr. Science" and "Mr. Democracy" in the same respectful tones formerly reserved for Confucius.

What encouraged such iconoclasm was the declining power of the Chinese government after 1895 and its virtual collapse after 1911. In this environment foreign and Chinese enterprise expanded rapidly and both became important agents of technological change, although the political uncertainty of the warlord period (1916–1927) often discouraged investment.[4] In the 1930s, political stability increased and, although the Nationalist government sought to extend its control over the economy, most technological change continued to originate in the private sector. Consequently, it was not until after 1949 that economic activity, including technological change, was once again powerfully shaped by political considerations—as it had been before 1895.

While there can be no doubt that the Communist Chinese are very different from the Confucian Chinese, it is also true that they are the inheritors of certain traditional attitudes that are of great significance for technology acquisition. One of these is a continuing anxiety about things Western and their capacity for corrupting the "purity" of things Chinese.[5] Another is the conviction that politics (and hence officials) should be in command. Because of the latter attitude many economic questions—including the pace, pattern, and source of technological change—become highly politicized. The history of Chinese technology acquisition since 1949 has been strongly influenced by both of these traditions.

The Need to Improve Human and Physical Capital

Cultural attitudes and political policies are basic determinants of the rate of technological change, but their operational significance lies in how they affect improvements in both human and physical capital. For in its simplest form technological change can be seen as a process that improves the quality of these two types of capital.

In China's case human capital can be enhanced by several means. First, it can be achieved by improving the educational system. Although the quality of primary and secondary education is important, the quality of higher education, especially in science and technology, is of more immediate concern. Furthermore, in order to provide a corps of teachers and develop a greater capacity to adapt and generate new technologies, high quality graduate education and research are also necessary. A second means is to send individuals abroad, either for short periods of technical training or for longer periods of undergraduate and graduate study. Finally, foreigners can be brought to China, either for short periods to provide on-the-job techni-

A Chinese-built, diesel locomotive engine crossing the Yangtze River Bridge at Nanking (September 1978).

cal assistance and training or for longer periods as teachers and researchers.

Improvement of the physical capital, on the other hand, is achieved by producing or importing new machinery and equipment that embodies the latest technology or by purchasing complete plants from abroad. In a large economy, such as China's, only a fraction of the needed improvements in physical capital can be achieved by means of imports. But the importance of these imports should not be underestimated, because the imported machinery is considerably more productive and has a greater impact on learning than does its domestically produced counterpart.

The rate at which China can improve its physical and human capital depends significantly upon its capacity to absorb foreign technology. This, in turn, depends upon the development of an effective set of institutions and incentives to promote the identification, modification, and use of those foreign technologies

Chinese freighters harbored in the Whampoa River near Shanghai (September 1978).

most productive in China. This important topic, however, is discussed elsewhere in this volume, so it need only be mentioned here.

Finally, it must be remembered that many efforts to improve China's technology will require foreign exchange. Thus, the rate of technology acquisition will also be influenced by the level of foreign exchange earnings and China's willingness to go into debt.

Technology Acquisition, 1949–1969

In order to perceive what is novel in Chinese technology acquisition since the Cultural Revolution it is necessary to examine briefly what went before. In doing so, we will pay particular attention to those developments that have affected human capital, physical capital, and the balance of payments.

From the establishment of the People's Republic in 1949 until the withdrawal of Soviet advisors in 1960, China received what one economist has called "the most comprehensive technology transfer in modern history."[6] More than 15,000 Chinese technicians and workers received training in Russia, and nearly 11,000 Soviet technicians worked in China.[7] In addition China imported a large quantity of Soviet and East European machinery and equipment, including about 157 complete plants. According to Robert Dernberger, these imports constituted about 27 percent of total Chinese investments in machinery and equipment in that period.[8] But in the course of these developments the Chinese also incurred a significant foreign debt, which, in the difficult years after 1960, proved painful to repay.

In the early 1960s Chinese technology acquisition ceased almost completely due to the combined effects of the Sino-Soviet split, reduced exports, and increased food imports. By the mid-1960s, limited purchases of complete plants, this time from the West, were resumed. But in 1966, just as economic conditions finally seemed favorable for an expanded program of technology acquisition, the Cultural Revolution began.

If the dates of the Cultural Revolution are taken to be 1966–1969, then during these years the acquisition of modern technology steadily declined. In an often chaotic atmosphere characterized by strong xenophobic overtones, the importation of machinery and equipment fell significantly and complete plant purchases ceased (see Table 6.1). Furthermore, much emphasis was put upon the development of small-scale industries that made little use of sophisticated technology. The educational system was greatly disrupted, and when schools reopened they stressed political attitudes and practical experience rather than academic excellence. Generally speaking, scholarly research and graduate education ceased and even the importation of foreign scientific journals was disrupted. In short, the immediate effect of the Cultural Revolution was to retard greatly Chinese efforts at technology acquisition. In addition, the attitudes exemplified in popular slogans (such as "self-reliance") together with certain reforms (such as those in the educational system) promised an even bleaker future. In the long run, however, promise and reality began to diverge.

Table 6.1

Chinese Trade and Complete Plant Purchases

($ millions)[a]

Year	Total Exports	Total Imports	Balance of Trade	Machinery and Equipment Imports	Complete Plant Contracts
1966	2210	2035	175	455	0
1967	1960	1955	5	380	0
1968	1960	1825	135	275	0
1969	2060	1835	225	240	0
1970	2095	2245	-150	395	0
1971	2500	2310	190	505	0
1972	3150	2850	300	520	0
1973	5075	5225	-150	860	1259
1974	6660	7420	-760	1610	831
1975	7180	7395	-215	2155	364
1976	7265	6010	1255	1770	185
1977	7955	7100	855	1200	80
1978[b]	10260	10650	-390	2500	6934

a. All figures in this paper are expressed in current dollars and consequently have an upward bias due to inflation and the decreasing exchange value of the dollar since 1973.

b. Preliminary.

Sources: CIA, China: International Trade, 1977-78 (Washington, D.C., 1978) and various earlier issues; Hans Heymann, Jr., "Acquisition and Diffusion of Technology in China" in U.S. Congress, Joint Economic Committee, China: A Reassessment of the Economy (Washington, D.C., 1975), p. 685; and Table 2 in this essay.

Technology Acquisition, 1969–1976

After the Cultural Revolution ended in 1969, Chinese imports of machinery and equipment again began to increase. More importantly, by 1971 a major political decision had been made (perhaps in connection with efforts to normalize relations with the United States) to contract for a large quantity of complete plant imports.[9] In the summer and fall of 1972 the Chinese carried out intensive discussions and negotiations with potential suppliers and by the beginning of the next year had started to sign contracts. During 1973, as the dollar amount of contracts approached $1.2 billion, it became increasingly obvious that a major policy shift had taken place. Not only were complete plant contracts unprecedentedly large—larger even than the Russian program in the 1950s—but their fulfillment required many Western engineers and technicians to reside temporarily in China and many Chinese to travel abroad.[10] In 1974 further contracts totaling $831 million confirmed that a policy shift had taken place.

In that same year, however, the program began to run into difficulties as worldwide inflation, combined with recession, led to rising prices for Chinese imports and shrinking markets for Chinese exports. The result was a $760 million deficit in the balance of trade. Still, this need not have led to a sharp cutback in imports and complete plant purchases had the Chinese leaders been more willing to use credit. But, even in the best of circumstances, being in debt to foreigners is a sensitive issue in China and in 1974 the Gang of Four was already mounting a major attack on the complete plant program.

In the course of 1974 and 1975 a growing number of articles appeared in the Chinese press opposing the "worship of things foreign" and warning against the adoption of a "slavish comprador philosophy." As Alan Whiting has shown, these articles, some couched as historical pieces, represented a growing attack on the complete plant policy.[11] For example, an August 1974 article critical of Li Hung-chang (read Chou En-lai) said, "Equipment, raw materials, and technology were imported as 'gifts' from the foreign imperialists, and foreign experts were hired to run the factories. In short everything became 'modernized.'"[12]

Similar articles, seemingly criticizing Chang Chih-tung, were in fact aimed at Teng Hsiao-p'ing. Finally, in September 1975, the entire technology acquisition program was repudiated in an article that pretended to be a criticism of the "self-strengthening" movement in the nineteenth century:

> Politically, "wholesale Westernization" meant loss of sovereignty and national humiliation, total sell-out of China's independence and self-determination. . . . Ideologically "wholesale Westernization" was meant to praise what is foreign and belittle what is Chinese and propagate national nihilism in order to undermine the national consciousness of the Chinese spirit. . . . Economically "wholesale Westernization" was aimed at spreading blind faith in the Western capitalist material civilization so as to turn the Chinese economy into a complete appendage of imperialism.[13]

Following the death of Chou En-lai in January 1976, the Gang's attacks on Teng and the technology acquisition program increased. And now a new criticism was added—the xenophobic indictment that Teng sought to barter away China's national resources (petroleum). Finally, in April, Teng was purged and the complete plant program ground to a halt. Contracts for few new plants were made despite a complete turnaround in the balance of trade. In September, however, Chairman Mao died and shortly afterwards the Gang itself was purged. The post-Mao era had begun.

Technology Acquisition Policy Since 1976

During the first nine months after the fall of the Gang, Chinese technology acquisition policy appeared to be similar to that of the early 1970s. But the rehabilitation of Teng Hsiao-p'ing in July 1977 and the Eleventh Party Congress in August made it clear that the Chinese leadership intended to embark on an expanded and considerably more pragmatic program of technology acquisition. Although it is risky to predict the future of China, current policies, if continued, suggest a rather radical break with the past. In all three of the ways that technological change can be furthered—improvement of physical capital, improvement of human capital, and relaxation of foreign exchange constraints—there have been dramatic new developments.

Physical Capital

Final data on China's imports of machinery and equipment for 1978 are not yet available, but there is little doubt that they will show a sharp recovery from the two-year decline of 1975–1977, when imports fell from $2,155 million to $1,200 million. This decline, as mentioned earlier, was caused by the combination of worldwide economic recession in 1974–1975 and increasing Chinese domestic political instability in 1975–1976.

It is in the area of complete plant purchases, however, that the most radical departure from the past has taken place (see Table 6.2). In 1978, after four years of steady decline, the Chinese signed contracts for complete plants totaling $6,934 million. Even discounting for inflation and the declining exchange value of the dollar (all values have been converted into dollars at current exchange rates), the real value of these contracts is certainly greater than that of the five previous years put together. Exactly how firm some of these contracts are, however, is open to question. In February and March 1979, for example, the Chinese indicated that the implementation dates of certain contracts would be delayed, but no contracts were cancelled at the time.[14]

Complete plant purchases are a particularly interesting indicator of technology acquisitions for several reasons. First, they indicate investment and technological priorities and forecast future machinery and equipment imports. Second, they constitute a technological package—technical assistance and training comes with them. Finally, they are highly visible. Table 6.2 shows the changing pattern for these contracts during the years 1973–1978. It should be recalled, however, that much imported machinery and equipment is unrelated to these complete plant purchases. In recent years, for instance, there have been extensive purchases of aircraft, machine tools, mining equipment, oil exploration and production equipment, ships, and telecommunications equipment—all of which embodied sophisti-

Table 6.2

Contracts for Whole Plants, by Industry

($ millions)

	1973	1974	1975	1976	1977	1978	Total
Petrochemicals	698	114	90	136	39	3325	4402
Iron and Steel		551		40		2978	3569
Fertilizer	392	120		8			520
Coal and Electric Power	161	46				202	409
Transport			200			79	279
Communications & Electronics						217	217
Non-ferrous Metals						127	127
Manufacturing	8		74	1	21	6	110
Petroleum and Gas					20		20
Total	1259	831	364	185	80	6934	9653

Sources: CIA, International Trade Handbooks (Washington, D.C. 1975-78); CIA, China: Post-Mao Search for Civilian Industrial Technology (Washington, D.C. 1979).

cated technology and yet were not part of any complete plant projects.

What does Table 6.2, and especially the data for 1978, tell us about Chinese priorities in technology acquisition? In his speech to the Fifth National People's Congress in February 1978, Chairman Hua Kuo-feng stated that the new Ten-Year Plan would be built around 120 large-scale projects.[15] Nineteen of these projects were to be in mining and metallurgy (10 iron and steel complexes and 9 nonferrous metals complexes), 48 in energy (8 coal mines, 10 oil and gas fields, and 30 power stations) and 11 in transportation projects (6 new trunk railways and 5 key harbors). The nature of the remaining 42 was not given. Thus, the contracts for complete plants listed in Table 6.2 are at least roughly consistent with Hua's outline.

But in early 1979 the Chinese announced that they were revising their priorities. A *Jen-min jih-pao* (People's daily) editorial of February 24 emphasized that economic policies in the next two years would stress restoration, readjustment, and consolidation.[16] First priority would be given to increasing agricultural output, while in the industrial sector, energy (oil, coal, and electric power), transportation, and building materials would receive greater attention. In general, it was stated, investment projects would be favored that could promise either quick results, earn good profits, or compete successfully in international markets. Increasing the production of consumers' goods was also given higher priority than before, and the iron and steel industry was given lower priority. In fact, the iron and steel industry appears to be the major casualty of the revised priorities as plans for new plants, mines, and beneficiation facilities have either been cancelled or postponed.

The rethinking of Chinese development strategy that became known in the first half of 1979 did not immediately manifest itself in a spurt of new contracts for foreign technology. Rather it indicated that Chinese economic development in the next few years will greatly depend on rationalization of the economy, more efficient operation of existing enterprises, selective technological upgrading, and gradual implementation of the contracts already signed in 1978. It does not indicate a significant modification of ends, then, but it does imply a much more realistic and pragmatic attitude toward means.

Finance

According to one estimate, Hua's February 1978 speech and Chinese shopping patterns since then indicated potential purchases of more than $40 billion worth of foreign plants, engineering assistance, and technology between 1978 and 1985.[17] To achieve this, according to one projection, would have required earnings on current account to increase at an unprecedented rate and debt owed to foreigners to become unprecedentedly large, i.e., $12–15 billion. Alternatively, if current account earnings were to grow at the rate actually achieved from 1970 to 1977 (i.e., 12 percent per year), still larger credits ($15–20 billion) would be required even to import a smaller ($25–30 billion) total of foreign plant and equipment. In the first (optimistic) case, debt service would rise to a peak of 10 percent in 1986, while in the latter it would rise to 21 percent in the same year.[18] As an examination of these calculations shows, it is not surprising that the Chinese have revised their plans, have slowed down the pace of plant purchases, and are now emphasizing the earning of foreign exchange, although their attitude toward the use of foreign credits remains favorable.

In an effort to obtain more foreign exchange (or to reduce the need for it) the Chinese are developing some novel approaches in addition to the more traditional ones, such as increased exports of goods and services. Among the more innovative means are cooperative investment projects, expanded tourism, and a more flexible attitude toward debt.

Beginning in 1978, Chinese firms entered into agreements with foreign firms in which the latter promised to supply them with machinery, special inputs, technical advice, and even whole plants in return for some of the output of these plants.[19] In one case, for example, the German firm of Konrad Hornschuch AG has agreed to build two petrochemical plants in China (total value $21 million) and to accept 50 percent of their annual output in the first five years as payment.[20] In another, Itoman & Company of Japan will provide materials, equip-

The new wing of the Peking Hotel, China's most modern tourist facility, completed in 1975 (September 1978).

ment, and advice to a Shanghai textile plant in return for the right to market its entire output.[21] These agreements allow the Chinese to increase the capacity and technological level of existing firms without increasing the demand for foreign exchange. They involve, however, direct foreign involvement in the operation of Chinese firms to an extent that the Chinese have previously found unacceptable.

The rapid expansion of tourism is also a novel method of financing the technological upgrading of Chinese industry. In 1978, more than 700,000 tourists visited China, of which 400,000 were Chinese from Hong Kong and Macao, 200,000 were overseas Chinese from elsewhere, and 100,000 were "foreigners."[22] The latter group was said to be three times as large as in 1977 and equal in size to the number of foreigners that visited China from 1963 to 1976. By 1985, China hopes to receive one million foreigners each year and an unstated number of overseas Chinese.

To accommodate these tourists will require a tremendous expansion of tourist facilities, such as hotels, restaurants, and curio shops, as well as a great improvement in the transportation system. Hotel expansion alone—an increase in the number of rooms from the present 30,000 to about 80,000 by 1985—will cost several billion dollars. The Chinese are exploring a number of forms of foreign equity participation in this industry in an effort to minimize the capital and foreign exchange requirements of such expansion.[23]

The anticipated growth of foreign trade and tourism implies an expanding market in the movement of people and goods to and from China, with related opportunities for China to increase its foreign exchange earnings. Consequently, negotiations are underway to purchase more foreign aircraft for use on international routes, and in the past two years there has already been a considerable expansion of China's merchant fleet.

More significant than these changes, at least in the short-run, is the changing Chinese attitude toward borrowing. In the past, China has made some use of foreign loans but preferred not to admit it, calling them instead "progress payments" or "deferred payments." But on December 6, 1978, the Chinese unashamedly signed their first admitted loan—an agreement with ten British banks for a $1.2 billion loan on which they intend to draw for capital goods imports.[24] The terms are 7.25 percent interest with five years to repay. In May 1979, the French agreed to extend a $7 billion credit to China and, together with credits extended by the Japanese and the Italians, it is clear that China will not lack for credit.[25] Loans at concessionary rates from the U.S. Export-Import Bank have also been proposed, but they will depend on congressional acceptance of a trade agreement with the Chinese. In addition to these sources the Chinese have also begun to receive financial and other assistance from such international agencies as the UN Development Program, WHO, and UNESCO.[26]

Even with an expanded ability to earn foreign exchange and borrow money, China's financial capacity to acquire foreign technology will continue to be influenced by its need to import a number of agriculturally related items, especially grain, cotton, and fertilizers.[27] In the past, China's purchase of these items has greatly reduced the import of capital goods. The recent trends of these imports can be seen in Table 6.3, which also clearly indicates that capital goods and agriculturally related items are substitutes for each other, i.e., when the percentage of one rises, the other falls. Obviously, then, China's capacity to acquire foreign technology, like many other aspects of its development, depends upon the degree of success it has in increasing agricultural output.

Human Capital

In the long run, however, the Chinese cannot simply import modern technology, no matter what capacity they have to finance it. Nor will they want to rely indefinitely on imported technicians and advisors who have numbered in the thousands in recent years. Instead, China must internalize the process of technological change—a need that Wang T'ao was among the first to perceive a century ago. Because of this, the reforms in education and research that have taken place in the past two years are extremely important and very basic. They will, however, be slow to take effect.

Among these reforms are the resumption of entrance examinations for university admission, the revival of graduate education, the selection of eighty-eight key universities for special attention, the revival of the Chinese Academy of Sciences, and the resumption of high-quality research. The most radical reform, however, is the decision to send Chinese students—both graduate and undergraduate—abroad for study and the invitations issued to foreign scholars to lecture in China. In 1978, more than 480 Chinese, aged twenty to forty-nine, were sent to twenty-eight foreign countries for two to three years of advanced study, mostly in science and technology. In the same year, approximately 100 foreign scholars were invited to China for lecture tours that lasted from one to three months and 140 more are expected in 1979.[28] This new policy of sending Chinese abroad for study and inviting foreigners to China seems likely to be an effective way to raise the abilities of Chinese scientists and engineers to international levels.

The fields of specialization selected by Chinese scholars sent to study abroad also indicate something of Chinese priorities with respect to technology acquisition. The data in Table 6.4

Table 6.3

Selected Chinese Imports

($ million)

	1970	1971	1972	1973	1974	1975	1976	1977
Food-Cotton-Fertilizer								
Foodstuffs	395	320	510	1,080	1,600	900	565	1,230
Natural Textile Fibers	95	125	215	450	520	260	190	350
Manufactured Fertilizer	140	135	145	210	220	405	230	345
(1) Subtotal	630	580	870	1,740	2,340	1,565	985	1,925
(2) Capital goods	375	420	445	725	1,650	2,210	1,840	1,290
(3) Total Imports	2,245	2,310	2,850	5,225	7,420	7,395	6,010	7,100
(4) (1)/(3) (percent)	.28	.25	.31	.33	.32	.21	.16	.27
(5) (2)/(3) (percent)	.17	.18	.16	.14	.22	.30	.31	.18

Sources: Richard E. Batsavage and John L. Davie, "China's International Trade and Finance" in U.S. Congress, Joint Economic Committee, _Chinese Economy Post-Mao_ (Washington, D.C., 1978), p. 738; CIA, _China: International Trade 1977-78_ (Washington, D.C., 1978) pp. 5, 15.

Table 6.4

Projected Chinese Students to U.S.: Fields of Interest 1978-79

Field	Number
Mathematics	30
Physics	58
Chemistry	30
Mechanics	10
Material Sciences & Technology	15
Astronomy & Astro-Physics	6
Meterology	7
Life Science	25
Medical Sciences	29
Radioelectronics	50
Computer Science & Engineering	45
Control Engineering	15
Aeronautical Engineering	15
Space Technology	15
Nuclear Engineering	10
Construction Technology	10
Mechanical Engineering	8
Metallurgical Engineering	10
Chemical Engineering	10
Agricultural Sciences	11
Other Subjects	24
	433

Source: Committee on Scholarly Communication With The PRC, Notes on Student Exchanges With China, 1 (November 1978), pp. 3-6.

show the areas of interest indicated for the first group of Chinese students slated to be sent to the United States during the year 1978–1979. Only sixty actually came for the spring semester, but their specialties were generally consistent with the interest expressed earlier.[29]

Conclusion

If the trends of the past two years continue, the present Chinese policies of technology acquisition will have to be regarded as a turning point in the history of the People's Republic. With respect to technology acquisition, and eventually perhaps to other things as well, it might not be facetious to label the current approach to modernization a Chinese "open-door policy." Such openness suggests a mixture of self-confidence and pragmatism that has rarely been seen in China since 1957. But while there are good reasons to expect that these policies will contribute effectively to Chinese economic development, especially in the near future, there are also some risks and problems that should be mentioned.

First, it is not clear how deeply the present policies are supported, nor is it clear that these policies will outlive the leadership of Teng Hsiao-p'ing. Now that Mao is dead it is unlikely that the Gang of Four and their supporters will make a political comeback, but it is possible that they, and the groups who gained from their egalitarian policies, could become a source of political instability. This could lead to considerable moderation of present policies. Furthermore, it is also possible that rising expectations, fueled by greater awareness of the non-Chinese world, may lead to frustration and internal tensions, again causing modification of present policies. Finally, given traditional Chinese anxieties about outsiders, the presence of thousands of foreign tourists, technicians, and scholars in China could lead to a xenophobic reaction. Still, if these and other sources of political instability can be avoided, the present policies should be extremely effective for the next few years.

In the longer run, however, technological change will primarily depend on the effectiveness of Chinese institutions in promoting the importation (or production), distribution, and use of new technologies.[30] In other words, China's ability to thoroughly internalize the process of economic change will be crucial. The Russian experience of the past twenty years suggests that their institutions have been a major impediment to technological change, and the Russian ancestry of China's economic institutions means that many of these impediments must have been inherited. Certainly the recently expressed Chinese interest in U.S. management techniques and the Yugoslav economic system, together with the initiation of interest charges on capital construction projects, suggest that institutional reform may yet be forthcoming in China. Whether such reforms are desired primarily for their effect on technological change or simply to improve the operating efficiency of enterprises is at present unclear. Together with the dramatic changes in technology acquisition already under way, however, they would certainly enhance the image of China as a dynamic society.

Notes

1. For a stimulating discussion of this problem see Joseph R. Levenson, "T'i and Yung—Substance and Function," in his *Confucian China and Its Modern Fate: The Problem of Intellectual Continuity* (Berkeley, Calif.: University of California Press, 1958), pp. 59–78.

2. Paul Cohen, *Between Tradition and Modernity: Wang T'ao and Reform in Late Ch'ing China* (Cambridge, Mass: Harvard University Press, 1974), pp. 196–197.

3. See Shannon R. Brown, "The Transfer of Technology to China in the Nineteenth Century: The Role of Direct Foreign Investment," *Journal of Economic History* 39 (March 1979):181–198.

4. Wang Ching-yu, ed., *Chung-kuo chin-tai kung-yeh shih tzu-liao, ti-ehr-chi, 1895–1914* [Source materials on the history of modern industry in China, second collection, 1895–1914] (Peking, 1957). John K. Chang, *Industrial Development in Pre-Communist China* (Chicago: Aldine, 1969), pp. 71–73.

5. This, in part, is the theme of Robert F. Dernberger's essay, "Economic Development and Modernization in Contemporary China: The Attempt to Limit Dependence on the Transfer of Modern Industrial Technology from Abroad and to Control Its Corruption of the Maoist Social Revolution," in Frederic J. Fleron, Jr., ed., *Technology and Communist Culture* (New York: Praeger, 1977), pp. 224–264.

6. Hans Heymann, Jr., "Acquisition and Diffusion of Technology in China," in U.S., Congress, Joint Economic Committee, *China: A Reassessment of the Economy*, 94th Cong., 1st sess., 1975, p. 678.

7. Alexander Eckstein, *China's Economic Growth and Foreign Trade* (New York: McGraw-Hill, 1966). p. 169.

8. Dernberger, "Economic Development," p. 243.

9. Allen S. Whiting, "Chinese Domestic Politics and the Importation of Whole Plants, 1971–76," (Paper for U.S. State Department, November 3, 1977).

10. Alexander Eckstein, *China's Economic Revolution* (Cambridge, England: Cambridge University Press, 1977), p. 261. Eckstein esti-

mates the annual rate of plant imports in the mid-1970s (in 1973 prices) to be $700 million as compared to $430 million in the 1950s.

11. Whiting, "Chinese Domestic Politics."

12. Ch'en Chin, "Worshipping Things Foreign and Betraying the Country," *Hung Ch'i* [Red flag], no. 8 (August 1, 1974), in *Selections from P.R.C. Magazines* [hereafter *SPRCM*], no. 738-788 (August 30–September 9, 1974). Cited in Whiting, "Chinese Domestic Politics."

13. Liang Hsiao, "The Yang Wu Movement and the Slavish Comprador Philosophy," *Historical Research*, no. 5 (October 20, 1975), in *SPRCM*, no. 859 (December 16, 1975). Cited in Whiting, "Chinese Domestic Politics."

14. *China Business Review* (hereafter *CBR*) 6, no. 2 (March–April 1979):4–5.

15. *New York Times* (hereafter *NYT*), March 7, 1978.

16. *Jen-min jih-pao* [People's daily], February 24, 1979.

17. *China: Post-Mao Search for Civilian Industrial Technology* (Washington, D.C.: Central Intelligence Agency, 1979), p. 9.

18. Ibid., p. 10.

19. For a list of cooperation agreements signed in 1978–1979, see *CBR* 6, no. 2 (March–April 1979):72–73.

20. *Wall Street Journal*, November 8, 1978.

21. *CBR* 5 (November–December 1978):68.

22. *Beijing Review*, nos. 2 and 11 (January 12 and March 16, 1979).

23. *CBR* 6, no. 2 (March–April 1979):21–27.

24. *CBR* 5, no. 5 (September–October 1978):77–79.

25. *NYT*, May 10, 1979.

26. Ibid., November 16, 1978.

27. In 1957, the last year for which good data are available, foodgrains, cotton, and soybeans occupied 89 percent of the total sown area of China. Nai-ruenn Chen, ed., *Chinese Economic Statistics* (Chicago: Aldine, 1967), p. 287. Since fertilizer is, in part, a substitute for land, these agriculture-related imports are related to China's land scarcity and the relatively low productivity of agriculture.

28. *Beijing Review*, no. 5 (February 2, 1979).

29. Committee on Scholarly Communication with the P.R.C., *Notes on Student Exchanges with China* 7, no. 2 (February 1979):7–8.

30. For a more detailed discussion on this theme see Shannon R. Brown, "Trends in China: Foreign Technology and Economic Growth," *Problems of Communism* 26, no. 4 (July–August 1977):30–40.

Commentary on Technology Acquisition

Robert F. Dernberger

In distinguishing between foreign and domestic technology, it would be a mistake to treat imports as the major source of technology. Foreign technology must inevitably be grafted onto a Chinese base. Moreover, indigenous technology determines what is to be brought in from abroad. Therefore, emphasis must be placed first on domestic Chinese capabilities and only then on China's ability to integrate these with foreign technology.

Second, imports of machinery, equipment, and complete plants do not constitute the transfer of technology. Once again, the emphasis should be on China's ability to integrate these into its domestic economy. Since the 1950s, Chinese attitudes toward technology acquisition have broadened to include participation in technical seminars, training abroad, and many other previously unused avenues. Nor is the acquisition of foreign plants necessarily any more important than the importation of raw materials or semifinished products that feed domestic technological capabilities.

Third, any meaningful discussion of augmenting human capital (via education) and physical capital (via imports of plants and equipment) must take into account what is perhaps the most important element—the effective adaptation of technology to local conditions. Paul Samuelson argued several years ago that you cannot look at a piece of technology and say whether it is augmenting your labor or whether it is augmenting your capital. What any particular technology contributes to factor productivity depends upon how it is used in a particular setting.

We now have available empirical proof of Samuelson's belief

that any technological innovation simultaneously affects the productivity of labor, the productivity of capital, and the economies of scale. This is relevant to our argument. England, at one time, sent identical textile machinery to several different countries. Japan managed to capture a large portion of the world textile market, not by any engineering adaptation of that technology, but by the way the factory managed and used its abundant resource of unskilled labor. India's textile industry failed due to its inability to adapt the same machinery to its local conditions.

China's technological acquisitions could similarly fail for the same reasons. So I would argue that the way in which the Chinese adapt technology to meet their particular needs and fit their available resources will determine whether a given technological input is labor saving or capital saving.

Fourth, it may be misleading to use trade statistics given in U.S. dollars to illustrate recent changes in Chinese technical import policy. Although analysts frequently use the figure of 60 percent for the increase in Chinese import spending during the first six months of 1978, fully one-third of China's imports during that period were purchased from Japan and were paid for with yen. When the dollar figures are adjusted, the increase, according to Japanese commentators, was only about 12 percent. Thus the 60 percent figure may reveal more about our domestic monetary problems than it does about what the Chinese are doing in terms of import trade. Furthermore, a close look at the composition of the commodity statistics will also help in putting some of the more spectacular Chinese import figures in perspective. Iron and steel constitute about one-half of China's imports from Japan, yet these grew by only 6 percent in the first half of 1978. Chemical fertilizers, on the other hand, dropped by 30 percent. Hence, to take the figure of 60 percent as the growth of trade and start arguing about large quantities of Chinese imports is a little premature.

An additional warning is necessary concerning China's foreign trade statistics. There is a big difference between *signing* contracts and *negotiating* contracts. As of December 1978, the Japanese claimed to have actually signed only eleven contracts, worth $400 million, a figure far below that frequently quoted by outside observers. In assessing the Chinese payments position, it is necessary to look at what contracts have actually been signed, what the delivery schedules are, and what the means of payment will be. It is certainly premature to be talking about a Chinese balance-of-payments crisis. Teng Hsiao-p'ing's experience with the political consequences of payments crises should place powerful restraints on his actions in this area.

Discussion

Hans Heymann posed the question of the long-term impact of the current program of technology acquisition on Chinese society. He observed that *Richard Baum* and others have suggested that the "struggle between two lines" in the modified form of a contest between the respective imperatives of "ideologic" and "technologic" persists. What will the ramifications of this struggle be? What will be the reaction of the "losers" in the new order—the former Red Guards, Party cadres lacking in technical skills, and youths who have spent their college years in the countryside learning from peasants?

Roy Hofheinz sounded a note of caution concerning China's potential political destabilization under the pressures of modernization. He specifically drew a historical analogy between the present period in China and the period from 1901 to 1911 when many of the policies currently being followed were first tried, including massive imports from abroad, economic reform, and the sending of students abroad. The collapse of this program after 1911 should not be taken lightly today, despite the tremendous changes in political consciousness China has undergone over the last seventy-five years.

Heymann, in an examination of Chinese criteria for technological choice, found three not always compatible desires: economies of scale (implying high capital and skill intensities), payment by compensation (implying a product up to world standards of technology), and self-reliance. Since these goals are not always compatible, different trade-offs will have to be made among them.

Carl Riskin suggested that the goal of relative self-reliance has already begun to reassert itself. The Chinese have become defensive about the acquisition of technology via complete plants and have "served notice" to the rest of the world that other, less expensive paths will be found as soon as their short-term priority needs, which only complete plant purchases can satisfy, have been met.

William Clarke raised a number of problems that the Chinese will have to overcome before they will be able to fully absorb and use acquired technology:

1. Lack of design tradition, evident in most factories.
2. Lack of precision necessary for mass production; their whole metrology is an order of magnitude short of what they need for mass production.
3. Lack of suitable infrastructure for specific problem-solving.
4. Lack of good production and inventory control. There is much waste in in-process inventory.
5. Lack of full utilization of existing capacity. Failure here is graphically illustrated by the seven or eight Boeing 707s one always sees sitting on the runway in Peking. Perhaps a better example of this is the Talien Locomotive Plant which, despite its enormous potential, operates far below capacity.

Clarke further suggested that perhaps the greatest danger is that the leadership does not fully perceive the difficulties or comprehend the complexity of what they are setting into motion. The Chinese are at this point readjusting their expectations somewhat. Part of this adjustment has clearly been necessitated by the inadequacy of the planning and technological infrastructure that exists in China. Under these circumstances, an 85 percent fulfillment of the current Ten-Year Plan would be a tremendous success; 50 percent might not even be judged a failure.

7
The Absorption and Assimilation of Acquired Technology

Rudi Volti

In assaying the prospects for technological development in the centuries to come, an informed observer of the early sixteenth century would most likely have looked to China as the most promising site for future progress. Chinese society had already manifested impressive levels of urbanization, entrepreneurship, managerial skill, and inventive ability. Demonstrating a striking promise of a modern economic order, China appeared to be poised on the threshold of a revolution in production. Yet the fruition did not come, and the following centuries of accelerated economic progress belonged to the West and not to China. The early promise was not fulfilled, and China as a civilization shared the fate of its peasants, who, in R. H. Tawney's famous summation, "ploughed with iron when Europe used wood, and continued to plough with it when Europe used steel."[1] By the nineteenth century, China's former technological lead served only to highlight the relative backwardness of a nation that proved pathetically incapable of resisting the aggressive intentions of more technologically advanced nations.

This absence of sustained technological development was certainly not due to a lack of inventive ability within the Chinese people. The fundamental problem lay in the inability and unwillingness of traditional political and social elites to create the appropriate climate for the development and assimilation of new things. Ironically, the lack of technological development finally proved fatal for the traditional elite and the political and cultural order that sustained them. Although the ancien régime had been a model of longevity, its shortcomings became all too apparent when Europe, the United States, and Japan began to press their demands. Solidly backed by the technological and organizational revolutions of the preceeding centuries, the imperialist powers were able to subjugate China in a strikingly short space of time. The penetration of these industrial nations may not have destroyed the traditional economy, but it seriously undermined the foundations of Chinese culture and society. China could no longer be supported by the verities of an honored past; it could only be concerned with redressing the present disparities of economic and political power.

In this venture, the application of new technologies was essential. This in turn necessitated a greater receptiveness to ideas, processes, and materials that had been developed elsewhere. But nagging doubts attended the effort to transform China's technological order: Could foreign things be assimilated into the Chinese way of life without a profound dislocation of Chinese culture? Efforts to achieve a rapprochement between imported modernity and indigenous patterns of life were not easily realized, for technological progress could not be pursued in complete disregard of its cultural consequences. China's recent history, as elegantly summarized by Joseph Levenson, can thus be seen as the search for "modernization with pride."[2]

The confrontation between the entrenched civilization of traditional China and the technological novelties introduced by the intruding West has long been a basic theme in modern Chinese history. It bears repeating here because a complete resolution has never been reached. Many of the key components of modernity have been imports from other lands and not the results of indigenous Chinese efforts. To be sure, all cultures have made heavy use of foreign products and processes, but rarely has importation come so suddenly and to so well-established and self-assured a civilization.

The initial response to evident technological incapacity came in the form of government-sponsored efforts at bolstering China's military capacity.[3] The importation of new technologies was at first confined to the government's armories and shipyards, but it soon became apparent that acquired technologies could not easily be restricted to the Kiangnan Arsenal and other military spheres. There was no escape from the fact that a modern military force required the supporting infrastructure of a modern, technologically progressive economy.[4] Even this did not mark the limits of modernization; for progressive Chinese thinkers, the assimilation of Western science and technology took on an importance that transcended the strengthening of military power and its economic props. Science and technology were to be the foundation of a new Chinese society erected over the remains of a crumbling civilization. Science and technolgy were more than the means of revitalizing the Chinese economy; as new sources of thought and behavior they became ends in themselves.[5]

Such avant-garde notions about the transcendent role of science and technology could not be taken as anything but a mortal threat to those whose identity and authority were bound up with the values and patterns of the traditional order. A culture founded upon scientific thinking and devoted to technological progress would be profoundly different from the one that had been the work of the preceding millennia. Some Chinese, however, endeavored to have it both ways, seeking to retain the essential features of Chinese civilization while at the same time acquiring and assimilating the foreign technologies necessary for China's resurgence. According to their prescription, new technologies and organizational structures could be incorporated for their utility value (*yung*) while leaving unchanged the essence of Chinese civilization (*t'i*). This *t'i-yung* synthesis, supposedly derived from the neo-Confucian philosophy of the Sung Dynasty, made an appealing package. But its surface plausibility was quickly challenged by the more unregenerate members of the Chinese political and cultural elite. To them, no easy distinction could be drawn between utility and essence; a China that took the path of technological and organizational modernization would soon lose its way in its pursuit of foreign novelties. Ironically, in their way of thinking, the traditional elite presaged the views of later generations of Western social scientists who were to find in industrialization and continuous technological change a "universal solvent" that dissolved and transformed all "premodern" cultures. For Confucian literatus and Western sociologist alike, a commitment to acquire and assimilate modern technologies could only result in the dissolution of the established culture.

These qualms were not enough to stem the tide of change, and there was little chance that the Confucian literati could maintain the world in which they had been so comfortable. By the beginning of the twentieth century, the old order and much of the traditional culture were on their last legs. The Communist rise to power could thus be seen as the last nail in the coffin that modern ideas had prepared for the debilitated body of old China. With its commitment to modernization and technological development, the People's Republic of China could be taken as simply the latest stage in the transformation of Chinese culture, a process that began with the Opium Wars in the mid-nineteenth century. The *yung* had devoured the *t'i* and in so doing had obliterated the last of the great preindustrial civilizations.

Yet such a summation is too facile, for the fundamental problems of technological assimiliation have not been completely resolved even today. Despite the ouster of the xenophobic Gang of Four and the apparently smooth accession to power by a phalanx of Chinese pragmatists, it is still premature to conclude that the balancing of imported technologies with indigenous Chinese culture has been achieved. A fundamental question still remains: Will Chinese experience for the remainder of this century simply confirm Marx's judgment that "the country that is more developed industrially only shows to the less developed the image of its own future"?[6]

New technologies and the manner of their assimilation can fundamentally alter the configuration of Chinese society and disrupt many cultural patterns, including many of those that are distinct to a Communist order. Changes in productive technologies can lead to concomitant changes in patterns of authority, ideological orientations, organizational modes, and habits of consumption. The looming possibility of technologically determined social development subsumes many of the basic issues that will shape the future of China. For the People's Republic of China the problem is particularly acute, for today's China is not only heir to an ancient cultural tradition, it is also manifestly committed to the construction of a socialist society. Both inside and outside China can be found the apprehension that the values that energized a long revolution will be eroded as Chinese society accommodates to the demands of economic modernization.[7] These inescapable tensions put a sharp edge on the familiar academic debates concerning the convergence of industrial societies.

Beyond these enduring problems of technological and cultural change, there still remain issues of political power and the ability to control technology and its assimilation. The onslaught of technological modernity has helped to speed the destruction of the traditional elite, but their fate and that of their culture is not identical with the fate of Chinese culture in general. Although the eclipse of elite culture is a matter of both intellectual interest and practical importance, it would be a mistake to extend to an entire society conclusions drawn from the analysis of its most elevated members. Sinologists and other outside observers have too often equated the achievements and concerns of the cultural and political elite with the Chinese "essence," thereby failing to take into sufficient consideration the great majority of the Chinese people who live outside the high culture mainstream. We must also look to these people if we wish to ascertain the impact of Western technology and to assess the process of assimilation. A fundamental fact of life for China's multitudes was their subordination to a political and cultural elite, a subordination that profoundly affected the course of economic and technological development. In today's China, the patterns of domination and subordination differ markedly, but they still are major determinants of the process of technological assimilation. In modern China, as in traditional China, relations of power and authority play a major role in determining patterns of change. Technological development does not occur in a political vacuum, for the assimilation of new technologies always reflects the goals, procedures, and values that have been created by the political process.

Technological Assimilation and Rural Development

Any analysis of the distribution of power and authority in contemporary Chinese society must begin with the fact that three-quarters of China's people reside and earn their livelihood in the countryside. An important goal of technological development should therefore be the incorporation of the countryside into the national political and economic system. It may even be said that a self-sustaining process of modernization should center on a progressive narrowing of the cultural gap separating city and countryside. The most effective technologies are those that help to close this gap and in turn make the countryside more receptive to further technological changes.[8]

Maoist policies have in general been characterized by their rural orientation, and the political culture of Maoism has been suffused with a populist suspicion of cities and all their creations.[9] Yet Maoist populism should not be seen as an atavistic response to the inexorable demands of modernization. Technologies that have been acquired by city-dwellers, be they private entrepreneurs or government officials, are often difficult to assimilate into the countryside, for all too often they have little relevance to the needs of rural people. The recent concern of Western developmental economists with "appropriate" technologies bears witness to the fact that technologies that have been established in modern urban settings may not be suitable to the needs of poor nations with large rural populations. The capital-intensive technologies that are typical of modern economies rarely make sense in an economy that has the factor endowments of a country like China. Although impressive gains can be made by enterprises and sectors that employ state-of-the-art technologies, diversion of resources to them may result in significant opportunity costs for other sectors and enterprises. As R. S. Eckaus has stressed, optimal technological choices cannot be reduced to maximizing the productivity of only one factor of production; rather, the goal should be "to maximize the total output that can be obtained from *all* the resources *available* to the country."[10] Technologies that increase productivity only in a certain set of enterprises may not be optimal for the economy as whole, for, again to quote Eckaus, "It is, after all, the productivity of the entire labor force and the output of the entire economy which is important for development."[11] Moreover, when the external effects of a given technology are taken into account, such as its capacity to stimulate the development of labor skills, the adoption of a "modern" technology becomes even more problematic.

The development of technologies appropriate to the needs of the labor-intensive rural sector is implicit in Maoist ideology, with its concern for the elimination of the "three great differences": the separation of industry and agriculture, city and countryside, and mental and physical work. Yet there have been times when this general orientation was not translated into effective technological policies for the countryside. On a number of occasions, efforts to bring technological change to the rural economy were overcentralized, resulting in the diffusion of inputs and techniques that were inappropriate for many areas. Inappropriate technologies were followed by insurmountable problems of assimilation. Thus, ill-considered attempts to widely diffuse double-share plows during the late 1950s met with stiff resistance,[12] and attempts to accelerate capital formation in the countryside during the Great Leap Forward all too often ended unhappily.

Bitter examples such as these underscored the hazards of attempting to administer agrotechnical change from afar. Due in part to these failures, a decentralized approach became a key fixture of rural technological policy. With regard to agricultural mechanization, for example, individual production units (rather than specialized tractor stations under centralized control) were to provide the basic organizational framework for the diffusion and assimilation of modern farm implements—for the premise of the Maoist approach was that a close connection between crop production and the use of new implements would generate the greatest degree of popular involvement with technological change.[13]

Current policies, however, present a more complex picture. As with many other Maoist approaches to the organization of technological change, local initiatives are being deemphasized in favor of a more centralized approach to the administration of agricultural mechanization. Assuming that local sources of capital and technical skills are not equal to the task of mechanizing farm tasks, the current regime has begun to turn to the establishment of state-sponsored tractor stations for the provision of services to surrounding communes and production

Handicraft factory at the Huangtu commune near Shanghai (May 1975).

brigades.[14] In the recent past, agricultural mechanization had been developed under the aegis of local administrative units; tractors and ancillary equipment were produced in every province, while the all-important task of maintenance and repair was taken on at county, commune, and brigade levels. Rural industries were of central importance for the process of agricultural mechanization. By 1977, 98 percent of China's counties claimed farm machinery repair stations and factories, with a full-time staff of 380,000 workers.[15] But impressive as these statistics seem at first glance, they translate to a full-time employment of fewer than 175 workers per county, a figure that hardly seems adequate to the enormous tasks of mechanizing China's age-old agricultural system. Moreover, the decentralization of farm machinery production resulted in the proliferation of models and a consequent lack of parts interchangeability.[16] It is therefore understandable why a greater degree of centralization is currently being sought. One of the prime tasks of agrotechnical policy will thus be to bring coherence to farm mechanization

Workers assembling electronics components at seventh electronics factory, Shanghai (September 1978).

while at the same time preserving local initiative and a responsiveness to the great variability of local crop-growing conditions. But whatever the exact mix of centralization and local responsibility, the Chinese are not likely to reproduce the sad history of agricultural mechanization in the Soviet Union, where tractors and mechanized implements were Trojan horses specifically employed to gain Party control over the countryside.[17]

Despite some centralizing tendencies, the production of other modern inputs, such as agricultural chemicals, remains decentralized to a considerable degree; for example, half of China's chemical fertilizer is currently produced in relatively small plants under local administration.[18] It can be fairly assumed that decentralized efforts help to create a closer nexus between production and use, thereby giving local peasants a stronger sense that new inputs are not foreign importations, but the product of their own local economy. New crop varieties and seed strains have also been locally produced and demonstrated in experimental plots before being used in the fields. These plots are set up as special "points," which make use of scientists and technicians sent from specialized research institutes. In this context, experimentation, demonstration, and propagation can be closely linked, thereby facilitating the absorption of new inputs and techniques for crop production.[19] There can be little doubt that the establishment of a close working relationship between research work, the production of new inputs, and their actual application can create a favorable climate for the assimilation of new farm technologies. In China, agricultural extension work has been predicated on maintaining a strong linkage between the development of new technologies and their subsequent application. Although basic agricultural research has at times been adversely affected by the fusion of theoretical research and practical application, the process has played a positive role in the assimilation of new technologies.[20]

Organizational Strategies and Technological Assimilation

The forging of a close connection between theory and practice has been a basic thrust of the Maoist approach to social change in general and technological change in particular.[21] In organizational terms, this merger of theory and practice has been stimulated by efforts to develop an administrative order through which local initiative and participation can be brought to bear on specific technological applications. In addition to being a cornerstone of Maoist political and economic strategy, widespread use of local initiative and effort is mandated by the diffuse nature of Chinese society, where the logistics of administering a largely rural nation of some 950 million people often preclude the centralized administration of new technological applications. China lacks many critical prerequisites of a modern administrative order and suffers from considerable deficiencies in the technical skills of its citizenry. It has only 400,000 college-trained scientists and technicians and, perhaps even more important, has severe shortages of middle-level technical personnel, skilled workers, and local administrators. Not only must new technologies be created and diffused, but the development of generally higher levels of administrative capability and increased technical sophistication of the Chinese populace as a whole are essential prerequisites for technological progress.

The development of these skills can best be achieved when technological change becomes part of a learning process and the application of specific technologies is made into an occasion for "learning by doing."[22] The often-reported overstaffing of many Chinese industrial enterprises can be construed as an indication of efforts to expose a large number of workers to advanced productive practices. In this regard, the Tach'ing oilfield can be taken as a leader, for it reportedly has trained 56,000 workers and cadres as well as 4,000 scientists and technicians for work in newly opened fields.[23] Similarly, the Shanghai No. 1 Machine Tools Plant, another industrial pacesetter, has trained hundreds of technicians, many of whom are graduates of its famous factory-run college.[24] Yet these figures and the policies underlying them must be put in perspective. The Chinese no longer see on-the-job training as the primary venue for the development of scientific and technical skills, for current educational policies have reasserted the primary role of universities and research centers for the development and application of advanced technologies. Even so, on-the-job training, both formal and informal, will remain an important contributor to the assimilation of improved ways of doing things. The need for well-trained workers and lower-level technicians cannot be overestimated. According to one Chinese report, two-thirds of China's industrial workers took up their work after 1968, and many of them had not received appropriate technical training beforehand.[25] There thus remains the critical task of developing an adequate level of specialized skills, skills that can be taken for granted only in an advanced industrial economy. Many of these skills will be developed at the workplace; they will not be of a high level, but they are nonetheless essential to the successful assimilation of new technologies on the shop floor.[26]

Few would argue that values, attitudes, and skills must be developed parallel with changes in material technology. Yet, for this to happen appropriate organizational structures must be set up as a matrix for both technological and cultural change. Technologies do not diffuse automatically nor are they assimilated by atomized individuals and economic units. The assimilation of a new technology requires administrative complexes to import, develop, screen, and aid in the implementation of new ways of doing things. Technological change is mediated by specific organizations, and the assimilation of new technologies reflects organizational patterns. Indeed, it has even been said that the organizational structure of the agencies involved in technological development will do much to determine the type of technologies employed as well as the manner of their implementation.[27]

The pivotal role played by organizations in the development and assimilation of new technologies creates a fundamental paradox for a society committed to the political direction of technological change. While specific organizations can be key instruments of technological advance, they can be self-serving entities as well. Each organization has its own set of goals, rules, and procedures that can substantially affect the choice of technology and the manner in which it is assimilated. General policies of social and technological transformation can be altered by the very organizations charged with putting them into practice.[28]

Although specific information on Chinese organizational behavior is still fragmentary, there are a number of indications that individual productive enterprises can exhibit some capacity to change general policies through their specific operations. Although many individual enterprises are directly linked to agencies of the central government (such as ministries, bureaus, and industrial corporations), many other agencies play a direct or indirect role in determining the performance of the enterprise. Not only are central ministries involved in the setting and monitoring of basic policies, but local administrative agencies (such as provinces or municipalities) can be heavily involved in economic administration. The presence of a multiplicity of agencies concerned with the work of a single enterprise can result in a certain degree of administrative confusion, leaving the individual enterprise some latitude in interpreting, executing, and even influencing policies.[29] Since the administration of productive activities is not monolithic, individual organizations can sometimes direct their activities in accordance with their own interests. For example, as David Lampton's study of the Chinese health care system has indicated, the interests and resources of specific medical organizations have been of major importance in determining how policies were implemented. Even at times when a distinct policy line was ascendent, as during the Great Leap Forward, established health care organizations continued to pursue their usual activities at an undiminished rate.[30]

The role taken by special-purpose organizations in the development and implementation of new ways of doing things is thus a key issue in any analysis of China's assimilation of new technologies. It is particularly relevant in today's China, where efforts are being made to plan economic development more exactly. In any planned economy, organizational structure and behavior determine to a significant degree the success of individual items of technological change. As Joseph Berliner has masterfully demonstrated, if new technologies are to be successfully assimilated, organizational structures and activities must mesh with other planned attributes of the economy, such as prices, incentives, and decision rules.[31] In sum, the formulation of policies is only part of the process of stimulating technological development; general policies must also be backed by organizational activities that harmonize with other attributes of the economic system in such a way that technological development can be stimulated and sustained.

The role played by special-purpose organizations in promoting technological and other changes has also long been a matter of considerable debate in the People's Republic of China. It has been hypothesized, for example, that the nub of contention between Mao and Liu Shao-ch'i was the extent to which social change was to be channelled through specific organizations.[32] In the area of technological change, the Maoist approach stressed popular initiative and comprehensive efforts to couple technological development with general social change. To Mao, leaving technological development as the work of specific organizations would encapsulate the process rather than diffuse it throughout Chinese society. Special-purpose organizations, according to Mao's way of thinking, were too narrow in their perspectives and too inclined to concern themselves only with the attainment of limited goals, having little regard for changing the values and capacities of the population as a whole. The Maoist prescription was to have all organizations—instead of being narrowly involved with either research, development, or the propagation of new technologies—assume responsibility for all facets of technological change in close conjunction with practical work.

The post-Mao era has seen an apparent retreat from these principles. A much higher degree of functional specialization has come to characterize the work of individual organizations.[33] Roles and mandates have been made much more specific; educational institutions have become more concerned with academic knowledge; research units have paid less attention to the propagation of new technologies; and so on. Moreover, where Mao sought to develop technical skills from the bottom up by diffusing responsibilities, his successors have been more inclined to vest power at the upper echelons of individual organizations. Organizations with close ties to the central government (such as ministries, departments of the Academy of Sciences, and elite universities) have been allowed to develop their programs with a much greater degree of insulation from other segments of society. In all likelihood, these individual organizations are gaining the capacity to shape technological policies with diminished concern for the larger issues of developing appropriate technologies and working for their assimilation at local levels.

Enlarged roles for selected organizations will necessarily alter the relationship between technological assimilation and the patterns of general social change. The extent of local and national self-reliance, the role of expertise, rural-urban balances, and many other crucial elements of social policy will be strongly affected by the technologies chosen and the manner in which they are assimilated into Chinese society. The connection between policy and implementation is an intimate one, and the process of technological assimilation will be heavily determined by the specific organizations involved, their operating procedures, goals, and connection to other elements of the society.

My expectation here is that the more centralized the organization and the more precise its internal division of labor, the more "modern" will be the technologies selected and the more their assimilation will be confined to preselected sectors. That is to say, centralized organizations with close links to established policymaking bodies will import or internally develop sophisticated technologies, which because of their complexity and "foreignness" will tend to remain encapsulated within specific economic units and will not be easily assimilated outside of them.

China's present leadership is apparently seeking to engender economic modernization by concentrating its efforts on a few key sectors. In so doing, it has greatly strengthened the role played by organizations under central control. This strategy will undoubtedly upgrade the technical level of many enterprises, but it may work to the detriment of technological assimilation in general by overemphasizing the importance of a relatively small number of industries and enterprises as vanguards of techno-economic advance. Productive improvements advance on many fronts, and not all of them require centralized administration for their development and asssimilation. In fixating too narrowly on the central administration of a few technological breakthroughs, the current leadership may be losing some other opportunities for economic advance. Even worse, such policies may exacerbate tensions between those enterprises and sectors that are the beneficiaries of up-to-date inputs and techniques and those that must make do with indigenous ways of doing things.

Policy, Assimilation, and Technological Dualism

Special-purpose organizations under central direction undoubtedly are needed when the technologies to be propagated are strikingly novel, when a good deal of planning is required, and when materials and skills have to be carefully coordinated. At the same time, many new technologies can be assimilated with less organizational support when they have some connection with existing ways of doing things. Incremental technological changes generate fewer demands on organizational capacities, yet they still can substantially contribute to a nation's development. Indeed, the net gains from many small improvements may outstrip those engendered by more complex and ambitious technologies that remain confined to only a few enterprises. In many areas, technological progress might best be served by decentralizing the organization of technological change and giving to many small enterprises the mandate for collecting and developing marginal improvements and stimulating their assimilation.[34] Technological breakthroughs of a revolutionary variety may be the ultimate source of profound economic change, but they become fully operative only when they are followed by countless improvements and refinements. Even a cursory survey of such diverse industries as construction, power generation, petroleum refining, and rail transportation underscores the vital importance of small cumulative technological improvements that go largely undetected outside the immediate industry. Moreover, these improvements have often been the achievement not of well-trained specialists but of a legion of unsung craftsmen, foremen, and rank-and-file workers, whose efforts may not have amounted to much individually but have cumulatively resulted in profound transformations in the way things are done.[35]

The emerging economic and technological strategy of the present regime seems to have resulted in a downplaying of the incremental approach to technological transformation in favor of a concentrated effort to bring key sectors of the Chinese economy up to advanced world levels through the importation or internal development of technologies that allow sharp breakthroughs. And, in line with our expectations, this effort has been paralleled by an increased emphasis on the key role played by central agencies as well as by more hierarchical organizational arrangements within these agencies. Ministries, universities, and industrial corporations have been given the major responsibility for technological development while grass-roots and shop-floor initiatives have been downplayed. Little is heard these days of worker innovations or of the activities of "three-in-one combinations" for the solution of specific technical problems. This, of course, does not mean that these efforts have completely disappeared. They remain submerged as the Chinese leadership and the media devote their attention to the more glamorous key projects that are to form the core of China's technological transformation. Yet again it must be stressed that these projects, for all their importance, are only half the picture.

A multifaceted approach to the development and assimilation of new technologies is dictated by the extreme diversity of the Chinese economy. As with all other countries that have come late to industrialization, China's economy exhibits sharp manifestations of dualism. Not only are there the aforementioned discontinuities between much of the agricultural sector and the more modern urban sector, but vivid contrasts can also be seen within many individual enterprises; modern industrial processes may make use of supplies brought in by hand-drawn carts, and automated production methods may employ materials that have been prepared by extensive hand labor.

Such dualism is often taken as an emblem of economic and technological backwardness. But dualism, while it results in considerable inequalities, does not condemn an economy to stagnation; from the standpoint of development potentials, the critical issue is whether or not there exist any linkages between the backward and the advanced. When backward enterprises and their personnel are not stimulated by systematic contact with those that are advanced, the result will likely be the continued relative stagnation of the former. If, however, these linkages can be forged, the result can be a "dualism of development"[36] through which new materials, techniques, and, above all, skills diffuse from the advanced to the backward.

This sort of diffusion creates obvious possibilities for enhancing technological assimilation. The accelerated technological development of advanced enterprises or sectors should not result in totally lopsided development if their work is conjoined with that of less-advanced enterprises. New technologies and skills can thereby be "spun off" for assimilation by more backward enterprises. However, as I have pointed out earlier, the organizational structures and processes of the advanced units can result in a narrowness of purpose that keeps them separate from less advanced units, thus attenuating a vital stimulus to the widespread assimilation of new technologies.

In many instances, of course, the technologies employed by an enterprise preclude any technological spin-offs to less-advanced units. In petroleum production, for example, there are few opportunities for generating such linkages.[37] Because of this, China's recent energy development strategy has resulted in the crystallization of distinct sectors with few interconnections: a high-technology one involving petroleum, and a low-technology one for such enterprises as biogas generation[38] and small-scale hydroelectric power.[39] But other sectors can benefit from a close working relationship between advanced units and less-advanced ones. A two-phase process of technological assimilation, whereby advanced technologies are imported or developed by advanced sectors and enterprises and then with appropriate modification diffused to more backward sectors, is the essential feature of a "dualism of development." It is not an easy process, for it requires flexibility of planning, the maintenance of communication channels between the two, and above all the will to generate technological development outside of the sector or enterprise to which one is directly responsible. Given present policies, it is not certain that these stipulations will be met. China, however, is fortunate in having a firm basis for this linkage in its uniquely rich heritage of indigenous technological virtuosity. The historic accomplishments of traditional Chinese technology were not always the creation of the "high culture," but were often the products of the "folk culture" of China's villages and small urban enterprises. The presence of this heritage means that the populist nativism that helped to shape Maoist policies can play a vital role in technological development. As long as there is an indigenous technological tradition onto which new technologies can be grafted, the process of assimilation will be much easier.

We can see this process most clearly in the realm of medical technologies, where an indigenous technological base has been combined with modern inputs and techniques to produce an effective system of medical care. Although most outside attention has been focused on the work of "barefoot doctors" and their "serve-the-people" ethic, it should be remembered that the successes of this program rest on the harmony between technologies employed and the manner in which they are applied. The strong commitment to making maximum use of indigenous materials and practices has aided the assimilation of new medical practices by making medical services less of a foreign intrusion for the local populace. This in turn has allowed a decentralized deployment of medical services, for improved medical techniques do not require the imposition of radically new technologies by centrally controlled organizations. To return to an earlier theme, technologies that do not totally negate indigenous technological accomplishments can help to resolve some of the problems of assimilation that emerged with China's confrontation with the industrialized world. Instead of mounting quixotic efforts to use foreign ways of doing things without affecting Chinese "essence," contemporary medical practices exhibit elements of a synthesis between the foreign and the indigenous.[40]

Given the vast store of Chinese technological achievements in the past, it is somewhat surprising that additional examples of this sort have not been more evident. Perhaps the superiority of imported technologies in most areas has been overwhelming, and there has been little room for incorporating indigenous ways of doing things. Then again, perhaps the existing organizational structure for the development and assimilation of new technologies has precluded a more extensive use of indigenous capacities. Centralization, division of responsibilities, and the separation of research and productive work can easily lead to the development of policies that implicitly discount the potentials existing at the basic levels of Chinese society. There can be little doubt that many technological achievements can be generated by modern organizational modes or that many of these achievements will percolate into the less-advanced segments of the dual economy. But it also may be the case that in attempting to accelerate the pace of technological and economic development, China's current policymakers are foreclosing some alternate opportunities for technological development and assimilation.

The next decade will be a critical period in the history of the People's Republic of China, with the technological policies chosen reverberating far into the future. In selecting specific technologies, the Chinese leadership will be faced with growing challenges of accommodating new ways of doing things with other social goals. China's long revolution was fueled by the desire for both social justice and the development of a nation that was prosperous and powerful, yet the technologies that help to generate the latter cannot always be squared with the former. The tensions between these two sets of goals have existed since the foundation of the People's Republic, but they have never been as acute as they are at present. In the final analysis, the patterns of technological assimilation will be shaped by both the technological directions taken and the manner in which they are implemented by specific organizations. Above all, it remains to be seen whether or not the formulation and execution of technological policy will give adequate consideration to popular initiative and indigenous capabilities. Upon this question rests the likelihood of a uniquely Chinese approach to the acquisition and assimilation of new technologies.

Notes

1. R. H. Tawney, *Land and Labor in China* (Boston: Beacon Press, 1966), p. 11.
2. See Joseph R. Levenson, *Confucian China and Its Modern Fate: A Trilogy* (Berkeley, Calif.: University of California Press, 1968).
3. See Barton C. Hacker, "The Weapons of the West: Military Technology and Modernization in 19th-Century China and Japan," *Technology and Culture* 18, no. 1 (January 1977).
4. See Benjamin Schwartz, *In Search of Wealth and Power: Yen Fu and the West* (New York: Harper & Row, 1969), p. 16.
5. James Chieh Hsiung, *Ideology and Practice: The Evolution of Chinese Communism* (New York: Praeger, 1970), p. 339.
6. Karl Marx, *Capital: A Critique of Political Economy* (Chicago: C. H. Kerr, 1906), p. 13.
7. See, for example, James Peck, "Revolution versus Modernization and Revisionism: A Two-Front Struggle," in Victor Nee and James Peck, eds., *China's Uninterrupted Revolution* (New York: Pantheon, 1975).
8. See Arthur Goldschmidt, "Technology in Emerging Countries," *Technology and Culture* 3, no. 4 (Fall 1962).
9. Maurice Meisner, "Leninism and Maoism: Some Populist Perspectives on Marxism-Leninism in China," *China Quarterly*, no. 45 (January–March 1971).

10. R. S. Eckaus, "Technological Change in the Less Developed Areas," in Stephen Spiegelglas, ed., *Economic Development: Challenge and Promise* (Englewood Cliffs, N.J.: Prentice-Hall, 1970), p. 173. Emphasis in original.

11. Ibid., p. 174.

12. "Why Does the Demand for Double-Wheel Double-Blade Plows Drop and Why Is Their Production Suspended?" *Chi-hua ching-chi* [Planned economy], no. 9 (September 23, 1956), in *Extracts from China Mainland Magazines,* no. 56, (November 13, 1956), p. 24.

13. William Hinton, *Iron Oxen: A Documentary of Revolution in Chinese Farming* (New York: Random House, 1971), pp. 215–225.

14. "China to Speed Up Agricultural Development," *Beijing Review,* no. 11 (March 16, 1979), p. 14.

15. New China News Agency (hereafter NCNA), "National Exhibition on Technical Innovation for Farm Machinery Opens in Peking," May 28, 1977, in *Survey of People's Republic of China Press* (hereafter *SPRCP*), no. 6356, p. 114.

16. Ching Hua, "How to Speed Up China's Agricultural Development," *Peking Review* (hereafter *PR*), no. 42 (October 20, 1978), pp. 10–11.

17. See Robert F. Miller, *One Hundred Thousand Tractors: The MTS and the Development of Controls in Soviet Agriculture* (Cambridge, Mass.: Harvard University Press, 1970).

18. *China: The Role of Small Plants in Economic Development* (Washington, D.C.: Central Intelligence Agency, 1974), p. 10.

19. *Plant Studies in the People's Republic of China: A Trip Report of the American Plant Studies Delegation* (Washington, D.C.: National Academy of Sciences, 1975), pp. 163–164.

20. Dwight Perkins, "A Conference on Agriculture," *China Quarterly,* no. 67 (September 1976), pp. 600–604.

21. Mao's general approach is contained in "On Practice," in *Selected Readings from the Works of Mao Tse-tung* (Peking: Foreign Languages Press, 1967), pp. 54–59.

22. See Peter Kilby, "Farm and Factory: A Comparison of the Skill Requirements for the Transfer of Technology," *Journal of Development Studies* 9, no. 1 (October 1972).

23. NCNA, "China's Largest Oilfield Trains Workers and Technicians," October 6, 1975, in *SPRCP,* no. 5959, p. 153.

24. NCNA, "Shanghai Builds Up Worker-Technician Contingent," May 1, 1976,, in *SPRCP,* no. 6093, p. 145.

25. "Raise Workers' Technical Level," *PR,* no. 36 (September 8, 1978), p. 20.

26. See Richard Baum, "Technology, Organization, and Social Change: Maoism and the Chinese Industrial Revolution," in *Proceedings of the Third Sino-American Conference on Mainland China* (Taipei: Institute of International Relations, 1976), pp. 827–828.

27. See Denis Goulet, *The Uncertain Promise: Value Conflicts in Technology Transfer* (New York: IDOC, 1977), p. 173.

28. See, for example, Seymour Martin Lipset, *Agrarian Socialism* (Berkeley, Calif.: University of California Press, 1950), pp. 255–275.

29. Barry Richman, *Industrial Society in Communist China* (New York: Random House, 1969), pp. 445–449.

30. David M. Lampton, *Health, Conflict, and the Chinese Political System* (Ann Arbor, Mich.: University of Michigan, Center for Chinese Studies, 1974).

31. Joseph Berliner, *The Innovation Decision in Soviet Industry* (Cambridge, Mass.: Massachusetts Institute of Technology Press, 1976).

32. See Jack Gray, "The Two Roads: Alternative Strategies of Social Change and Economic Growth in China," in Stuart R. Schram, ed., *Authority, Participation, and Cultural Change in China* (Cambridge, England: Cambridge University Press, 1973).

33. These principles are embodied in the "Thirty-Point Decision on Industrial Development." Its essential features are summarized in *PR*, no. 28 (July 14, 1978), p. 3.

34. William W. Lockwood, *Economic Development of Japan: Growth and Structural Change* (Princeton, N.J.: Princeton University Press, 1954), pp. 198–199.

35. See Nathan Rosenberg, "Technological Interdependence in the American Economy," *Technology and Culture* 20, no. 1 (January 1979):32–40.

36. See David S. Landes, "Japan and Europe: Contrasts in Industrialization," in William W. Lockwood, ed., *The State and Economic Enterprise in Japan: Essays in Political Economy of Growth* (Princeton, N.J.: Princeton University Press, 1965), pp. 173–174.

37. To be sure, the Tach'ing oilfield is famous for its subsidiary factories, which make use of old machinery and scrap materials, but these are strictly sideline efforts. See NCNA, "New Type Socialist Oilfield," January 6, 1973, in *Survey of China Mainland Press*, no. 5297, p. 92.

38. See Vaclav Smil, "Non-Fossil Fuels and Intermediate Technologies," in Thomas Fingar, ed., *China's Energy Policies and Resource Development* (Palo Alto, Calif.: U.S.-China Relations Program, Stanford University, 1976), pp. 14–15.

39. NCNA, "Chinese Peasants Build 56,000 Small and Medium-Sized Hydroelectric Power Stations in Ten Years," June 14, 1976, in *SPRCP*, no. 6122, pp. 198–200.

40. Kazuko Tsurumi, "Some Potential Contributions of Latecomers to Technological and Scientific Revolution: A Comparison of Japan and China," in Ramkrishna Mukherjee and Radovan Richta, eds., *Scientific-Technological Revolution: Social Aspects* (Beverly Hills, Calif.: Sage Studies in International Sociology, 1977), vol. 8, pp. 157–160.

Commentary on Technological Absorption and Assimilation

Jack Baranson

I would like to focus on two basic points, the rural-urban dichotomy and the whole question of "What is technology?" Rudi Volti rightly points out the existence of a basic distinction between urban and village technologies. It must be remembered that the rural sector constitutes 70 or 80 percent of China's society and economy. Hence, rural industrialization will continue to be important as an adjunct to agricultural production and as an employment-generating device. However, this does not necessarily mean, as Volti has implied, that rural development in China is bound to be fundamental for decades to come. The rural sector is a very different world and has an entirely different set of problems than that of the urban sector.

There is no question that there are certain linkages between the two sectors. For example, the process of mobilizing manpower, materials, and tools in rural villages and turning them into factories eventually creates linkages. Something that was a blacksmith shop may eventually become an automotive parts manufacturer. Nevertheless, it is a very different world and I think it poses a very special set of problems.

I think that the major policies and the considerable ferment in China today are largely centered around the modern urban sector. There is no question that the development of the rural areas continues to be a nagging problem. However, my guess is that the development of the rural sector will be put aside for the time being and that the leading edge of change and economic development will come from the effort to modernize the urban sector.

Turning to the subject of technology, there is a difference between practitioners—people who have been in factories and know what technology is—and people who talk about this sort of thing from the top down. To understand the process of technological acquisition and absorption, we need more input from people of the former type—industrial practitioners.

A diesel engine is a very complicated industrial artifact. It involves anywhere from 40,000 to 80,000 separate little techniques. To understand the question of technology acquisition and absorption, one must understand what it takes in the way of mobilizing people, materials, and tools to turn out a finished product like a diesel engine. The process requires system design and manpower training, recipe givers and recipe absorbers. The naïve assumption that you can go to laboratories and recreate 80,000 little techniques and put them all together is just not realistic.

China, in its recent development history, has gone through three phases of technological acquisition. In the Soviet period, up through 1960, they had a major technical partner essentially as a technology supplier. In the period 1961–1971, China turned to new "friends" as technology partners. They went to other socialist countries they could deal with, as well as to countries like France. They made an ineffective effort to use the French to set up a truck plant. It never came to anything. It was a very insufficient, inadequate type of what I would call "back-door acquisition." During this period, the Chinese used trade fairs to acquire prototypes and then used reverse engineering to try to duplicate the system. This also is a very inadequate way of going about the process of technology acquisition. Certainly some of the present managers and authorities in China must have learned from this experience that this approach to acquisition was not going to get them anywhere in a definitive way.

The model that the Chinese have recently adopted closely resembles that of nineteenth-century Japan. The new program is geared to a massive infusion of professional technical cadres of the highest possible caliber. The emphasis is on selection, technological training, and the sending of people abroad, i.e., on fostering technological skills, not on political theory.

The distinction that Mao drew between intellectual and manual labor has now been diminished. From Teng's point of view there is no contradiction here. As long as a person serves the revolution, the distinction between intellectual and manual labor is not significant.

A highly trained and competent technical class is fundamental to technology acquisition. In order to train such a class and to motivate them, Chinese leaders have placed renewed emphasis on material prerequisites and on training people abroad. The opportunity to go abroad must be a strong incentive for technical trainees to behave and study diligently.

An important part of the new program will be the dependence on foreign capital in terms of technology and credit. Certainly, this was counter to Mao's fundamental principle of remaining independent of capitalist countries. Teng insists that China can import foreign technology while maintaining its political-cultural system. However, the new policy thrust—the creation of an urban technical elite as well as increased dependence on outside sources for educational, technical, and financial assistance—will inevitably create a new set of stresses and strains in the political system.

Discussion

Hans Heymann suggested that while the Chinese may have learned a great deal from the failed technological policies of the late 1960s, particularly with regard to the limits of self-reliance, those years were also a period of blossoming for the rural sector. Thus, the danger now (when the center seems to be totally preoccupied with the advanced sector of the economy) would be a failure to pay sufficient attention to the energies of the rural sector.

Jon Sigurdson claimed that the Chinese leadership is still very much concerned with the rural sector, at least judging from the statements contained in the circular of the National Science Conference of March 1978. Implementation might be another matter, he conceded.

Lucian Pye saw less cause for optimism about the ability of the Chinese to eliminate dualism and facilitate the trickle-down of technology from the advanced modern sector to the countryside because the Chinese lack anything approaching the equivalent of the market to direct the decentralized yet integrated acquisition of a multitude of new techniques. The Chinese have no financial institutions like the Japanese business empire, the *zaibatsu*, which has the ability to tie money and investment together in the most productive fashion. Nor do the Chinese have entrepreneurs who could function as the communicators of technological needs and innovations. These elements of rural/urban integration lie behind the much admired Japanese model of the early twentieth century. In particular, the Chinese strategy of industrialization via large industrial units under authoritative management fails to achieve the critical Japanese linkage between thousands of small rural suppliers contributing not only to agriculture but also to urban industry.

Thomas Fingar, in response to Pye's comments, claimed that Chinese banks and financial organizations are now playing an increasingly important role in monitoring both investments and the performance of industries and individual plants. This relationship between banking and industry may yet develop along the Japanese lines.

Ralph Miller remarked that the secret of industrial development and of technology assimilation is not in the import of expensive turnkey plants from abroad but in the orchestration of the myriad details into a harmonious whole. He pointed out that there are no secrets in the automotive business, but there are good reasons why countries are willing to pay hundreds of millions of dollars to Western manufacturers to come in and license them. These manufacturers are not licensing the design; they are licensing the *system* and the *processing*. What they need is not the prototype to copy but the drawings with the materials specifications and the tolerances, the routing sheets, and the basic understanding and expertise to orchestrate everything so that all the millions of things can come together to make a truck.

Stanley Lubman seconded Miller's observations, saying that the Chinese now realize, to a greater extent than ever before, that technology assimilation is a *process* rather than an outcome. However, the Chinese remain somewhat confused, or at least ambivalent, about this process. He went on to cite recent changes in Chinese commercial policy to exemplify this new awareness (e.g., the Chinese acceptance for the first time of "cost-plus"—as opposed to "fixed-fee"—contracts and the establishment of new Chinese corporations with the aim of fostering closer relations between buyers and sellers).

Fingar noted that there was another side to the new Chinese approach to technology assimilation. He described a program in "systems engineering" (a combination of operations research and industrial engineering) set up within the First Ministry of Machine Building in 1978. The program was set up explicitly for the purpose of training managers to think in the terms described by Miller. The Canadian who is setting up this program has said that it will be at least five years before it even begins to be functional.

8
China's Energy Technology

Vaclav Smil

China's development of its energy resources in the past three decades has been quite impressive. It is now the world's third largest producer of raw coal (and will shortly surpass the United States to become the second largest producer after the Soviet Union). China's crude oil extraction, negligible in 1949, has been expanding by more than 10 percent annually so that it now ranks behind Venezuela, and its natural gas flow is approaching 60 billion cubic meters, placing China in fifth place worldwide.[1]

But, as must be expected, the image is quite different in relative comparisons. Per capita consumption of primary energy is currently just above 600 kilograms of coal equivalent annually, a value characteristic of a poor developing country. And quantitative comparisons of Chinese energy technology with current advanced world standards reveal serious gaps and deficiencies in practically every exploration, extraction, transportation, and conversion activity.[2]

The Chinese are, naturally, aware of this considerable technological lag, which they estimate to be at least fifteen to twenty years, and they also admit the relative weakness of the whole energy sector in the swiftly expanding national economy. For these reasons, accelerated development of energy resources has become, together with farm production, the most important task among the eight comprehensive spheres singled out for

This chapter is an abridged and slightly modified version of the author's contribution to Leo Orleans, ed., *Selective Review of China's Science and Technology* (Palo Alto, Calif.: Stanford University Press for the National Academy of Sciences, forthcoming). It appears here with the permission of the National Academy of Sciences.

special attention during the Ten-Year Plan (1976–1985) of scientific modernization.[3]

The following comprehensive review of China's energy technologies attempts to present a large variety of specific information in international perspective to convey an appreciation of both the existing technological lag and the magnitude of the future tasks facing the Chinese.

Coal

Coal is China's most important fossil fuel, providing some 60 percent of the nation's primary energy use, and China's extraction of around 600 million metric tons of raw coal annually is surpassed only by that of the U.S.S.R. and the United States. Yet, the coal industry has been repeatedly labeled a weak link in China's economy, and inadequate coal supply has been one of Peking's most serious and intractable economic problems. Chronic underinvestment and the lack of modern technology in the coal industry have resulted in low rates of mine mechanization and coal processing. New policies, designed to modernize the coal industry, are now in effect, but it will take at least fifteen years for China to raise its coal mining technology to the current level of the Soviet Union or the United States.

Production

The single most important characteristic of China's coal production is its low level of mechanization. There are no recent official figures on the degree of mechanization, but a good estimate can be derived by considering a variety of relevant information. Mechanized extraction in 1958, the last year for which a reliable nationwide breakdown is available, accounted for 31.76 percent of total production in the mines operated by the Ministry of Coal Industry.[4] In K'ailan, China's largest and most modernized coal mining region, production by mechanized workfaces accounted for nearly 50 percent in 1975 and was reported to be slightly lower than that in spring 1978, when it had not yet fully recovered from the damage caused by the 1976 earthquake.[5]

Considering the fact that one-third of China's coal production comes from local small mines where there is little or no mechanization (on the average certainly no more than 20 percent), the highest conceivable share of currently mechanized coal extraction in China is about 40 percent, but the figure is more likely around one-third of the total. In comparison, extraction is virtually 100 percent mechanized in the other two coal superpowers, the Soviet Union and the United States.[6]

While manual extraction with picks or pneumatic drills, blasting with dynamite, and loading with shovels into carts remains the predominant coal mining method in Chinese mines, many individual collieries are using advanced, efficient technologies. The room-and-pillar method, which has been traditionally used with both conventional and continuous mining, has been mostly displaced in large, modern mines by longwall retreating, which was introduced by the Soviets in the 1950s.[7] Another modern method used at several experimental mines and workfaces is hydraulic mining, which now operates with equipment designed by the T'angshan Coal Machinery Research Institute.

Most of the equipment in Chinese coal mines is domestically produced, although only a few plants turn out coal machinery exclusively. Serially produced equipment (which includes drills, cutter-loaders, scraper-conveyors, belts, winches, hoisting machinery, carrying cars, air compressors, water pumps, electric mine locomotives, small power shovels and conveyors for surface mining, and a variety of automatic control devices) is largely based on the Soviet and East European designs of the 1950s and on even older Western prototypes.[8] Moreover, the coal-mining machinery industry continues to suffer from shortages of high-quality steels.

Consequently, there were major purchases of foreign equipment during the 1970s. In 1973 and 1974, the Chinese bought at least $116 million of advanced equipment from Poland, Britain, West Germany, and the United States and during 1978 they initiated negotiations that might ultimately lead to purchases totalling nearly $5 billion.[9] The greatest part of this money (about $4.2 billion) may eventually go to Krupp, Demag, Thyssen, and Ruhrkohle of West Germany to set up five new deep mines, to modernize a sixth mine, and to open two large surface mines; a British consortium and Mitsui Mining of Japan are to develop other mines and deliver various items of machinery.

Current Chinese plans are "to basically mechanize work in the mines in ten years, with the major mines equipped with coal-cutters and tunnelling machines, continuous transport facilities, automatic coal lifting, washing and dressing machines and computerized communications and dispatching systems."[10] This will require not only further imports and substantial expansion of domestic machinery production capacities but also mass training of technicians and miners to handle the sophisticated equipment.

Planned doubling of the 1977 output in a decade will necessitate the opening of a large number of new shafts. This is an area of coal technology in which the Chinese have become fairly experienced: in 1977, they put forty-two pairs of new shafts into production; in 1976, more than fifty; and in 1975, twenty-two.[11] The deepest mine in China has a main shaft 925 meters deep, twenty kilometers of corridors, and an output of 600,000 metric tons a year. It was built by Peip'iao's mining bureau (Liaoning Province) between August 1966 and the autumn of 1973.[12]

Chinese experience and capabilities in opening and operating large surface mines are much more limited. While more than 50 percent of U.S. coal and some 30 percent of Soviet production originate in open mines, only 7 percent of China's coal was produced in open mines in 1958 (this figure includes only modern mechanized operations and small-scale rural outcrop mines), and that figure does not surpass 10 percent today.[13]

The small proportion of efficient surface mining, the low level of deep mine mechanization, and high reliance on rural small mines result, obviously, in low labor productivity. In 1957 and 1958, the last two years for which official figures are available, the average output per man per day in the large Ministry of Coal Industry was (including aboveground labor) between 1 and 1.8 metric tons (underground only), values roughly comparable with West European performance at that time, though much below U.S. production.

Recent Chinese disclosures on raw coal output and on the

mining labor force make it possible to calculate the productivity for K'ailan. The output per man per day before the T'angshan earthquake of 1976 was less than 1 metric ton when all 100,000 workers on the mining bureau's payroll are included and about 2 metric tons counting underground miners only.[14] The Shansi Province figure, depressed by a large output from inefficient small mines, is only 0.69 tons per man per day.[15] In contrast, the current U.S. rates are 10.75 tons for underground mines and 30.50 tons for surface operations; West European deep mine figures float between 3 and 4 tons per manshift underground.[16] These comparisons show clearly the potential for major improvements in the years ahead.

Preparation

Another area of coal technology where the Chinese need to make substantial progress is coal preparation. Coal preparation usually involves removal of associated rocks by crushing and washing the raw coal, gravity separation of coal and incombustible foreign material, and sorting the coal into fractions of consistent size and quality for different markets. While virtually all solid fuels extracted in developed nations go through some kind of processing before marketing, coal preparation has been a segment that has consistently lagged in China's coal technology.

In 1949, only four plants with an annual capacity of 5.2 million metric tons were in operation; a decade later forty-six installations could handle 41.4 million tons, and the 1970 output was estimated at 83.6 million tons.[17] Even assuming a sustained 10 percent growth since 1970, the 1977 coal preparation capacity would be no more than 200 million tons. This means that the share of China's coal output prepared before marketing rose from 10 percent in 1949 to 20 percent in 1959, 30 percent in 1970, and about 40 percent in 1977.

A very important recent development concerns the unavoidable byproducts of the coal extraction and preparation process—the large amounts of coal waste and mine tailings. A nationwide effort is now under way to use these wastes in a variety of ways.[18] Those tailings with a higher energy content are burned in mine boilers and by local industries or made into briquettes for household use. The combustion of wastes and tailings leaves, naturally, large quantities of slag and ash, and these, in turn, may become useful commodities. Reports mention their use in producing cement, building materials, fertilizers, and molding powder as well as for the extraction of many valuable elements and compounds (germanium, gallium, indium, vanadium, molybdenum, nickel, copper, lead, sodium silicate, aluminum chloride, and ferrous sulphide).[19]

Transportation

Due to large regional disparities in coal production, China has always had to move large amounts of coal from the North to the South. The task has been somewhat eased with the development of new small and large mines in the nine provinces south of the Yangtze River, but the South must still import one-third of its needs and coal is thus easily the most important commodity hauled on China's railroads, amounting to nearly 40 percent of the total tonnage.[20] Although many Chinese railroads and much of the rolling stock are relatively new, there is no special coal transportation technology akin to the U.S. or European system of unit trains, where several powerful diesel engines, pulling permanently coupled assemblies of large cars (weighing around 100 metric tons) with total loads far exceeding 10,000 tons, continuously move between the mine and the consumption point, backed by automated loading and unloading facilities.[21]

The Chinese move their coal in ordinary gondola or hopper cars, with an average load of around 40 tons per car (new cars of modern design have a capacity of 50 to 65 tons, the older ones, 33 tons or less) and a total train load of no more than 3,000 tons.[22] Moreover, they are still pulling most of their trains with steam locomotives, which are energy-inefficient and give performance inferior to that of modern diesel or electric engines. As a part of the nationwide technological modernization, railway transportation is to make considerable progress by 1985. Major north-south lines are to be double-tracked and electrified, electrical and diesel locomotives are to haul more than 60 percent of the total load, bigger freight cars are to be introduced, and automation of traffic control and mechanization of loading are to be gradually extended. If accomplished, this modernization would go a long way toward improving the status of China's coal transportation.

Oil and Gas

Since the mid-1960s, hydrocarbon production has been the most successful extractive branch of China's energy development. Soviet-aided oil and gas exploration during the 1950s resulted in the discovery of the huge Tach'ing field in Heilungkiang in September 1959. Discoveries of other large fields followed shortly; major natural gas strikes were also made at that time in the Szechwan basin.

As a result, Chinese hydrocarbon extraction started to register very high increments. Between 1967 and 1977, crude oil production grew at an annual rate of nearly 19 percent, while natural gas output climbed at 16.6 percent per year.[23] Most of this unsustainably fast expansion has been achieved with technology based on antiquated Soviet designs. As exploration and production now move into deeper strata, less accessible locations, and offshore waters, the industry faces the need for extensive technological modernization and the acquisition of advanced foreign equipment.

Exploration and Production

Modern hydrocarbon exploration and production technology was introduced to the P.R.C. by the Soviets during the 1950s. Later, China received substantial imports from Rumania and recently it has benefited from purchases of advanced Western and Japanese equipment. The largely Soviet-oriented technology has been a source of important limitations. Inadequate seismic equipment and the lack of computerized field units hinder the location of deep structures; reliance on old turbodrills and shortages of high quality drill bits, drilling and casing pipes, mud pumps, and gas treating facilities have resulted in inefficient field operations.[24] But the Chinese have at least mastered serial production of almost all essential components for shallow drilling in relatively soft formations and are now focusing on improvements in performance and quality.

Virtually all basic types of onshore hydrocarbon exploration equipment are now produced in China. Sian Geophysical Instruments Plant is the principal supplier of gravimeters, seismographs, radiometers, magnetometers, geophones, well-logging devices, isotope well-testing instruments, and gas analyzers.[25] The sophistication and performance of these devices are much behind the Western levels; for example, the factory turned out the first experimental, digital seismograph only in 1976, about a decade after its introduction in the West.[26]

A complex of plants at Lanchow is China's main producer of oil and gas drilling equipment. The Petrochemical Machinery Plant produces medium-depth (up to 3,200 meters) drilling rigs and oil-fracturing machines with pressures up to 1,200 atmospheres.[27] The Paochi Petroleum Machinery Plant has been producing small drilling rigs, drill pipes, collars, and tool joints since the 1950s and is now making lightweight links, elevators, and pipe tongs.[28] Various Shanghai and Peking-Tientsin area plants supply light drilling rigs, drilling bits, oil valves, control equipment, engines, and pumps. In recent years, the Chinese have devoted increased attention to the introduction of improved drilling bits. The first fine-grain synthetic diamond drill bit was developed between 1969 and 1974 in Peking's Research Institute of Powder Metallurgy and has since been widely used.[29]

Improved drilling technology led, obviously, to deeper wells. Exploratory drilling was limited to 1,000 to 2,000 meters in the 1950s. Depths of 4,000 to 5,000 meters were reached in the early 1970s. In 1978, the deepest Chinese exploratory drilling in Szechwan reached 7,175 meters, two decades after wells over 7,000 meters deep were completed in the United States.[30] As for field production, the Chinese have repeatedly claimed that they devised the method of injecting water into different oil-bearing formations in the early stage of production to maintain oil pressure. In reality, water flooding was introduced into China by the Soviets. Thus, it is not surprising that the Chinese used in their fields the line-drive waterflooding technique predominantly used in Soviet practice and have only recently turned toward the five-spot or nine-spot arrangements commonly used in the West, which increase recovery efficiency but slow down the rate of production.[31]

Offshore exploration started from earthen causeways in Po Hai Bay in the late 1960s. China's first offshore rig, Po Hai No. 1, drilled its first well in May 1971. A small jack-up with four legs, the rig can drill in water up to thirty meters deep.[32] In 1972, the Chinese bought the Fuji from Japan Drilling Company—a secondhand jack-up rig that can drill in up to 54 meters of water. During 1974, a Shanghai shipyard pieced together two hulls of old Liberty cargo vessels to build China's first drill ship capable of working in waters eighty meters deep.[33]

In June 1974, the Chinese commenced a large-scale aerial magnetic survey of their coastal waters, which lasted nearly four years and resulted in a series of 1:500,000 and 1:200,000 maps.[34] During this period, they also purchased seismic instruments and an advanced geophysical survey ship from France and acquired French and U.S. geophysical data-producing equipment. The survey and the new equipment have given the Chinese the ability to start assessing accurately their offshore hydrocarbon resources.[35]

The potential in Po Hai Bay and in the East and South China seas has been promising enough to prompt the steady expansion of China's offshore drilling fleet, which included a dozen drilling rigs by the summer of 1978. Recent purchases have included a large semisubmersible from Norway, two National Supply rigs, and a Bethlehem jack-up; the Japanese have won orders for two semisubmersible Hitachi rigs.[36] Clearly, the Chinese are very serious about swiftly expanding their offshore drilling and production capacities.

Transportation

Development of modern crude oil transportation in China started only during the early 1970s. Until the end of the 1960s, virtually all of the country's crude oil was moved in the most expensive, wasteful, and clumsy manner—by small railway tank cars and trucks. Although an extensive oil pipeline construction program started in 1970 (so that by mid-1976 3,200 kilometers of new trunk lines had been completed and another 2,000 kilometers were under construction), the total length of China's long-distance oil pipelines in 1977 was still less than 6,000 kilometers, or about 42 kilometers per metric ton of extracted crude, while the corresponding relative values were about 120 kilometers in the Soviet Union and 675 kilometers in the United States.[37] According to an NCNA release, just half of China's crude oil was moved by pipelines in 1977,[38] while most of the rest had to be transported from the oilfields by more than 30,000 railroad tank cars.

Chinese long-distance pipelines are twenty, twenty-five, thirty, and sixty-one centimeters in diameter, are welded together in eight-to-twelve meter sections, and are wrapped in six alternating layers of plastic cloth and bitumen before emplacement. Chinese-made pipes are mostly less than thirty centimeters in diameter; the larger sizes are spiral formed and, consequently, do not withstand high pressures.[39] An added difficulty is imposed by the high pour-point and high paraffin content of many Chinese crude oils, which must flow in heated pipelines in winter. Chronic shortages of high-quality steel and inadequate capacity of domestic pipe factories have necessitated continuous imports of large-diameter, seamless pipe imported mostly from Japan, West Germany, France, and Italy.

Pipe laying has recently benefited from imports of modern machinery, and the Chinese are now able, though with much arduous labor, to build the lines in difficult terrain and harsh weather in a relatively short time. The most difficult line of all—and certainly one of the most ambitious projects in the world—is the recent construction of a strategic pipeline 1,100 kilometers long from Tsinghai to Tibet.[40] Natural gas pipelines are much less extensive than crude oil lines and have been primarily concentrated in Szechwan, where more than 1,000 kilometers of gas pipelines had been laid by 1975, supplying mainly the local iron and steel, fertilizer, and power generation industries.[41]

Tanker transportation is relatively even less advanced than pipeline technology. After the first two 15,000-dead-weight-ton vessels were launched in 1969, it took another five years to design and build China's first 24,000-ton tanker in 1974.[42] A number of ships of identical size (1,878 meters long and 25 meters wide) have since been built in Lüta (Liaoning), where China's first—and so far only—50,000-dead-weight-ton tanker, powered by the country's largest marine diesel engine, was launched in 1976.[43] These vessels are still too small, however, to take advantage of economies of scale, which rise greatly between 50,000 and 200,000 dead-weight tons.

To construct larger ships (i.e., of at least 100,000 dead-weight tons), the Chinese not only lack the necessary shipyard facilities and construction expertise but, until recently, did not even have any deep-water ports to accommodate them. The only facility capable of handling tankers of up to 100,000 dead-weight tons is the new Lüta pier completed in 1976; it is a terminal of the Tach'ing pipeline and loads large foreign vessels with export oil.[44] The only deep-water dock in the South is Chanchiang in Kwangtung, which can receive ships up to 70,000 dead-weight tons.[45] Since 1974, the Chinese have been expanding their tanker fleet by purchases of secondhand ships from Norway and Japan and negotiations to purchase more Japanese ships are again under way.

Little is known about China's oil storage. Strategic oil supplies stored in anticipation of an armed conflict with the Soviet Union must be relatively large but are most likely dispersed in thousands of small oil storage tanks throughout the country.[46] China's first large underground stone cave oil tank—10,000 cubic meters—was completed at an undisclosed location only in 1977, and construction of the first large aboveground steel tank of the identical volume to store oil for large power plants was finished in Lüta in 1977.[47]

Refining

Modern Chinese crude oil refining had its origin in Soviet technology, as did other principal sectors of the hydrocarbon industries, which, in turn, were derived from earlier U.S. experience. Before the Soviets withdrew their technical assistance in 1960, they designed and built China's first large modern refinery in Lanchow, aided in the reconstruction and expansion of other smaller installations, and introduced basic techniques of atmospheric and vacuum distillation, thermal cracking, and coking.

After the Soviet withdrawal, the Chinese bought complete refineries from Italy, a heavy oil-cracking installation and an olefin extraction unit from West Germany, and they also gained access to U.S. catalytic cracking and platforming expertise via the Esso-Shell refinery in Havana.[48] These acquisitions enabled them to start work on the first two fully Chinese refineries: Tach'ing, whose initial phase was completed in 1966, followed by numerous expansions; and the Peking Petrochemical Plant, which began operating in 1969.

By 1973, a majority of refineries had catalytic cracking, platforming, and delayed coking installations, whereas only a few had this equipment in the mid-1960s. In the early 1970s, the first Chinese direct computer controls of distillation columns were also put in operation in a Shanghai refinery and they appear to be of modern design and well laid out.[49] Technologies introduced in 1974 included molecular sieve separation for normal paraffin and the hydrofining of lubricating oils. The first domestic equipment for transfer line catalytic cracking was installed in 1975, and the first large, completely Chinese catalytic cracking unit went on stream only in 1978. In general, Chinese refining technology of the late 1970s resembles Western capabilities of the late 1950s.

Advances in the Chinese refining industry can be illustrated by the increasing number of final products. Only ten basic varieties were made in the early 1950s, eighty had been added by 1960, and more than one hundred new kinds were introduced between 1965 and 1974, so that today's refineries turn out a nearly complete range of important fuels, lubricants, and petrochemical feedstocks.[50] The depth and the quality of products from a typical Chinese refinery still lag behind the output of a similar Western or Japanese installation, however. With the growth of crude oil production the size of refineries has been steadily increasing. The Soviet-built Lanchow refinery had an annual capacity of only 0.5 million metric tons; the largest installations in the late 1960s reached 2 to 3.5 million tons, and in 1978 the Tach'ing and Lüta refineries had annual capacities in excess of 5 million tons each. Even these refineries are very small in comparison to the world's giants, which can process in excess of 500,000 barrels of crude oil a day (more than 25 million metric tons a year).

Electricity

The Chinese are producing an inadequate amount of electricity in relation to their total energy needs and, according to official admissions, power generation is "a weak link" in the national economy. The number of installed generating units has been falling short of plan; much of the equipment is obsolete, overloaded, and in bad repair; power generation does not meet the growing needs of industry and agriculture.[51] Major technological advances are needed in the manufacture of generating equipment and in the construction of large power plants, as well as in upgrading an extension of transmission lines.

Generating Equipment

Chinese capabilities of producing modern power-generating equipment remained very limited until the late 1960s. The acquisition of power technology from the U.S.S.R. and from Czechoslovakia initiated the growth of thermal generating units from 3 megawatts in 1953 to 50 megawatts in 1959. But the first 100-megawatt unit, designed in 1965, was put into operation only in 1969 and a prototype 125-megawatt set was completed in 1969.[52] In comparison, the first 100-megawatt unit was introduced in the United States before 1930 and in the U.S.S.R. in 1939. Between 1949 and 1969, the ratings of the relatively less sophisticated hydro-generation equipment increased substantially. Harbin plants produced a 6-megawatt set in 1953, a 72.5-megawatt unit in 1959, and 150-megawatt set in 1968, and China's first 225-megawatt unit in 1969.[53]

Construction of the first 200-megawatt thermal unit commenced in 1971, but the equipment only went on stream at Peking's Chinghsi station in 1975. In 1971, work also started in Shanghai on China's first 300-megawatt thermal turbogenerator; it was installed at the Wangt'ing coal-fired power plant (Kiangsu) between the summer of 1973 and September 1974, and it achieved full capacity in January 1976.[54] The only rating advance in hydrogeneration in the 1970s was the completion of the first 300-megawatt unit installed at Liuchiahsia in Kansu Province. Thus, in both types of generation, 300-megawatt sets are now China's largest domestically designed power equipment, while the world's top capabilities are 1,380 megawatts for thermal and 700 megawatts for hydro turbogenerators. Typical sizes of new thermal units in China are between 50 and 125 megawatts. In comparison, median ratings of new U.S. thermal units are 500 to 750 megawatts; new large Soviet power plants have serialized 400 or 800 megawatt sets, and ratings above 400 megawatts are common in Europe.

In aggregate terms, the Chinese produced only about 6,600 megawatts of generating equipment in 1976 (about equal to the same year's total for Italy), and its production appears to be nowhere near the available plant capacity. Moreover, a comparison of annual production totals and actual capacity increases leads to the conclusion that about one-third of all new units are used to replace overloaded, inadequately maintained, damaged, and obsolete equipment.[55] Not surprisingly then, potential import needs are enormous. Between 1972 and 1976, about 4,500 megawatts of power-generating machinery were bought abroad and the goals of the Ten-Year Plan for modernization in electricity generation—construction of thirty large power stations—will require further imports of complete power plants or large generating units.

Chinese capabilities are also considerably behind world levels in gas turbine generation. Currently the largest Shanghai-made prototype unit has 10 megawatts—one-tenth the size of serially available Western and Soviet gas turbines.[56] Yet another area of deficiency is in pumped storage generation. While the capacities of the largest European storage units surpass hundreds of megawatts and the two biggest U.S. projects top 1,500 megawatts, the first Chinese pumped storage installation at Miyün reservoir near Peking has had, since 1973, a mere 11 megawatts.[57]

There is at least one area of power generating technology, however, where the Chinese have been claiming world primacy: direct water cooling of both thermal and hydraulic generators. They constructed the world's first 12-megawatt thermal generator with inner rotor and stator water cooling in 1958 and over the years applied the technology in their larger sets, including those of 300 megawatts.[58] The advantages of water cooling as opposed to air cooling of hydraulic units are an increased output of approximately 60 percent at a given speed, a more uniform temperature distribution in the machine parts, and a longer insulation life on a physically smaller machine. Consequently, some of the world's largest hydraulic units outside China have been built with water cooling, but there is no compelling engineering need or overwhelming advantage in the use of water cooling for relatively small machines, as the Chinese use it.

Power Plants

In 1977, China had at least 178 thermal and hydropower plants of 30 megawatts and up, several thousands of small fossil-fueled installations, and more than 70,000 small rural hydro stations; the aggregate installed capacity of these stations was 40,500 megawatts, equal to about 8 percent of the U.S. total, 18 percent of the Soviet capacity, and about 1.8 times India's total capability.[59] About 62 percent of China's generating capacity is in thermal power plants, and, in turn, 119 fossil-fueled stations of 30 megawatts and up housed at least 69 percent of the total thermal rating in 1977. Most of these stations do not exceed 100 megawatts in capacity, and China's largest thermal power plant is the 1,000-megawatt coal-fired Chingho station in K'aiyüan county in Liaoning.[60] In contrast, the largest U.S. and Soviet thermal power plants have topped 3,000 megawatts and there are scores of stations worldwide of more than 2,000 megawatts.

Coal was the only fuel for the Chinese power plants during the 1950s and much of the 1960s and even now it generates some 75 percent of all thermal power. Expanded construction of mine-mouth power plants is one of the main goals for the next decade. The only large natural gas-fired stations appear to be in Szechwan, while oil-fired plants are mostly located at or near the large oilfields.

The relatively small size of thermal stations equipped with outdated machinery results in considerable fuel waste. The last reliable published average national heat rate—604 grams of standard coal per kilowatt hour in 1957—was some 20 percent above the comparable Soviet value and nearly 50 percent larger than the average U.S. consumption.[61] Since then this wide gap has been somewhat narrowed by the introduction of more efficient units and also by increasingly frequent attempts to use waste heat to preheat the feedwater.

No recent figures are available on power plant load factors. The best capacity and production estimates give an average annual usage of 3,849 hours per installed thermal kilowatt in 1977 (i.e., load factor of 43.9 percent). This is about equal to the recent Indian load factors and 10 and 25 percent lower, respectively, than comparable U.S. and Soviet usage. Power plant controls and safety are also behind the Western standard. China's first computer-controlled 100-megawatt steam turbogenerator was installed near Peking only in 1975.[62]

The first large hydro stations in China—Sup'ung in Liaoning and Fengman in Kirin—were built by the Japanese during their occupation of Manchuria. Fengman with 564 megawatts remained by far the largest Chinese hydro station until 1965 when Hsinanchiang in Chekiang reached 652.5 megawatts. Hsinanchiang was one of a handful of more than thirty large and medium hydro projects started with Soviet and East European aid and advice during the Great Leap years, and it was completed more or less according to plan. Most of the other large projects were simply abandoned when the Leap collapsed and were finished only in 1973–1975. These delayed projects include several of China's largest power stations. Liuchiahsia on the Yellow River in Kansu with 1,225 megawatts is the largest of all; its concrete gravity dam is 147 meters high and 100 meters long, spanning the narrowest part of a steep gorge and creating a reservoir holding as much as 5.7 billion cubic meters of water.[63] Other large stations completed during this period include a 900-megawatt station at Tanch'iangk'ou (Han Shui in Hupei), a 300-megawatt station at Yenkuohsia, a 225-megawatt station at Chingtunghsia, and a 180-megawatt station at Papanhsia, all on the Yellow River. Altogether, sixty-six hydroelectric stations of 30 megawatts and up were identified as of 1977; the two largest stations under construction are Lungyang (1,600 megawatts) on the Yellow River and Kochoupa on the Yangtze.[64]

About one-third of the nation's hydraulic power capacity is installed in small rural power plants whose number grew from a mere 50 in 1949 to 86,000 in 1979.[65] While the available provincial figures show the weighted average size of about 45 kilowatts per station, most of these village projects are smaller than 25 kilowatts. The dams for these small stations were built with local materials by mass labor using traditional tools.

Transmission

In 1949, the P.R.C. inherited only 11,410 kilometers of high-voltage (110 kilovolts) transmission lines but the basic domestic technology developed fairly quickly during the 1950s with Soviet, Czech, and Hungarian aid. Thereafter, little progress occurred until the late 1960s, except for the completion of the first fully Chinese-made 220 kilovolt tie from Hsinanchiang hydro station (Chekiang) to Shanghai. The first transmission of power at 330 kilovolts over short distances started in 1972, but China's only 330-kilovolt line (just 534 kilometers long) was only completed in 1975.[66] In contrast to China's sole 330-kilovolt tie, even small European countries have been linked for more than a decade with 440-kilovolt interconnections. Moreover, the United States and the Soviet Union operate long-distance lines of 765 and 750 kilovolts, respectively, and are preparing to introduce 1,200 to 1,500 kilovolt lines. China's alternate-current transmission technology thus appears to be lagging somewhere between 15 to 25 years behind advanced Western performance. In addition, the Chinese do not have any direct-current transmission links, which have become essential for transferring large blocks of power over long distances.

Yet another weakness of China's transmission system is the lack of interconnections among the regional and provincial power grids. The two largest regional power grids, the Northeast and the North, are only connected by a single 220-kilovolt line and individual provincial networks in the East and in the South are completely separated, except for the Anhwei-Chekiang-Kiangsu system.

Main provincial transmission lines have 110 kilovolts and are being increasingly upgraded to 220 kilovolts. Long-distance lines are carried on steel towers and often on concrete pylons due to the shortages of steel. Interprefectural lines are now built at 110 kilovolts, and typical country distribution lines are 35 kilovolts, carried mostly on locally-made concrete poles through China's largely deforested countryside. Chinese engineers are now developing a 500-kilovolt alternate-current system, and 500 to 750 kilovolt lines should appear in China before 1985.[67]

Alternative Technologies

The search for alternatives to fossil fuels and hydroelectricity has become a major preoccupation of energy technology research in Western nations as they try to ease their dependence on the increasingly more scarce and costly traditional resources. Nuclear energy has, of course, played a key role in this search for the past quarter century, but direct and indirect uses of solar radiation, as well as geothermal energy, are becoming ever more prominent.

In comparison, the Chinese, with their still very abundant and largely undeveloped fossil fuel resources, do not have any pressing need to search for alternatives. Nevertheless, the Ten-Year Plan for modernization calls for "great efforts" in "exploring new sources of energy in order to change China's energy pattern gradually." As yet, the Chinese have no nuclear power installations and their greatest success in alternative energy has been with rural biogas generation.

Biogas

Without any doubt, the P.R.C. can now claim the world lead in small-scale biogas energy technology. There were more than 5.76 million methane digesters in more than 1,000 counties as of May 1978,[68] and the national total has been growing recently by hundreds of thousands each year. Most of the digesters are family units with a capacity of 10 cubic meters, and they are fed by a mixture of pig manure, human excreta, crop residues or grasses, and water.[69] Various digester designs have been tried in China, but by far the most popular type is the water-pressurized tank developed in central Szechwan; it is a rather simple structure consisting of intake, fermentation, and outlet chambers. Spent material is removed from the sludge compartment at least once a year and is applied on fields as an excellent organic fertilizer.

As long as the digester is tightly sealed, a variety of construction materials can be used. Cheap, locally available materials are always preferred, and the digesters are built from mortared rocks, bricks, and cement. The typical ten-cubic meter capacity unit requires about 100 kilograms of lime, 100 to 200 kilograms of cement, 1 meter of steel or PVC pipe to serve as the gas outlet and a few meters of plastic or bamboo tubes to deliver the biogas to the nearby house.[70] A simple glass safety valve is connected to the digester gas outlet to monitor for tank leaks, estimate the quantity of stored gas, and protect the digester from cracking.

The waterproof and gasproof structure gradually fills with aerobically predecomposed material. When gas production starts, proper care must be taken to maintain the suitable liquidity and desirable carbon-to-nitrogen ratio of the newly added digestible matter and to keep the temperature and pH of the digester fluid within the relatively narrow bounds that are optimal for methanogenic fermentation. Keeping the optimum temperature (around 30°C) during the cold season without heating the digester content is impractical, and thus biogas production either stops altogether or is greatly reduced during the winter months. Biogas is burned in simple stoves and lamps made of a clay and carbon mixture for cooking and lighting. In some places, gas from larger digesters is used for powering crop processing machinery and irrigation pumps or for generating electricity. Although not all of the nearly 6 million digesters in 1978 were used for methane generation (some are simply built to decompose manure), China's edge in rural biogas technology is considerable. In relative terms (per 1,000 families) China has about eight times as many digesters as South Korea and nearly 300 times as many as India.[71]

Solar Radiation and Wind Energy

Solar radiation reaching China is able to provide energy equivalent to 100,000 electricity generating plants with a 12-million kilowatt capacity,[72] but, as anywhere else, only a tiny fraction of this immense flow can be practically harnessed. Thus, China's use of solar radiation is much less advanced than its use of indirect solar energy (hydropower, biogas).

Infrequent Chinese reports have mentioned both small solar

stoves and relatively large solar water heaters. The first series of 1,000 small parabolic solar stoves was experimentally manufactured in Shanghai in 1974 to be used by peasants in the surrounding communes; it will boil 3 liters of water in twenty minutes and cook a kilogram of rice in fifteen minutes—a performance comparable to that of a small coal stove.[73] A reflector type solar stove used in Tibet for boiling water has twenty-square-meter mirror reflectors and an average capacity of 200 liters of boiled water a day when both summer and winter performance is taken into account. Similar devices are now used in several other provinces, but no nationwide figures or technical details are available.[74]

Reports on large-scale solar water heaters come from Peking and from Tibet and Sinkiang. Solar water heaters in Peking have been set up in many hotels, barber shops, and bath houses. In Lhasa, where annual sunshine averages 3,000 hours in clean mountain air, a 280-square-meter glass absorber heats bath water for 300 people daily in summer and 100 in the cold winter and similar baths have been built elsewhere in the Lhasa area. In Sinkiang, a bath train with solar-heated water has been in operation since 1978.[75]

The only information available on wind-harnessing technology comes from the Inner Mongolian Autonomous Region where the Prairie Research Institute, in cooperation with a Shanghai factory, built a small wind-powered, 100-watt electric generator.[76] This simple and cheap device can easily be taken apart and moved with the migrating herdsmen. A much larger 2,000-watt generator has also been developed for small settlements.

Geothermal Energy

Most of China is influenced by the continuing collision between Indian and Asian plates, and this condition gives rise to abundant geothermal phenomena throughout the country, especially on the Tibetan plateau.

China now has three small low-pressure experimental geothermal power stations and a larger high-pressure steam plant. The first station was put into operation in Fengshun county in Kwangtung in 1970. Hot water (92°C) is drawn from a well; after degassing, it is vaporized in two low-pressure expansion containers and the steam is introduced to an 86-kilowatt turbogenerator.[77] Naturally, the overall thermal efficiency of such a plant is rather low; internal electricity consumption is quite high; and, as the Chinese admit, problems with gas elimination and corrosion have yet to be solved. The second small station was constructed in Huailai county (Hopei Province) in 1974.[78] Hot water pumped from a well vaporizes an intermediate fluid of low boiling point (chloroethane or isobutane), which then runs a low-pressure turbine. The third hot water station was built between 1972 and 1975 at Huichang spa (Ninghsiang country, Hunan); it apparently uses low-pressure vaporization of the 92°C water to propel a 300 kilowatt generating set.[79]

China's first large steam field is in the Yangpaching area, 4,300 meters above sea level, 90 kilometers northwest of Lhasa. In 1978, the field became the site of the country's first geothermal steam–power plant. Underground steam temperature is more than 300°C, and the generating capacity of the first unit is 1,000 kilowatts.[80]

Nuclear Energy

China has maintained a relatively large-scale research and development program for nuclear weapons for more than two decades, has adequate supplies of both natural and enriched uranium, and now has a valuable opportunity to rely on substantial foreign experience in acquiring nuclear power systems. The first step in this direction was a preliminary agreement in 1978 to purchase two 900-megawatt power reactors from France, but this agreement was reportedly tabled by the P.R.C. during the economic readjustment of 1979.

The Chinese have no qualms about safety problems; they see nuclear power as having "outstanding merits," with an "accident rate . . . lower than that in other sectors of industry . . . basically a clean energy source."[81] Consequently the Ten-Year Plan for modernization envisages acceleration of scientific and technical research in nuclear energy and contains plans to "speed up the building of atomic plants."[82] The Chinese are also expanding their thermonuclear research, which started with the construction of the first small experimental Tokomak-type device by the Institute of Physics in Peking in 1973–1974. According to a Japanese report, work is underway on the construction of a four-story structure to house a medium-sized Tokomak facility at the Hsinan Institute of Physics, one of China's newest nuclear fusion research centers in Loshan (Szechwan).[83]

Conclusion

The Chinese plan that accelerated development will propel China's economy to the front ranks of the world before the end of this century. Previous timetables of the Communist leaders —Soviet or Chinese—for "catching up and surpassing" other world powers have shown a uniform tendency to go awry. When taken literally, Chou En-lai's call for the Four Modernizations, adopted by Hua and Teng as one of their main slogans, is destined to meet a similar fate. One of the few key reasons for this almost inevitable outcome is the state of China's energy technology.

Energy is, naturally, the principal mover of economic development, and I have endeavored to show that China's current capabilities to extract, transport, and convert its energy resources are, if one is to choose a single indicative figure, some twenty years behind advanced world performance. But, obviously, it will not be enough simply to close this gap in the remaining two decades of this century. Research and development of new energy technologies are among the most intensive intellectual and engineering undertakings in industrialized societies, and major breakthroughs and advances are inevitable, which will present additional challenges to China's ability to modernize.

The Ten-Year Plan of scientific modernization in energy technology presents a most desirable list of tasks. Gasification and liquefaction of coal and high voltage transmission are explicitly singled out as important research and development areas. Heightened research effort is to focus on hydrocarbon drilling and recovery, large dam construction, improvements in the efficient use of energy in power generation, and on the iron and steel, chemical, and metallurgical industries. Such improvements are indeed imperative. On the basis of the best available data, I have shown that Chinese steel production is as much as

3.86 times more energy intensive than its Japanese counterpart and China's small nitrogen fertilizer industry uses nearly twice as much energy per unit mass of output as modern large factories.[84]

The gaps are too large and too many, however, to be eliminated or even shrunk to marginal differences. Undeniably, the quantity will be there. During the next two decades China will become the world's second largest coal producer, will move forward in the ranks of oil- and gas-producing nations, and will greatly enlarge its power generation. But the variety, sophistication, and performance of its energy technology will, with a very high probability, remain much behind the world's top level.

Notes

1. Vaclav Smil, *China's Energy Achievements, Problems, Prospects* (New York: Praeger, 1976), and "China's Energetics: A System Analysis," in U.S., Congress, Joint Economic Committee, *Chinese Economy Post-Mao*, 95th Cong., 2d sess., 1978, pp. 323–369.

2. Department of Economic and Social Affairs, *World Energy Supplies* (New York: United Nations Organization, annually).

3. Fang Yi, "Report to the National Science Conference," Foreign Broadcast Information Service [hereafter FBIS], March 29, 1978, p. 2.

4. I. I. Bazhenov, I. A. Leonenko, and A. K. Kharchenho, *Ugolnaya promyshlennost Kitaiskoi Narodnoi Respubliki* [Coal industry of the P.R.C.] (Moscow: Gosgortekhizdat, 1959), p. 254.

5. New China News Agency (English) [hereafter NCNA] in *Summary of World Broadcasts* [hereafter *SWB*], no. 978 (May 3, 1978), p. 10.

6. Tsentralnoye statisticheskoie upravleniye, *Narodnoe Khozyaistvo SSSR* [National economy of USSR] (Moscow: Statistika, annually); National Coal Association, *Bituminous Coal Facts* (Washington D.C.: National Coal Association, biennially).

7. Yuan-li Wu with H. C. Ling, *Economic Development and the Use of Energy Resources in Communist China* (New York: Praeger, 1963), pp. 44–48.

8. J. Craig, J. Lewek, and G. Cole, "A Survey of China's Machine-Building Industry," in U.S., Congress, *Chinese Economy Post-Mao*, p. 314.

9. *China: The Coal Industry* (Washington, D.C.: Central Intelligence Agency, 1976), pp. 10–11.

10. Hsiao Han, "Developing Coal Industry at High Speed," *Peking Review* [hereafter *PR*] 21, no. 8 (February 24, 1978):7–8.

11. NCNA (English) in *SWB*, no. 950 (October 12, 1977), p. 15; and *SWB*, no. 965 (February 1, 1978), p. 9.

12. NCNA (Chinese), in *SWB*, no. 786 (July 31, 1974), p. 5.

13. Smil, "China's Energetics," p. 341.

14. Peking Home Service, *SWB*, no. 860 (January 14, 1976), p. 7; Anonymous, "A Heroic People, a Heroic Army," *PR* 19, no. 34 (August 20, 1976):6; NCNA (English), *SWB*, no. 978 (May 3, 1978), p. 10.

15. Shansi Provincial Service, *SWB*, no. 970 (March 8, 1978), p. 10.

16. National Coal Association, *Bituminous;* also, *Energy in Western Europe—Vital Role of Coal* (London: National Coal Board, 1977), p. 39.

17. A. B. Ikonnikov, "The Capacity of China's Coal Industry," *Current Scene* 11, no. 4 (April 1973):1–9.

18. Chekiang Provincial Service, *SWB*, no. 927 (May 4, 1977), p. 2; NCNA (English), *SWB*, no. 970 (March 8, 1978), p. 8.

19. NCNA (English), *SWB*, no. 956 (November 23, 1977), p. 7; and *SWB*, no. 959 (December 14, 1977), pp. 10–11.

20. Kang Chung-mou, "A Study of the Energy Sources on the China Mainland," *Issues and Studies*, 11, no. 4 (April 1975):60.

21. J. C. Kneiling, *Integral Train Systems* (Milwaukee: Kalmbach, 1969); R. C. Rittenhouse, "Fuel Transportation," *Power Engineering* 81, no. 7 (July 1977):48–56.

22. Craig, Lewek, and Cole, "A Survey," p. 309; P. W. Vetterling, and J. J. Wagy, "China: The Transportation Sector, 1950–71," in U.S., Congress, Joint Economic Committee, *People's Republic of China: An Economic Assessment*, 92d Cong., 2d sess., 1972, pp. 159–160.

23. Smil, "China's Energetics," p. 367.

24. A. A. Meyerhoff and J.-O. Willums, "Petroleum Geology and Industry of the People's Republic of China," *United Nations ESCAP, CCOP Technical Bulletin* 10 (1976):178.

25. NCNA (English), *SWB*, no. 828 (May 28, 1975), pp. 10–11.

26. NCNA (Chinese), *SWB*, no. 876 (May 5, 1976), p. 13.

27. NCNA (English), *SWB*, no. 949 (October 5, 1977), p. 14.

28. NCNA (English), *Survey of People's Republic of China Press* [hereafter *SPRCP*], no. 5749 (December 9, 1974), p. 26.

29. NCNA (English), *SWB*, no. 979 (May 10, 1978), p. 7.

30. NCNA (English), *SWB*, no. 999 (September 27, 1978), p. 19.

31. Meyerhoff and Willums, "Petroleum Geology," p. 205.
32. NCNA (English), *SWB*, no. 830 (June 11, 1975), pp. 10–11.
33. NCNA (English), *SWB*, no. 810 (January 22, 1975), p. 15.
34. NCNA (English), *SWB*, no. 987 (July 5, 1978), p. 2.
35. W. R. Scheidecker, "Petroleum Developments in the Far East in 1976," *American Association of Petroleum Geology Bulletin* 61, no. 10 (October 1977):1835.
36. Kyodo (English), *SWB*, no. 991 (August 2, 1978), p. 20.
37. *China: Oil Production Prospects* (Washington, D.C.: Central Intelligence Agency, 1977), p. 25; Vaclav Smil, "China Reveals Long-Term Energy Development Plans," *Engineering International* 15, no. 8 (August 1978), p. 25.
38. NCNA (English), *SWB*, no. 963 (January 18, 1978), p. 13.
39. CIA, *China: Oil Production Prospects.*
40. Ibid.
41. NCNA (English), *SWB*, no. 814 (February 19, 1975), p. 14.
42. Liaoning Provincial Service, *SWB*, no. 776 (May 24, 1974), p. 13.
43. NCNA (English), *SWB*, no. 893 (September 1, 1976), pp. 10–11; Peking (for South East Asia), *SWB*, no. 888 (July 28, 1976), p. 7.
44. CIA, *China: Oil Production Prospects*, p. 26.
45. NCNA (English), *SPRCP*, no. 5702 (September 11, 1974), p. 76.
46. NCNA (English), *SWB*, no. 770 (April 10, 1974), p. 1.
47. Lüta City Service, *SWB*, no. 960 (December 21, 1977), p. 2.
48. B. A. Williams, "The Chinese Petroleum Industry: Growth and Prospects," in U.S., Congress, Joint Economic Committee, *China: A Reassessment of the Economy*, 94th Cong., 1st sess., 1975, p. 245.
49. S. Yuan, "An Inside Look at China's HPI," *Hydrocarbon Processing* 53, no. 4 (April 1974):106.
50. Williams, "The Chinese Petroleum Industry", pp. 244–245.
51. Chien Cheng-ying, "Electric Power Should Play a Pioneering Role," *SWB*, no. 956 (November 23, 1977), p. 4.
52. R. Carin, *Power Industry in Communist China* (Hong Kong: Union Research Institute, 1969), pp. 84–85.
53. W. Clarke, "China's Electric Power Industry," in U.S., Congress, *Chinese Economy Post-Mao*, p. 411.
54. NCNA (Chinese), *SWB*, no. 883 (January 23, 1976), pp. 11–12.
55. Craig, Lewek, and Cole, "A Survey," p. 307.
56. Clarke, "China's Electric Power Industry," p. 408.

57. NCNA (English), *SWB*, no. 761 (February 6, 1974), p. 13.

58. NCNA (English), *SWB*, no. 795 (October 20, 1974), p. 13; NCNA (Chinese), *SWB*, no. 883 (January 23, 1976), p. 11.

59. U.N.O., DESA, *World Energy Supplies.*

60. Anonymous, "Huge Power Plant," *PR* 21, no. 49 (December 8, 1978):31.

61. Smil, "China's Energetics," p. 313.

62. NCNA (English), *SWB*, no. 813 (February 12, 1975), p. 16.

63. Anonymous, "China's Biggest Hydro-Power Station," *PR* 18, no. 7 (February 14, 1975):11–12, 21.

64. NCNA (English), *SWB*, no. 1019 (February 21, 1979), p. 5; Anonymous, "Building a Dam on the Changjiang River," *Beijing Review* 22, no. 12 (March 23, 1979):17–18.

65. Smil, "China's Energetics," pp. 85–86.

66. NCNA (English), *SWB*, no. 814 (February 19, 1975), p. 13.

67. Peking Home Service, *SWB*, no. 1006 (November 15, 1978), p. 3.

68. NCNA (English), *SWB*, no. 983 (June 7, 1978), p. 13.

69. Anonymous, "Questions About Marsh Gas Tank," *K'o-hsüeh shih-yen* [Scientific experimentation] (hereafter *KHSY*), no. 7 (July 1974), p. 30.

70. Anonymous, "Construction of the Fixed Top Fully Enclosed Biogas Plant," in *Compost, Fertilizer, and Biogas Production from Human and Farm Wastes in the People's Republic of China* (Ottawa: International Development Research Center, 1978), pp. 56–57.

71. A.K.N. Reddy and K. K. Prasad, "Technological Alternatives and the Indian Energy Crisis," *Economic and Political Weekly*, special issue (August 1977), p. 1484; National Academy of Sciences, *Methane Generation from Human, Animal, and Agricultural Wastes* (Washington, D.C.: National Academy of Sciences, 1977), p. 5.

72. Anonymous, "Umbrella-Shaped Solar Disks," *KHSY*, no. 10 (October 1974), p. 31.

73. Anonymous, "Solar Energy Stoves," *PR* 17, no. 40 (October 4, 1974):38.

74. NCNA (Chinese), *SWB*, no. 866 (February 25, 1976), p. 10.

75. NCNA (English), *SWB*, no. 1019 (February 21, 1979), p. 3.

76. Anonymous, "Use of Wind Energy in Inner Mongolia Explored," *Kuang-ming jih-pao* [Illumination daily], August 10, 1977, p. 2.

77. Geothermal Power Generation Experimental Group of Kwangtung Province, "An Experimental Geothermal Power Station," *KHSY*, no. 6 (June 1971), pp. 36–37.

78. Anonymous, "Geothermal Power Station," *PR* 17, no. 20 (May 17, 1974):31.

79. Hunan Provincial Service, *SWB*, no. 886 (July 14, 1976), p. 7.

80. Ko Tze-yüan, "Tibet's Abundant Geothermal Resources," *Ta-kung pao* [Great harmony daily], April 8, 1976, p. 13; Chang Ming-tao, "Tibet's Geyser," *China Reconstructs* 26, no. 11 (November 1977):44–46.

81. Feng Tse-chun, "Nuclear Power," *KHSY*, no. 12 (December 1976), pp. 29–31.

82. Fang Yi, "Report," p. 10.

83. Kyodo (English), *SWB*, no. 963 (January 18, 1976), p. 4.

84. Smil, "China's Energetics," pp. 356–357.

Commentaries on China's Energy Development

William Clarke

Although the Chinese will remain behind in per capita energy consumption, they will show impressive progress, attaining state-of-the-art levels in some areas by the end of the century.

The immediate problem is the conversion of primary energy into electric power. Though in the long run supplies of primary energy should not prove to be a problem for China, current per capita output is on a par with that of Bolivia. This is not a problem that can be patched up with imports. The manifestations of the lack of electric power are felt by all industrial and nonindustrial consumers alike in the form of staggered hours of industrial operation, brownout effects, and the inability of the steel industry to produce at capacity.

Other serious problems involve the lack of reserve capacity for variations in peak demand, a situation that characterizes most thermal power plants in China. The power plants usually operate at 90 percent of capacity. The frequent instability of electric power can cause great damage to industrial machinery (fluctuations run 180 to 250 volts).

Many of these failings seem to have been recognized in the current Ten-Year Plan: 30 of 120 major new projects are power plants (20 of them hydro and 2 nuclear). Moreover, planners have begun to situate new thermo-power plants at the mouths of coal mines, thereby taking the burden of hauling coal off the railroads and placing it on transmission lines. Chinese hydro potential is the greatest in the world, but most of it lies in the South and the Southwest, far from many of the major industrial centers. Thus, long-distance high-voltage power transmission lines will be essential if this capacity is to be developed.

In order to reach 1985 goals, the Chinese will have to increase their power capacity by more than 60,000 megawatts, or 2.3 times their 1978 capacity. Hydropower will play a large role in this projected increase, and imports of equipment and technology will be sought to make it a reality. The Chinese have been very frank in stating that they will need a lot of help with their large hydro projects over long construction periods, particularly in the development of electrical and mechanical equipment as well as in extra-high-voltage transmission equipment. The scope of hydro projects already begun and in the planning stages is enormous. The Yangtze River dam at Kochoupa near Ichang is the largest construction project under way in China today. The 30,000-megawatt dam planned further upstream in the Yangtze River gorges will be the largest hydroproject in the world. The Chinese will look primarily to the United States for help with the Yangtze gorge project, possibly to the U.S. Army Corps of Engineers, the Bureau of Reclamation, and Bonneville Power.

Alfred H. Usack, Jr.

An "installation gap" exists as the Chinese have the appearance of being able to build a great deal of their own power-generating equipment with their two large foreign-built turbogenerator plants and two large domestically built plants. Yet, a high proportion of the new equipment turned out by these plants is not going for new capacity. This may be because much of it is going to replace old, obsolete, or faulty equipment already in service, or because the highly touted water-cooling mechanism developed by the Chinese is not functioning as it should. Low annual usage rates further indicate that there are serious problems in this area.

In natural gas, the figures indicating an impressive national endowment are, once again, deceptive: 80 percent of Chinese natural gas is produced and used in Szechwan, a province that produces only 5 percent of the national industrial output and 10 percent of grain output. Moreover, Szechwan is also a major center for coal and biogas production. How is this vast disparity between local supply and demand to be accounted for?

In petroleum, the developmental timetables are especially

tight. There is evidence that Tach'ing, China's largest oil field, producing more than half of the nation's oil, is peaking out. New fields are being opened onshore, and, with large investments in transport, several additional fields could be developed in the Far West. However, the production from these may not be sufficient to meet Chinese needs in the future, much less leave a surplus for export. There are still many questions about the productive potential offshore, too—even of the Po Hai Bay.

Still, it will be possible for the Chinese to do a lot in a short period of time, but phasing energy supplies with the demands made by other sectors will be crucial. The current ambitious hydro development plans are too costly, have excessively long lead times (the large ones will not come on stream until after 1985), and are too dependent on expensive advanced transmission systems, which China currently cannot supply. The Chinese should be giving higher priority to natural gas, where resources are extensive but distribution is poor, and where there is waste through flare-off of oil-associated gas.

In the critical area of energy transportation, the Chinese seem to be moving in too many directions at once: coal-mouth power plants, hydroelectric plants and nuclear power plants tied to large-capacity electricity transmission, the expansion of oil pipelines, the dieselization and electrification of railroads. In the short run, it might be more effective to concentrate on one or two forms of energy transport. This is only one of the many trade-offs of economic efficiency, timeliness, and the capacity to absorb modern technology involved in China's energy development. Whether a strategy of gradual build-up or a leapfrog, stage-skipping approach is followed is another question. And education, training, and management will be crucial to the success of any approach.

K. P. Wang

With simple, well-learned techniques, the prospects for Chinese energy production are excellent, even if the Chinese do fall short of their own projections. The gap between the present state of mining technology and what will exist in the near future is not nearly so large as it might appear.

In coal, Chinese technology differs from U.S. technology because of differing local conditions: Chinese coal, lying in relatively deep and slanted seams, has led to the use of longwall techniques rather than the continuous mining techniques prevalent in the United States. Whether or not the Chinese succeed in doubling production, coal production will certainly go up quite a bit over the next few years. Before the Cultural Revolution, there were about thirty technical training schools run by the Ministry of Coal Industry. These have been reduced to about seven over the last five years. Current plans are to once again reach the figure of thirty schools within a few years and then go on to establish thirty additional schools.

Discussion

The discussion ranged broadly over a number of issues.

Richard Baum set the initial direction of discussion by rejecting the question, "Is the Chinese energy glass half full or half empty?"—a question implicit in much of this session. Baum suggested, rather, that attention be concentrated on the entire Chinese developmental continuum and that the questions to be asked are: What have the Chinese achieved to date? What do they hope to achieve in the future? How will they get from here to there? What is the likelihood of success in their own terms? What social and economic spin-offs will Chinese energy development have?

Doak Barnett responded by pointing out that the Chinese are pursuing what will, in the long term, prove to be an eminently rational policy. Their interests are best served by a diverse energy mix at home, stressing coal, while relying on oil exports for foreign exchange earnings. However, there is a calculated risk involved in the assumption that there is a lot of oil offshore and that it can be obtained fairly quickly. In fact, the entire economic program may rest on the assumption that, by the mid-1980s, the Chinese will export oil at a rate of something like 50 to 100 million metric tons a year.

Other discussants expressed concern over future energy bottlenecks, the provision of energy for the rural sector, and

Chinese energy for export.

Nicholas Lardy wondered how much of a constraint energy will prove by 1985, especially if the projected 10 percent industrial growth rate is achieved. *Thomas Fingar* pointed to the possible bottlenecks that may affect fundamental energy goals, particularly in engineering education.

William Clarke strongly disputed Usack's contention that Chinese hydro efforts may be misdirected, stating that currently 80,000 local hydro plants play an invaluable role in the transmission of power to 50,000 communes. In the light of insufficient power-transmission facilities, this represents a major contribution. Moreover, larger hydro projects for the future are exactly what the Chinese need most, even though they will require substantial outside help to build and the payoff will not come until after 1985. Nor should Chinese dam-design capabilities—success with concrete gravity arch design, for example—be overlooked.

C.H.G. Oldham wondered about the balance of concern between energy for industry and the need to meet rural energy needs. Biogas expansion may play an important role in this area. *Genevieve Dean* and *Jack Craig* also focused their comments on the rural sector, Dean asking whether increased rural needs might be met by the expansion and interconnection of local power grids, and Craig pointing to the internal transfer of dated power equipment from larger to smaller plants.

John Hardt, turning to energy and exports, suggested that the Chinese should look at the energy embodiment of their exports so as to maximize the foreign exchange returns on their energy endowment.

On the question of the outlook for China's offshore oil, *J. Ray Pace* assessed the geological prospects as being generally favorable, both in the Po Hai Bay and the Gulf of Tonkin. He cautioned, however, that more up-to-date seismological data are needed and that there will be a minimum lead time of five years between discovery and production, compounded by an additional year to establish adequate supply bases. In sum, it will take longer than the Chinese think. Pace predicted that Chinese oil will not be exported in significant amounts before the mid-1980s, and that even then there will be no massive imports by the United States. U.S. companies will play a role, although Pace did not expect to see any major contracts signed immediately. Pace said that the critical constraints on offshore production will be: (1) the availability of sufficient credits to keep technical imports coming until output is self-sustaining in terms of the foreign exchange it brings in, (2) skilled manpower, and (3) the accuracy of Chinese planning.

9
The Modernization of National Defense

Jonathan Pollack

The modernization of Chinese national defense capacities has long been a preoccupation of decision makers in China. Both in terms of the specific content of various efforts to enhance Chinese military power and the major consequences deriving from such decisions, modernization encompasses a diverse and complex range of political, economic, and organizational choices. Modernization denotes more than simply selecting among various advanced technologies, although such choices are an integral part of this process. Decisions related to military acquisition also exert a major and direct influence on basic industrialization strategies and the resource allocation process, the manpower and training requirements for China's armed forces, and the defense doctrines espoused by the P.R.C.'s military leadership. Less directly, but no less critically, debates over defense modernization have served as the vehicle for elite political conflict at the highest decision making levels. Thus, a comprehensive view of this issue must pay heed to the entire range of decisions, issues, and programs involved in (and affected by) such a policy objective.

Our concerns in this chapter are more modest. Rather than review the full spectrum of China's military needs or analyze recent leadership debate on security issues in any detail,[1] a variety of basic considerations related to defense economics will be addressed. The choices and dilemmas that Chinese military planners have had to confront (both recently and over the past three decades) are far from unique. For China as for all states, decisions related to national defense are ultimately ones of allocation. Toward what end, and with what degree of effort, are organizational capabilities most appropriately devoted? What amount of investment and expenditure does a given security need require, and how should alternative choices be weighed? If a given defense need seems particularly acute or pressing, what are the possible consequences for competing budgetary and technological requirements, whether military or nonmilitary?

While each of these questions is central to any allocation decision, the actual process of determining "how much is enough" is not nearly as rationalized or cooly analytical as the label implies. Indeed, beyond a minimal consensus on the necessity of enhancing China's defense capabilities, substantial diversity in opinion and outcome has long been apparent—on what to acquire, how much, how quickly, by what means, and for what purposes.[2] More importantly, China remains a labor-intensive economy with a growing, but still relatively small, advanced industrial sector. As a U.S. government study has noted, "The Chinese military in many ways mirrors the economy that supports it."[3] China's heavy reliance upon its large reserves of manpower and low-technology weaponry no doubt reflects past political and organizational decisions. Even more fundamentally, however, it accords with the nation's actual economic circumstances. Such constraints will only be overcome by a prodigious, long-term development effort not only in the defense sector, but throughout China's economy.

This is not to slight China's accomplishments in military research, development, and production. While the P.R.C.'s current military strength does not even begin to rival the technological sophistication of U.S. or Soviet power, it does constitute a substantial and significant combat force within East Asia. Much of this strength, to be sure, derives from sheer numbers rather than the qualitative characteristics of specific weapons systems. At the close of the 1970s, for example, China continues to maintain the world's largest land army (presently numbering more than 3 million) and an armed militia estimated at 7 million.[4] Through a process of unobtrusive if somewhat uneven development and procurement, Peking's naval and air forces rank as the world's third largest. The output from China's defense plants also enables the People's Republic to transfer significant quantities of arms to various Third World states.[5] According to U.S. estimates, Chinese military expenditure in 1976 totaled $32.8 billion, the third highest figure globally.[6] In addition, the acquisition and development of nuclear and thermonuclear weaponry have been a major policy objective for twenty years, with modest but growing delivery systems now in operation.

No matter how impressive these achievements might first appear, the qualitative attributes of Chinese capabilities in virtually all categories of weaponry lag severely behind those of the military forces arrayed against China by the Soviet Union. Even more telling, in particular areas of weaponry China could well begin to lag behind potential or actual rivals in the Third World. For example, India's recently signed contract to acquire the Jaguar, a Franco-British deep-penetration aircraft, will give the Indian air force a plane clearly superior to any in the present Chinese inventory. Since the autumn of 1976, however, Chinese military planners have shown increased concern for China's military preparedness. Frank and worried assessments of China's defense readiness and its vulnerabilities have appeared in the Chinese press and are being conveyed to visitors from abroad. There has also been a renewed receptivity to the possible introduction of advanced defense technology from abroad, manifested principally by the visits of numerous Chinese military delegations to various European armaments plants and active-duty military units and by widespread expectations (thus far not realized) of Chinese purchases of modern weaponry from France, the United Kingdom, and other supplier states.[7]

No attempt will be made in this essay to assess the seriousness or political consequences of these inquiries. The absence of any major agreements, despite years of intermittent reports to the contrary, should caution against the likelihood of Peking becoming a major market for advanced defense technology from the West in the near future. This judgment is reinforced by the decided P.R.C. preference for indigenous production of military hardware, an issue to be explored further below. Moreover, notwithstanding the inherent sensitivity of the defense modernization issue and the absence of any detailed official statements about its relationship to China's development plans in other key sectors, the needs of national defense clearly remain a lower overall priority than the other three modernizations in Peking's economic plans. The 1970s have been marked by a sustained military confrontation between the Soviet Union and China, yet U.S. estimates of P.R.C. defense spending indicate that Chinese military expenditure remained virtually constant between 1972 and 1977, despite the fact that overall industrial production during this period grew by more than one-half.[8] Given the recently promulgated policy of "consolidation and adjustment," and the consequent diminution in the emphasis to be given to heavy industrial development between now and 1985, this pattern seems likely to persist for the foreseeable future.

In a more long-term sense, however, leaders in China are likely to become increasingly more conscious and explicit about the shortcomings and possible vulnerabilities of the Chinese armed forces in relation to their various regional rivals and adversaries. Regardless of whether Chinese military inquiries abroad soon yield any major agreements, such activity has greatly increased the exposure of senior military commanders and defense production personnel to an extensive and impressive range of modern weaponry, particularly for the ground and air forces. Over time, therefore, the proponents of heightened attention to the defense sector could well become more voluble and well informed in their policy advocacy. And, notwithstanding the belief that national defense ranks at the bottom of China's Four Modernizations, many of the P.R.C.'s present targets and goals in both industrial development and in science and technology will bear very directly on future Chinese military capacities. The engineering and manufacturing skills that are now being upgraded can be applied to defense as well as civilian production; research developments in areas such as lasers, metallurgy, optics, communications, and computers will also be critically important in the defense sector.

Thus, it is possible and even likely that leadership sentiment will ultimately coalesce in pursuit of more extensive and more advanced military preparations. Military modernization, however, will only progress as far as available industrial, technological, and budgetary capacities permit. This observation in particular holds true for defense sectors that are especially deficient or outmoded—that is, those that depend heavily on various advanced technologies, where China's economy is weakest. Indeed, U.S. government sources believe that the proportion of China's advanced industrial sector committed to defense production is already "far larger . . . than is the case in the U.S. or the U.S.S.R."[9]

Such considerations lend some perspective to the obvious dilemmas and difficulties that currently face China's economic and military planners in terms of basic investment strategies and specific allocation priorities. No matter how essential particular defense needs might be judged by some decision makers, the consequences of investing the requisite manpower and budgetary resources to accomplish a given task could adversely affect other goals in China's national development program. Outright purchases of completed weaponry from abroad represent another possibility, but they have not been undertaken on an extensive scale since the early years of the Sino-Soviet alliance. Two principal reasons explain why the latter policy is now generally avoided, and both factors will continue to apply during the next decade or more. First, the staggering costs of such purchases, given the sheer size of the Chinese armed forces, would rapidly deplete China's currency reserves available for purchasing technology from abroad. Even exempting any possible purchases in the defense area (where several contracts reportedly under negotiation are valued well in excess of $1 billion), China's foreign technology budget for the 1978–1985 period is already estimated as being between $52 and $59 billion.[10]

Second, for two decades China has made a major effort to develop an indigenous arms industry so as to avoid the possible complications and dependency that outright purchase of end items from abroad might well engender politically, economically, and technologically. The latter policy, however, creates its own dilemmas. While there is a decided preference for manufacturing needed components within China, the items one is able to produce will reflect the overall levels of China's technological and engineering competence. These levels obviously lag well behind the achievements of China's principal rivals, thereby potentially leaving the P.R.C. at a pronounced military disadvantage in various conflict situations.

It is clear that there are no entirely satisfactory solutions to these recurrent policy dilemmas. China's leaders (both military and civilian) have never been very forthcoming about their efforts to resolve such choices; thus it is not possible to provide a full account of the strategies that have been adopted. Nevertheless, even partial reconstructions of the policies relied upon in the past offer the most reasonable guide to present and future planning. How have decision makers sought to minimize the potential negative consequences of substantial investment in the defense industries, without unduly jeopardizing Chinese security?

It cannot be emphasized too strongly that Chinese defense planning and weapons-acquisition policies have always been oriented toward the long term. So construed, a truly "quick fix" option for Chinese security (except in the sense of abrupt political changes) does not exist. Those responsible for such policies have always recognized that there is a logical but incremental progression in the development of an independent defense industry. Attention must be devoted on a sustained basis to developing a range of scientific and technical capabilities. Thus, defense modernization encompasses far more than gaining access to particular types of equipment or defense items.[11] For a full-scale, autonomous industry to develop, one must cultivate and gain considerable practical experience with a broad range of technological, engineering, and manufacturing skills. A scientific and managerial infrastructure for research, development, and production must be assembled. To fully equip and maintain a modern military force will also require the extensive training of military personnel to use such equipment appropriately, and the necessary technical expertise and familiarity to maintain, repair, or otherwise refurbish modern weaponry.

Thus, the overall level and degree of competence achieved in these realms is a good measure of the extent of a given nation's independence in national defense production, not to mention in industrial development more generally. By such criteria, China has advanced further toward military self-sufficiency than any other Third World state. Though it is fashionable to dismiss Chinese weapons as antiquated and militarily suspect, such commentaries lose sight of several key considerations. In selected realms and for particular needs, Chinese factories produce more than representative military equipment. The AK-47 rifle, for example, is widely considered among the finest infantry weapons in the world. In addition, the available Chinese weapons have in many (if not all) instances proven generally adequate to the combat requirements of the People's Liberation Army (PLA). Moreover, success or failure in warfare is not wholly attributable to the sophistication of available military technology. And, regardless of the shortcomings of specific weapons, it is hardly insubstantial (either militarily or politically) that China currently possesses its own network of defense industries across the entire spectrum of military needs.

The significance of this latter point becomes clearer by quickly reviewing China's progress in defense production since the establishment of the People's Republic. In 1949, Chinese weapons inventories consisted exclusively of captured Japanese, U.S., and Kuomintang stocks, combined with whatever production domestic factories could furnish as well as modest amounts of Soviet aid. Through grants, transfers, and purchases during the Korean War, China rapidly began the transformation to a modern national defense force—with especially pronounced results in the creation of an air force and modern infantry and armored units. Following the end of the Korean War, attention turned to the creation of manufacturing facilities under Soviet license. By the late 1950s, these plants were producing military equipment in virtually all categories of need, including jet aircraft. With the abrupt cessation and withdrawal of Soviet advisory assistance in 1960, Chinese scientists and engineers had to undertake rapidly the independent management of all arms plants. Though serious setbacks and difficulties were encountered, by the mid- to late-1960s China had resumed production in all key defense facilities, and these were obviously independent of foreign management or control.[12] Thus, by this time China had acheived self-sufficiency (if not an independent design capability) in most areas of defense manufacture. This included the ability to "reverse engineer" key weapons systems for which only prototypes or limited supplies were available, such as the TU-16 intermediate bomber.[13]

To move beyond such production capacities and toward a self-sustaining design and manufacturing effort is far more difficult, and only modest beginnings have been made in this realm. The first such step is the ability to undertake modifications and improvement of preexisting designs. This goal has been pursued by Chinese scientists and engineers in certain areas of defense production since the late 1960s, but with very uneven results. The felt urgency to break free of past restraints and demonstrate an ability to undertake self-sustaining design and manufacture is understandable in the context of asserting national independence, but not easily realized. China's experience with the F-9, the nation's first domestically designed and produced fighter-aircraft, offers an instructive example. Since first appearing in 1970, the aircraft has been produced only in limited numbers and is judged a failure (or at best a partial success) by outside military observers. Indeed, whether the aircraft should be deemed wholly Chinese or simply a modified MiG-19 remains an open question.[14] Comparable difficulties in improving upon available Soviet technology in both the naval and ground forces provide further evidence of this recurrent problem. Only in the area of strategic weaponry, where the P.R.C. in the 1960s made an enormous commitment of time, money, and manpower, has China gradually begun to develop weapons systems that depart significantly from the components initially furnished by the Soviet Union. China's experiences in defense production, therefore, amply illustrate the long-term effects of technological dependence, given the disparate, highly complex skills that are called upon in the manufacture of sophisticated weaponry. The capability for truly indigenous design and production requires the development of an industrial infrastructure with both the technical sophistication and incentive structure to move beyond existing models and systems. This level of scientific and technological competence still remains the exclusive preserve of the major industrial powers and seems certain to remain so for the foreseeable future. Chinese military planners are under no illusions about the potential sources of technology for their current effort to upgrade the nation's defense capabilities. Now, as in the past, China must look abroad.

But on what bases—political, managerial, or economic—are such technology transfers to be undertaken? For Chinese decision makers, the maintenance of indigenous control over production capabilities remains a paramount consideration. The enormity of China's military needs and the sheer size of its armed forces make the outright purchase of weapons from abroad—even on an extended credit basis—a costly and risky long-term policy. Undue reliance on grants, purchases, and transfers could leave China potentially vulnerable to the vagaries of the supplier state's policies and production capacities. Rather than risk such dependence, planners must attempt whenever possible both to broaden the sources of supply and to acquire the ability to manufacture components of completed weaponry on Chinese soil. Thus, ideally, the Chinese will seek more than mere prototypes or outright transfers of finished weapons systems. By acquiring the means of production itself—through the building of indigenous production facilities and the training of Chinese scientists and engineers to oversee such operations—military planners will be able to maintain their autonomy from external control.

It is in this context that the Sino-British jet engine agreement of late 1975 is most appropriately viewed.[15] Negotiations were initially undertaken as early as 1972, proceeded sporadically for some time, and developed more fully during 1974 and 1975. The final agreement includes contractual obligations in three separate areas: (1) the supply of fifty supersonic Spey jet engines (the RB 168-25R, presently used in the British version of the F-4 Phantom and the Vought A-7 Corsair II close-support aircraft), (2) a license to manufacture these engines in China in a plant being built near Sian, and (3) the furnishing by Rolls Royce to the P.R.C. of facilities and technical expertise for engine testing and maintenance. Although various press reports suggest that there have been difficulties and delays in completing the third segment of the agreement,[16] once completed the project will have advanced Chinese jet propulsion technology well beyond current levels. More importantly, British engineers will have furnished China with the facilities and training necessary to manufacture these engines independent of external assistance.

The ultimate result will be to advance Chinese jet engine technology by at least a half-dozen years and to provide China with the requisite equipment and experience to produce and maintain such engines on an independent basis by the early or mid-1980s. With Chinese personnel ultimately assuming full responsibility for managing these production and maintenance operations, there will be little possibility of undue or unexpected leverage being applied by the supplier state. China's air force will then for the first time possess an engine for a fighter aircraft whose capabilities and limitations are not intimately understood by their Soviet counterparts.

There seems little doubt that the negotiations during the past several years between China and various Western European defense firms for selected modern weapons systems have included discussions of comparable arrangements. For example, Chinese officials have reportedly been negotiating an agreement with France for the purchase of several thousand HOT antitank missiles. Such an initial purchase would be intended for testing and training purposes but would be followed by parallel agreements to manufacture the missile under license within China.[17] China's prolonged negotiations with Great Britain for the Harrier vertical take-off and landing (VTOL) aircraft, by far the largest and potentially the most significant agreement under serious negotiation, reportedly involve comparable arrangements. According to accounts in the Western press, the P.R.C. would initially purchase at least seventy of these aircraft along with various spare parts (a contract reportedly worth $1.2 billion). Such a sale would then be followed by agreements on technical training and construction of an aircraft factory in China, where another 250 planes might be produced with British assistance over the next decade.[18]

Despite these reports—some of which have claimed that agreements had already been reached—as of mid-June 1979 there was no official confirmation that any such negotiations had been successfully concluded. Numerous reasons have been suggested to account for the continuing uncertainties and delays related to these agreements. Despite the apparent seriousness of such inquiries, Chinese negotiators may well be more interested in examining and acquiring extensive familiarity with state-of-the-art military technology than actually purchasing any equipment. Alternatively, the delays in reaching any agreements may well reflect continued disagreement among Chinese defense experts about the appropriateness and costs of various weapons systems whose purchase is under consideration. Others feel that the P.R.C. is conducting such inquiries far more for political effect vis-à-vis the Soviet Union than for the purpose of acquiring advanced military systems.

Not all the possible factors explaining such delays pertain to Chinese calculations. The P.R.C.'s undeniable insistence on gaining exposure to (and experience with) the design, engineering, and fabrication processes for such weaponry could well be encountering resistance from defense firms more intent on selling end items than providing Peking with the technological wherewithal to produce such equipment within China. Alternatively, the extreme political sensitivity of technology transfer to the P.R.C. (especially in the defense realm) continues to leave many in the West somewhat wary about the wisdom of entering into such agreements. Whatever the reasons underlying these delays—and it could be an amalgam of these factors—the negotiation of long-term defense arrangements are clearly matters of enormous cost, complexity, and sensitivity.

Given the extreme complexity and expense of any such agreements, it should be little surprise that China during the 1950s turned so fully and unequivocally to the Soviet Union for precisely such assistance. The absence of alternative sources of supply and the willingness of Soviet policymakers to furnish such aid more than explain China's extreme dependence upon Soviet technology. Indeed, Chinese armaments production in the late 1970s is still based almost wholly on Soviet designs, some of them initially transferred more than two decades ago.[19] This fact illustrates the enormous difficulties of incorporating new designs and manufacturing facilities into a preexisting industrial structure of such size and consequence. It also indicates the irregularity with which defense modernization has been pursued over the past decade. Finally, it suggests the understandable reluctance of Chinese planners to commit themselves unequivocally to new plant investment before being persuaded that old weaponry will simply no longer suffice.

While Chinese writings no longer discuss the full extent of Soviet support for China's earlier defense modernization efforts, both official and unofficial sources in the U.S.S.R. continue to describe such aid. During the Korean War, according to one of the more detailed accounts, "the cost—repaid by the Chinese side—of the arms equipment supplied to China by the U.S.S.R. . . . amounted to only 20 percent of the total value of the Soviet military credits." Moreover, more than half the military credits granted during the 1950–1955 period were purportedly used not for service in the Korean War, but as part of the PLA's overall modernization effort. Additional claims in this particular article seem wholly credible and merit extensive quotation:

> Over the period 1950 through 1963, 71 enterprises of the military industry [out of more than 100 that had been pledged] were built in China with the participation of the Soviet Union. . . . The U.S.S.R. Government set aside for China from its own available stocks sufficient weapons and military-technical equipment to reequip 60 PLA infantry divisions. Equipment which was located in Port Arthur was also handed over to the PRC. At the same time, the Soviet Union gave China documentation for organizing the production of new models of practically all types of modern military equipment, and sent a large number of specialists there who gave assistance both in setting up the production of new types of military equipment and also mastering the armaments which the PLA military units had received. Thanks to Soviet military assistance the PRC was able, prior to 1960, to devote less than 10 percent of its budget to military purposes.[20]

The scope of such assistance may well be unprecedented in the history of alliances. This conclusion is even more apparent when one adds the very substantial assistance given by the Soviet Union to the Chinese nuclear program—aid that was vital to Chinese successes in the strategic weapons area.[21] There is little doubting Khrushchev's rather regretful conclusion that "all the modern weaponry in China's arsenal [in the early 1960s] . . . was Soviet-made or copied from samples and blueprints provided by our engineers, our research institutes. We had given them tanks, artillery, rockets, aircraft, naval and infantry weapons. Virtually our entire defense industry had been at their disposal."[22]

Indeed, notwithstanding the total rupture of Sino-Soviet defense relations in the early 1960s, one should not rule out the possibility that newer Soviet weaponry might ultimately (if rather unconventionally) find its way into Chinese inventories. Several Japanese press reports bear directly on this question.[23] According to these sources, Egypt and China reached an agreement in 1976 whereby China would receive a variety of Soviet armaments originally furnished to Cairo in exchange for spare parts and maintenance help for Egyptian MiG-17s and -21s damaged in the 1973 war. Some cash may also have been involved. The transaction supposedly included an unspecified number of MiG-23 aircraft, surface-to-air missiles, antitank weaponry, and T-62 tanks.

Assuming the truth of such reports, intriguing possibilities become available to Chinese defense engineers, especially in fighter aircraft. A hybrid fighter-plane (tentatively designated the F-12) is purportedly being based on an improved model of the Spey engine, with numerous other components being drawn from the MiG-23. If more advanced Soviet technology in areas such as airframes could be used for such an aircraft, it could be easily adapted to preexisting defense industry facilities originally built by Soviet engineers. Comparable prospects would seemingly exist in other areas where such weaponry might be available. Should such efforts bear fruit, they would lend even greater support for arguments favoring continued development of indigenous defense industries, since their existence alone makes these possibilities feasible.

Access to and experience with various technologies, therefore, exerts a singular influence on the pace and direction of China's military modernization. But this objective cannot be separated from the development process as a whole. As noted earlier, Chinese writings now regularly discuss the ambitious goal of the Four Modernizations, but attention to the complex interrelationships among these four overall areas remains highly guarded. Rather than consider this topic in any detail, we will only indicate some of the more vital considerations that continue to affect Chinese defense decision making.

If a single conclusion should be apparent from our analysis, it concerns the specialization inherent in advanced defense technology. Some (though by no means all) of the needs generated by national defense requirements necessitate the investment of time, funds, and manpower that will be of only modest benefit to other industrial sectors. Thus, a key consideration in resource allocation is how best to integrate China's overall economic needs with the perceived imperatives of national security. This issue was less of a concern in the first two decades of Communist rule, for several reasons. During the 1950s, the Soviet Union (as previously discussed) gave China access to an exceptional range of defense technologies, including the basic infrastructure for an entire modern defense industry. Soviet assistance, therefore, enabled China to reduce vastly the percentage of state expenditure committed to national defense.[24] While Chinese investments in machine building and other defense-related industries were substantial, they were not nearly so dislocating as they would have been had Soviet aid not been available.

Although the Soviet withdrawal of 1960 had a very pronounced effect on both civilian and military programs in China, it still did not fundamentally alter the institutional arrangements established in the 1950s. Thus, the defense plants already built with Soviet help or then under construction could (once they were fully operational) produce weaponry deemed adequate for China's perceived national security needs. Moreover, by concentrating principally on security needs in terms of deterrence (i.e., the development of nuclear delivery systems and reliance on a mass militia), China avoided the vexing decisions that would have been required if intermediate defense technology needs had been judged more pressing.

It is precisely such choices, however, that Chinese policymakers have had to consider increasingly during the 1970s. As early as the spring of 1971, articles in the Chinese press acknowledged that the highly specialized requirements of nuclear delivery systems and advanced weaponry clashed directly with more basic investment needs in industrial development.[25] The posing of two alternatives ("electronics versus iron and steel") was somewhat disingenuous in that Lin Piao was accused of overemphasizing the former at the expense of the latter. It would have been more accurate to admit that, insofar as Chinese defense needs focused very heavily on the nuclear weapons program, this tended to somewhat restrict the range of technologies (and the amount of investment) that a more expansive defense modernization program would have entailed.

By the mid-1970s, Chinese military planners were beginning to look far more candidly toward their vulnerabilities in "middle-range" defense considerations. Attacks on Teng Hsiao-p'ing in 1976 focused on his supposed assertion that "fighting a modern war means fighting a war of steel."[26] Teng's opponents recognized that greater attention to a more differentiated national security agenda would unquestionably pose the issue of investment priorities in far more dramatic and consequential fashion than at any previous time.

This judgment has been amply borne out by the greatly heightened attention to military modernization apparent since the autumn of 1976. To be sure, most analyses in the Chinese press (including those with military authorship) continue to assert that China's defense modernization still must follow overall improvements in economic construction. But some articles now voice with increasing candor and explicitness a rather different argument. In general, they suggest that a militarily secure China in the 1980s cannot depend on the investment priorities that have heretofore been deemed adequate. As one particularly pointed article has stated:

> In any future war against aggression, if anyone still thinks it's possible to use broadswords against guided missiles . . . then he evidently is not prepared to possess all the weapons and means of fighting which the enemy has or may have. This is a foolish and even criminal attitude.
>
> Any future war against aggression will be a people's war under modern conditions. The suddenness of an outbreak of modern war, the complexity of coordinating ground, naval, and air operations, the extreme flexibility of combat units and the highly centralized, unified, planned, and flexible command structure—all these factors make it necessary for our army to have appropriate modern equipment.

> For example . . . our armed forces must have an automatic computerized countdown, communications, and command system and rapid, motorized, modern transportation facilities. They must also be armed with conventional and strategic weapons so they can take quick and effective retaliatory action against any invading enemy. . . . Once [our armed forces] are armed with modern weapons, they will be like winged tigers and will become more invincible than ever.[27]

Quite clearly, the consequences of such altered priorities would be profound. Even assuming substantial growth in the Chinese economy as a whole, the structural implications of attending to such investment needs would fundamentally affect the orientation of the P.R.C.'s overall modernization program.

How are the potential conflicts between the expressed needs of defense planners and the more basic requirements of Chinese industrialization to be reconciled? It is still too early in this process to offer conclusive judgments. Nevertheless, several more refined policy arguments have already surfaced. One, voiced by numerous civilian decision makers, is to assert that defense needs, no matter how urgent they might appear, must still await sustained growth and improvements in basic industries and in science and technology.[28] A second opinion, voiced in articles under military authorship, while acknowledging the importance of the development of the national economy as a whole, further asserts that "the defense industry . . . has considerable independence and initiative . . . [which] will inevitably continue to make new demands on other industries and on science and technology, thus motivating the development of the entire national economy."[29] A third viewpoint, aired by leaders charged with somehow reconciling such rival claims, offers the prospect of achieving simultaneous development: "Serious efforts should be made to implement the policy of integrating military with non-military enterprises and peacetime production with preparedness against war, and fully tap the potential of the machine-building and national defense industries."[30] All such arguments, however, are necessarily somewhat self-serving. They reflect the increasingly complex interactions between technology, economics, and national defense that will continue to preoccupy Chinese policymakers in the coming decade, and for which no intermediate solutions or compromises are readily discernible.

Even assuming the prospect of political consensus on such complex and potentially divisive issues, three key conditions could still be left without adequate resolution. First is the issue of competing defense choices within the Chinese armed forces. The increasingly visible arguments advocating enhanced military expenditure have only begun to touch on an equally difficult question: Which specific defense needs ought to take precedence? China's security needs remain vast *and* diverse. Competing military needs will require decisions on technology transfer and resource allocation that are highly divergent. At present, at least four overall areas of need are under debate in Peking: infantry modernization; the upgrading of the air forces, including air defense; naval acquisitions; and the strategic weapons program. A further consideration that tends to cut across all these issues is the systematic development of modern capabilities related to command, control, and communication. Each of these areas constitutes a compelling defense need, but it is extremely doubtful that China can contemplate simultaneous or equivalent efforts in all these realms. The choices and dilemmas related to acquiring modern military technology are often far too consequential to expect adequate attention to each. As a result (not unlike the Soviet experience of the 1950s), there is increasing evidence of debate and cleavage on such basic choices for China's national defense.[31]

The second key question is less political or economic than managerial and institutional. Simply stated, can the Chinese economy absorb and fully integrate a major infusion of sophisticated defense technology over the next decade? Will there be sufficient supply of highly trained scientists and engineers to operate and maintain new defense facilities and equipment? At a related level, do the Chinese armed forces have sufficient, adequately trained manpower that can appropriately use such equipment? Notwithstanding the sheer absolute size of the PLA and of individual service sectors, the answer is far from certain.

Finally, and perhaps most importantly, is it in fact realistic to expect China's armed forces to approximate the technological proficiency of the P.R.C.'s past or potential military rivals by the year 2000? China is now seeking to purchase weaponry that represents current state-of-the-art technology. Given the very prolonged process of fully integrating modern military equipment into a preexisting force structure, it could be the late 1980s or even later before such technology of the early and mid-1970s is adequately introduced into the Chinese armed forces. Yet advances in military technology continue without letup. China's security planners may then find themselves in the unenviable position of having invested billions of dollars on improved military capabilities, only to find that the P.R.C. continues to lag several generations behind the Soviet Union and the United States. To be sure, technology alone will not determine Chinese perceptions of the P.R.C.'s future security requirements any more than it has in the past. But decision makers in Peking must surely wonder whether the current military modernization effort has a reasonable chance of achieving success. The absence of any unambiguous or certain answer no doubt remains a cause for continuing concern among those planning the future of Chinese military power.

Notes

1. For a more detailed review of these questions, see my "The Logic of Chinese Military Strategy," *Bulletin of the Atomic Scientists* 35, no. 1 (January 1979):22–23., and "Rebuilding China's Great Wall," ibid., forthcoming.

2. For a more detailed overview of these dilemmas and choices, see my "China as a Military Power," in Onkar Marwah and Jonathan D. Pollack, eds., *Military Power and Policy in Asian States: China, India, Japan* (Boulder, Colo.: Westview Press, 1979).

3. Statement of George Bush (then director of the Central Intelligence Agency), May 27, 1976, in *Allocation of Resources in the Soviet Union and China—1976,* U.S., Congress, Joint Economic Committee, Hearings Before the Subcommittee on Priorities and Economy in Government, Part 2, 94th Cong., 2d sess., 1976, p. 31.

4. Both figures are taken from *The Military Balance, 1977–1978* (London: International Institute for Strategic Studies, 1977), pp. 53–54.

5. According to U.S. government data, between 1967 and 1976

China transferred approximately $2.6 billion (in 1975 constant dollars) in arms to Third World states, thereby making the P.R.C. the world's sixth leading arms exporter for this overall period. *World Military Expenditures and Arms Transfers, 1967–1976* (Washington, D.C.: U.S. Arms Control and Disarmament Agency, 1978), p. 126.

6. Ibid., p. 39. No doubt this figure in part reflects the sheer size of China's armed forces, given a military force of such enormous absolute numbers. But it also suggests how serious a preoccupation national defense has been for China. Although comparisons are not wholly apt, the 1976 data on the other major military spenders offer some perspective on this figure: U.S.S.R., $141 billion; United States, $87 billion; Federal Republic of Germany, $15 billion; and France, $14 billion. Ibid., p. 6.

7. For a useful review of these activities, see Paul H. B. Godwin, "China and the Second World: The Search for Defense Technology," *Contemporary China* 2, no. 3 (Fall 1978):3–9.

8. This information derives from an analysis of Chinese defense expenditures undertaken by the Office of Strategic Research of the Central Intelligence Agency, to be published by the Joint Economic Committee of the U.S. Congress during 1979.

9. Bush, *Allocation,* p. 31.

10. See the table in *The China Business Review* 6, no. 2 (March–April 1979):57.

11. For recent Chinese sources that show an explicit awareness of central dimensions of this modernization process, see "March Toward the Modernization of Science and Technology for National Defense," *Chieh-fang-chün pao* [Liberation army daily], editorial, September 24, 1977, in *Jen-min jih-pao* [People's daily, hereafter *JMJP*], September 25, 1977, p. 3; "Integration of 'Millet Plus Rifles' with Modernization" (article written by the theoretical group of the National Defense Science and Technology Commission), in Peking Domestic Service (Mandarin), January 20, 1978, in Foreign Broadcast Information Service, *Daily Report—People's Republic of China* [hereafter FBIS—P.R.C.], January 23, 1978, pp. E1–6; and *Chieh-fang-chün pao* newsletter, in Peking Domestic Service (Mandarin), March 22, 1978, in FBIS—P.R.C., March 24, 1978, pp. E12–13.

12. For a detailed overview of Chinese efforts in machine-building generally, but with additional attention to the military realm, see Jack Craig, Jim Lewek, and Gordon Cole, "A Survey of China's Machine-Building Industry," in U.S., Congress, Joint Economic Committee, *Chinese Economy Post-Mao,* 95th Cong., 2d sess., 1978, vol. 1, pp. 284–322.

13. Hans Heymann, Jr., *China's Approach to Technology Acquisition: Part I—The Aircraft Industry* (Santa Monica, Calif.: Rand Corporation, R-1573-ARPA, February 1975), pp. 18, 23–24. Only two prototypes of the TU-16, a mainstay of China's nuclear delivery systems, were originally available to the P.R.C.; they had been transferred to China in 1960.

14. Nikolai Cherikov, "The Shenyang F-9 Combat Aircraft," *International Defense Review* 9, no. 5 (October 1976):714–16.

15. This paragraph derives principally from "Breaking with the Past," *Far Eastern Economic Review*, 90, no. 52 (December 26, 1975):9; U.S., Congress, House, Subcommittee on International Relations, *Export Licensing of Advanced Technology: A Review*, Hearings, 94th Cong., 2d sess., April 12, 1976, pp. 7–8, 26–27; and "U.K. Assisting China in Spey Production Plan," *Aviation Week and Space Technology* 5, no. 2 (July 12, 1976):16.

16. See, for example, the report in *Far Eastern Economic Review* 98, no. 47 (November 25, 1977):5.

17. "Peking Said to Buy Missiles in France," *New York Times*, May 3, 1978; Jim Browning, "France Moves Ahead on China Arms Sales," *Christian Science Monitor*, October 24, 1978.

18. *The China Business Review*, November–December 1978, p. 68; Dinah Lee, "The Harrier Men Jump In," *Far Eastern Economic Review* 103, no. 7 (February 16, 1979):28.

19. See, for example, statement of Morton I. Abramowitz, [then] deputy assistant secretary of defense, East Asia and Pacific affairs, April 6, 1976, in U.S., Congress, House, Subcommittee on Future Foreign Policy Research and Development, Committee on International Relations, *United States–Soviet Union–China: The Great Power Triangle*, Hearings, 94th Cong., 2d sess., 1976, pp. 182–187; and Drew Middleton, "What the Chinese Forces Lack: Most Types of Modern Weapons," *New York Times*, June 24, 1977.

20. All the above citations are taken from O. Ivanov, "Peking's Falsifiers of the History of Soviet-Chinese Relations," *Mirovaya Ekonomika i Mezhdunarodnyye Otnosheniya* [World economics and international relations], no. 12 (November 19, 1975), trans. in FBIS, *Daily Report—Soviet Union*, January 14, 1976, pp. C8–9.

21. This issue is discussed much more extensively in my "China as a Nuclear Power," in William H. Overholt, ed., *Asia's Nuclear Future* (Boulder, Colo.: Westview Press, 1977), pp. 38–41.

22. Nikita Khrushchev, *Khrushchev Remembers—The Final Testament*, trans. Strobe Talbott (Boston: Little, Brown, 1974), p. 269.

23. See the Kyodo report from Peking, November 14, 1977, in

FBIS—P.R.C., November 15, 1977, p. E1; and a second Kyodo report from Tokyo (allegedly based on information from Japan Defense Agency sources), January 19, 1978, in ibid., January 20, 1978.

24. Ivanov, "Peking's Falsifiers," p. C9.

25. See "Develop China's Iron and Steel Industry Under the Guidance of Mao Tse-tung Thought," *JMJP*, May 12, 1971, p. 3; and "A Criticism of the Theory of Making the Electronics Industry the Center," ibid., August 12, 1971.

26. See, for example, Peking Domestic Service (Mandarin), August 4, 1976, in FBIS—P.R.C., August 10, 1976, pp. E4–5; and the article by Shen Ping in *Hung-ch'i* [Red flag], no. 8, (August 1976), in FBIS—P.R.C., August 24, 1976, pp. E1–7.

27. "Integration of 'Millet Plus Rifles' With Modernization," pp. E3–4.

28. See, for example, Li Hsien-nien's speech to the National Conference on Learning from Tach'ing in Industry, April 20, 1977, in *JMJP*, April 23, 1977.

29. "The Strategic Policy of Strengthening Defense Construction," *Kwang-ming jih-pao* [Enlightenment daily], January 20, 1977, p. 2. The authors of the article are identified as the theoretical group of the National Defense Industry Office.

30. The citation is from Hua Kuo-feng's "Report on the Work of the Government" delivered at the First Session of the Fifth National People's Congress, February 26, 1978, in *Peking Review*, no. 10 (March 10, 1978), p. 23.

31. On these issues, see my analysis in the articles in the *Bulletin of Atomic Scientists*.

Commentary on National Defense Modernization

Almon R. Roth

There is no question in my mind that China is interested in acquiring military equipment. The Chinese are also interested in acquiring the technology and expertise that will permit them to move beyond the confines of 1950s Soviet technology, enabling them to manufacture what they refer to as "modern equipment." This is very basic. At present, however, they do not even have the metallurgical technology to make turbine blades for the Spey engines purchased from England. They realize that they have exhausted the technology that they acquired from the Soviets. There is nowhere they can go to really make small incremental improvements. To further illustrate their basic problem, the Chinese apparently had difficulties in producing the MiG-21 engine, yet they are now moving to build the Spey engine, which is ten years in advance of the MiG-21.

I would argue that they are not likely to catch up, even with the Russians. The technology that they may acquire now, the Spey engine or the HOT antitank missile, is technology of the 1960s. I believe that they are trying to keep pace in order to prevent the gap from widening. They will be extremely fortunate if they can do this. I would say that they are likely to continue to be about twenty years behind throughout the foreseeable future.

I also would like to add a word of caution for those who read about these topics in the press. China's acquisition of military technology from the West is a very intriguing topic. Most military editors, in the *New York Times* and elsewhere, talk excitedly about the topic at great length. Do not be misled. When the Chinese acquire the HOT technology from France, and I believe they will, you might see something on the order of a few thousand missiles being acquired, in addition to the basic technology. Yet, a few thousand antitank missiles are insufficient; tens of thousands are needed if the Chinese are going to make a significant improvement in their capability. A few thousand are needed simply for familiarization, training in their use and maintenance, and as prototypes. They will not provide an adequate defense capability.

It is commonly suggested that the Chinese might acquire as many as 300 Harriers from the United Kingdom. This figure has been reported in the press since 1972. It boggles the mind to think that the Chinese would want such an aircraft at all. I suppose that they could use the aircraft to improve their ground attack capabilities, but I wonder if they really envision what they are getting into. The U.S. marines have had a high accident rate with the aircraft, principally due to difficulty in training pilots. The British, who are the principal users of this aircraft at present, have had special problems in operating it—for example, for putting in forward supply bases, not to mention ground maintenance. Moreover, for the Chinese to build a similar aircraft of their own would represent a quantum jump in their existing aerospace technology.

Again, I would like to caution people not to be too quick to jump on the bandwagon in anticipating China's acquisition of large quantities of military equipment from the West. What they will buy and how much they will buy are open questions. They may end up buying very little. But they have already accomplished several things in their recent drive to acquaint themselves with Western military technologies. The armories of Western Europe have been opened to them. They have acquired reams of invaluable technological information from on-site inspections as well as publications and textbooks; this is a tremendous advantage to them. In addition, they have accomplished one other purpose. They have used their well-publicized quest for Western arms to agitate the Soviets.

Discussion

David Lampton asked Jonathan Pollack to clarify his claim

that the acquisition of military technology, translated into productive capacity, would reduce, or even ultimately eliminate, Chinese military dependency. Lampton argued that the technology that is sold to the Chinese is significantly beyond their capability to effectively produce, absorb, and use. In his view, the acquisition of technology is not likely to eliminate dependency. It may narrow its scope somewhat, but continued borrowing will still be necessary.

Pollack responded by stating that he did not intend to give the impression that foreign purchases of military technology would eliminate the dependency problem. Obviously, this will not be the case. Purchasing equipment abroad from a variety of sources simply opens up the possibility of avoiding undue dependence on any one source of supply. On the other hand, Pollack argued that if the Chinese, in the next three to five years, were to make some basic decisions on what kinds of hardware they would like to obtain, they might well become locked into dependence on that particular system.

Rensselaer Lee inquired as to the existence of an internal debate in China over military doctrine. What, for example, does the doctrine of the inevitability of war currently mean in China? *Pollack* responded by stating that at a public level there is virtually no Chinese debate over what one would call strategic or military doctrine. There are bits and pieces of information, but these are very partial and episodic. We simply do not have the kind of coverage in the Chinese media that would enable us to study those questions the way we can in the Soviet case.

On the inevitability of war, *Pollack* stated that, if we read their statements carefully, the Chinese never say that war is inevitable between them and anyone else. The idea is that war between imperialist states is inevitable.

Almon Roth stated that China has traditionally done the best it could with what it had. Certainly, the P.R.C. is not going to go to a forward defense strategy in the near future. They have no way to implement such a strategy. They could not possibly cope with a Soviet attack by stopping Russian troops at the border. China's leaders are well aware of this.

John Hardt noted that, according to several East European analysts, the Chinese military were so important in the accession to power of the present leadership that they may have greater influence than is commonly supposed. If this is true, the army may exert greater influence over technological choices than might otherwise be considered rational, given China's current developmental priorities.

Roth responded by arguing that, although military influence is strong in the Chinese government, there is an apparent consensus among China's leaders that military modernization should receive the least stress among the Four Modernizations. In other words, China needs to build up the other three modernizations before military modernization, defined in terms of the acquisition of equipment, can go forward.

Roth also pointed out that the Chinese have been incrementally modernizing their military forces for years. For one thing, they have been producing increasing amounts of existing equipment. Moreover, as part of the current modernization drive, which began in late 1976, they reopened the military schools, brought experienced military people in from the field to serve as instructors, introduced examinations for the people accepted into the schools, and began to teach modern warfare tactics. Although we do not yet know the extent, they have also begun to demobilize those officers who could not adapt to modern warfare. In these areas, then, the Chinese have already begun their military modernization program.

10
Conclusion: The Four Modernizations Reconsidered

Jeffrey Schultz

When U.S. Ambassador Leonard Woodcock asked Vice-Premier Teng Hsiao-p'ing what he would like to see on his path-breaking January 1979 trip to the United States, Teng's reply was immediate and unqualified: "Space and your advanced technology."[1] During the course of his visit, Teng spent some time engaging in diplomatic activities, such as the acceptance of a pair of silver spurs from the mayor of Houston and a good deal of time digging those spurs into Soviet flanks. However, true to his word, most of his time was spent in the likes of Ford Motor Company's Atlanta plant, marveling at the way windshields are installed on Ford LTDs; in Houston, "playing astronaut" in the space shuttle flight simulator at the Johnson Space Center; and at Seattle's Boeing 747 plant, inspecting the landing gear on the jumbo jets that will soon be delivered to China. As one U.S. official traveling with Teng commented, "They [the Chinese] perceive us as the most advanced society, and they idealize us and look for magic coming out of their new [U.S.] connection."[2]

Teng's visit clearly indicates that, in the surge of post-Mao ambitions and plans that have been pouring out of China since 1977, the most dizzying have been those directed at industrial science and technology (S & T). S & T is acknowledged to be the basis for the other three of the Four Modernizations—agriculture, industry, and national defense—first outlined by Chou En-lai in 1975 and now the major blueprint for Chinese economic policy. Nor are S & T policies strictly limited to the laboratory or the shop floor. They directly involve a broad range of agricultural, industrial, military, and social policies, as well as conventionally defined R & D policies.

China's importation of foreign technology—much publicized in the West since 1978—has a central but supportive role to play in this process of S & T modernization. Peking has flirted with Messrs. Science and Democracy many times in the past with ambiguous results. Technology imports certainly have the potential for easing certain bottlenecks and for accelerating industrial growth in certain sectors, but the cultural and organizational infrastructure onto which foreign machinery, equipment, and expertise are grafted do not always prove well suited—or hospitable—to wholesale technological transplantation.

Even if the selection and financing of the most advanced S & T that the West has to offer posed no problem for China, the goal of technological modernization would nevertheless remain problematic and elusive. For there are at least three dimensions to the process of technological transformation—acquisition, absorption, and dissemination. Bottlenecks or failures in any one of these areas will do much to nullify progress in the other two. It is one thing to import and assemble a modern steel mill "out of the box." It is quite another to make it work properly and to coordinate it with vital supply, marketing, and planning networks.

An examination of the wider meaning that the current ferment in China's S & T policies has for Chinese society as a whole raises a number of questions. Through what sort of program do the Chinese propose to implement their far-ranging S & T goals? What are the continuities and discontinuities between present and past S & T policies in China? How will current organizational structures serve to promote or hinder technological development? What are the implications ("spin-offs") of S & T modernization for Chinese society as a whole? Finally, what effects will S & T modernization have on the core of values bequeathed to this generation by the Chinese revolution?

The Program

The details of China's overall plan for S & T modernization which are implicit in much of the current Ten-Year Plan, were spelled out explicitly in late 1977 and early 1978 in a rapid succession of meetings and national conferences, in particular the National Science Conference of March 1978, which was highlighted by speeches by Hua Kuo-feng and Teng Hsiao-p'ing.[3]

The Ten-Year Plan targets eight comprehensive areas of S & T modernization: (1) energy resources, (2) materials, (3) electronic computers, (4) lasers, (5) space science, (6) high energy physics, (7) genetics, and (8) agriculture. In his speech at the March 1978 conference, Fang Yi outlined four major goals to be achieved by 1985:

1. The training of 800,000 professional research workers
2. The creation of a number of up-to-date centers of scientific research
3. The completion of a nationwide system for S & T research
4. Success in reaching advanced world levels of the 1970s in a number of branches of S & T

A multitude of individual educational, manpower, R & D, legal, trade, financial, industrial, and international policies have been designed to achieve these and other S & T goals. The most important ones are summarized on the following pages.

Educational Policies

1. Educational elitism has made a comeback in the designation of eighty-eight "key" universities to which places must be won via competitive examination.

2. Thousands of students are being sent abroad to study.

3. Academic S & T exchanges with Western countries have been greatly accelerated.

4. The "July 21 Universities" for second-track technical education are being upgraded.

5. Special attention is being shown to gifted children.

6. Postgraduate education and research at the university level have been reestablished.

7. Graduate students and junior faculty who entered the universities during the Cultural Revolution are being displaced from the system, while promising middle school students, finding it easier to bypass a stint in the countryside, are being

recruited directly into the universities.

8. Standard textbooks are being compiled for nationwide use.

9. Training in management and other social sciences is receiving renewed emphasis, with programs in such areas as operations research and systems analysis.

Manpower Policies

1. Thousands of S & T professionals who were sent to the countryside or to factories during the Cultural Revolution have been rehabilitated and restored to their former titles and positions of employment.

2. Technical criteria and peer reviews have replaced political criteria for promotions.

3. The technical competence of S & T administrators, researchers, and academics has been strengthened through the removal of supporters of the Gang of Four.

R & D Policies

1. Researchers have been guaranteed that they will be able to spend five-sixths of their time on scientific (as opposed to political) work.

2. Much more emphasis is now being placed on basic science and theoretical research than in the past. These no longer need be directly related to production.

3. Past policies emphasizing innovation and practical research have not been slighted by any means. Both in Hua's pronouncements[4] and in the conclusions of the January 1978 National Conference on Technical Innovation,[5] practical research has been brought to the fore.

Legal Policies

1. Article 12 of the new Chinese Constitution adopted in March 1978 by the Fifth National People's Congress explicitly endorsed state support for S & T, the promotion of technological innovation, and the combination of professional and mass, native and foreign efforts in S & T.

2. A uniform commercial code containing sections on foreign investment, taxation, and labor law was debated at the Second

Session of the Fifth National People's Congress in June 1979.

Foreign Trade

1. International commercial practice has been gaining increased acceptance in China, witness the signing of "cost-plus" contracts with foreign firms, the inclusion of standard force majeure provisions in contracts, and the provision for third country arbitration of disputes.

2. The 1960s policy of purchasing a limited number of prototypes of sophisticated Western machinery for "reverse engineering" purposes is giving way to longer-term consultative associations between individual Western experts and firms and the Chinese consumers.

3. An increasing variety of industrial cooperation agreements—barter, compensation trade, joint ventures, and so on—are being signed by Chinese technology purchasers. The objective of such schemes is the maximization of technology imports within the very tight constraints imposed by China's limited hard currency reserves.

4. Foreign businessmen, traditionally limited to dealing with China's ten Peking-based foreign-trade corporations, are, with increasing frequency, dealing directly with provincial and municipal branches of these corporations as well as with a growing number of end-user corporations, some of which are linked directly to industrial ministries and some to factories. Thus, closer links connecting production, foreign trade, and technological advance are being fostered.

5. In April 1979, a contract was signed for the design of a Peking foreign-trade center—an edifice that will be more than twice the size of Peking's tallest building (the Peking Hotel) and that will serve, by the mid 1980s, as the focal point of Chinese commercial and technical exchange in the capital.

Financial Policies

1. After repeated denials that they would avail themselves of world credit markets, the Chinese, beginning in December 1978, entered the international bank markets with a vengeance, negotiating more than $10 billion[6] in loans and credits by mid-April 1979; much of these funds have no doubt been earmarked

for technology imports.

2. The central government is now using economic criteria in granting loans and investment funds to individual enterprises.

3. Requirements governing the use of profits retained by individual enterprises have been revised, permitting the retention of up to 10 percent of enterprise profits for product improvement.

Industrial Management Policies

1. Comprehensive enterprises are being dissolved in favor of more specialized, rationalized forms of industrial organization.

2. The revolutionary committees that ran most industrial enterprises during the Cultural Revolution are being replaced by enterprise party committees as the leading enterprise-based managerial bodies. Other managerial models—German-style codetermination among them—are under study.

3. The contract system between enterprises has been strengthened to give impetus to specialization and to insure reliable sources of intermediate inputs in the production process.

4. Consistent with the decentralization of industrial organization, individual factory managers are being given more power in the everyday running of factories.

5. Small inefficient workshops that cannot cover their costs of production are being eliminated; comprehensive enterprises are being dissolved in favor of more specialized, rationalized forms of industrial organization.

6. Wages at the middle and lowest end of the wage scale have been raised and an effort is being mounted to increase the supply of consumer goods. Both moves act as incentives to increased productivity.

7. An Institute of Management has been established within the Chinese Academy of Social Sciences to facilitate the absorption and development of more efficient management techniques.

International S & T Policy

Formal economic and scientific-technological agreements were reached with a number of technologically advanced countries besides the United States in late 1978 and early 1979, among them France, Germany, Britain, Italy, and Sweden.

The Future of the Program

The above policies represent only the tip of the iceberg. After sifting through the details, however, certain themes become clear: the desire of the Chinese to accomplish, if not everything, then certainly a great deal, all at the same time; a renewed emphasis on the basic sciences; the replacement of political imperatives by the goals of higher productivity, specialization, standardization, serialization, and higher quality; calls for a more technically competent leadership; exhortations to recognize "objective economic laws" and learn from advanced capitalist countries; the creation of new institutions and the revival of old ones tailored to the demands of technological efficiency. All of these add up to a new recipe for Chinese S & T modernization.

Thomas Fingar's paper has dealt with many of the specific problems—attitudinal, organizational, technical, manpower, managerial, and financial—that are inherent in this program. Perhaps in the broadest sense, the leadership's foremost task will be political. It must amass popular support for this program even at the sacrifice of such consumer goals as providing each household with a color television set by 1985. It is already apparent that the rising expectations of the last two and one-half years—for higher living standards, more personal freedom, and more political democracy—will pose a difficult problem for China's rulers. The February 1979 slowdown in foreign purchases and the reordering of development priorities away from iron and steel toward agriculture and light industry came at least partially in response to this realization: "Agriculture and light industry require smaller investment, but they produce quicker results and this meets the needs of the people."[7]

For obvious reasons, no detailed military plan has been made public. However, as Jonathan Pollack has pointed out, the military mirrors the economy as a whole in its technological dualism, educational and absorptive bottlenecks, dependence on in-place Soviet technology, and reliance on manpower and easily manufactured low-technology equipment. An additional problem for the military is the integration of well-learned Maoist strategies with the more recent emphasis on achieving technological parity with the West. The exhortation to be prepared for a "people's war under modern conditions" embodies with particular clarity the difficult choices that Chinese planners now face. In the past, military electronics and the Chinese nuclear program claimed privileged status in budgets and in planners' priorities. Now that full-scale economic development is being taken more seriously, these and other more specialized military sectors will find it increasingly difficult to compete with agriculture, light industry, and a host of other sectors for scarce foreign exchange and investment funds. It is thus not surprising that foreign military procurements are receiving relatively low priority on China's current technological shopping list.

Continuities in Chinese S & T Policy

The previous section—indeed, most of what is being written about Chinese S & T policy today—is concerned with what is *new* in Chinese S & T policy. Yet Genevieve Dean has convincingly argued that China's current S & T push

> is basically a crash program for catching up with an earlier timetable, not a new approach to technological development. . . . [The] basic elements of current policy are the same as those in China's First Five-Year Plan (1953–1957): initial concentration of highly efficient, imported technologies in a "key" industrial sector, with minimal investment outside this sector until domestic industry can supply capital goods embodying new technologies.[8]

Mao never objected to modernization per se—quite the contrary. What he opposed were the technological imperatives that seemed somehow to creep into the modernization process, affecting such socially sensitive areas as income distribution, worker status, and the organization of the workplace. These forces came into direct conflict with his cherished egalitarian principles.[9]

Nor has the essential "struggle between two lines"—the ideological and the technological—lessened since it was fought by Mao and Liu Shao-ch'i in the mid 1960s. Jon Sigurdson wrote in 1978:

> The new technology and science policy now emerging in China may be an element which is at least partly antagonistic to the objective of reaching the socialist society conceived by Mao . . . to meet the technology requirements of the modern industry the emphasis must be on large systems with a high degree of vertical division of labor with apparent nonegalitarian consequences for management in production enterprise as well as in the related R & D institutions.[10]

What have been the constants in Chinese S & T policy? Most obviously, politics is still very much in command. Current modernization efforts are being directed by the firm hand of planners in Peking. Capital investment and technology allocation are likewise still centrally planned; most major production decisions are made jointly by enterprise management and the organs of the state planning apparatus. The basic tenet that technological innovation can be inspired by a top-down system of scientific administration remains essentially unchallenged, although there has been some tinkering with incentives as has also occurred in other areas.

Secondly, as Rudi Volti and others have pointed out, technological dualism ("walking on two legs") is likely to be a basic feature of the Chinese economy for some time to come. In many sectors technological parity with world levels can only be achieved through either massive imports or intensively developed domestic technologies. In either case, the result must inevitably be the creation of modern economic and technological, if not cultural, enclaves within a larger, relatively less advanced society.

Perhaps the most telling similarity between the current wave of S & T reforms and previous movements in the same direction is the still-current belief that technology can be transferred through the importation of machinery, plants, managerial techniques, and even institutions—all of which will maintain their perfect neutrality in a Chinese context and will, therefore, have no contaminating effect on socialism in China. This was one of the assumptions that led to Liu Shao-ch'i's downfall in the mid-1960s. Teng and Hu Ch'iao-mu (president of the Chinese Academy of Social Sciences) seem to be working under many of the same assumptions today.

As Richard Suttmeier and Genevieve Dean have observed,

planners have, over the last two years, essentially restored many of the S & T organizational structures of the early 1960s.[11] At least three major revivals occurred in 1977–1978: the State Scientific and Technological Commission at the top to coordinate Chinese S & T; many of the research institutes that were closed during the Cultural Revoluton, including many under the Chinese Academy of Sciences and a number of ministerial institutes; and the professional societies, under the leadership of the Chinese Science and Technology Association. The latter organizations, where China's top S & T professionals can meet for discussions, perform elite as well as "mass" functions. Again, these are *revivals* of institutions that in many cases flourished during the 1960s, only to be crippled or destroyed during the Cultural Revolution.

Self-reliance, by all appearances, is rapidly evaporating in China's rush toward modernization. Yet here, too, precedents suggest that current policies are far from new. The essence of self-reliance is, after all, independent control over technological decision making. There are no signs that this is about to be given up. To be sure, there have been significant recent marginal alterations in Chinese receptivity to certain forms of Western penetration: foreign technical seminars, resident foreign technicians, and training abroad for Chinese technical people have all been on the increase. These were certainly inimical to self-reliance as practiced by the Gang of Four. It is still not clear how compatible they will be with some form of self-reliance in the future. As cooperation between China and foreign governments and commercial entities continues to expand, the delicate balance between self-reliance, selective borrowing, and outright dependency is bound to be dynamic and, at least in the short run, highly unstable.

Financially, China has yet to prove itself willing to go as far as some of the Eastern European nations in opening its heart to the West. On January 26, 1979, the *New York Times* announced that the Polish government will permit Western creditor banks to monitor its economy. China may be heading in this direction, but it is not there yet.

In education, alongside the recent elitist trends noted above, there has been an upgrading of the mass-oriented "July 21

Universities."[12] Although skeptics claim that these are now little more than "paper organizations,"[13] these centers of "second-track" technical education, designed to complement the contributions of the 88 "key" institutions of higher education, may yet have a role to play in promoting educational equality. The First Ministry of Machine Building currently runs 800 such schools; the Fourth Ministry of Machine Building runs 200. The difficulty in making them an effective educational force is that the financial, logistical, and teaching support, which theoretically should be coming from the indivdual industrial ministries and university faculties, has been difficult to muster. Moreover, no financial incentives have been offered to encourage worker participation. It will be interesting to see whether the demands of current production completely undermine these vestiges of egalitarian education.

Egalitarianism has not been stricken from the workplace either, where the recent rise in wages for those in the lowest and middle ranges of the scale has brought about a partial compression of the wage structure.

Mao, one suspects, would have approved. True, a few substantial bonuses—amounting in some cases to more than 1,000 yuan—have been offered to technological innovators and even to translators of foreign technical books, and more material incentives are being promised to all in the form of consumer goods, which will come mainly from domestic light industry. Nevertheless, worker bonuses for higher productivity or upgraded skills are still rather small, generally amounting to around 12 percent of the industrial wage bill or an average of about 7 yuan per worker per month. Nonmaterial incentives are certain to remain an important part of the picture for some time to come.

The Chinese Approach to S & T Modernization

In 1964, the Chinese began work on the world's second largest automotive plant: the Wuhan No. 2. Designed to turn out 100,000 six-ton cargo trucks a year, it employs 160,000 people in twenty-six separate factories. Starting with massive imports of the latest Western technology, the complex was designed and constructed entirely by the Chinese. The Western-educated chief engineer is a former assistant chief engineer at the Ford Motor Company. Leaving nothing to chance, he brought in 5,000 experienced technicians, foremen, and workers from the smoothly running No. 1 plant at Changchun. Despite such careful preparation, however, the Wuhan No. 2 Automotive Plant did not produce its first truck until 1977. It produced no trucks at all in 1978; its managers hope to get it up to 14 percent of capacity by the end of 1979. The moral of the story: *Growth is not modernization: technology acquisition is not technology assimilation.*

The Chinese are not at all inexperienced in the three-dimensional process of technology acquisition, absorption, and dissemination. However, as Rudi Volti pointed out, since the earliest efforts of the "self-strengtheners" to Westernize Chinese armaments production in the nineteenth century, the constant stumbling block to success has been Chinese culture, which has proven somehow unconducive to the effective absorption of science and technology. An "appropriate culture" would encompass a set of institutions and attitudes conducive to the creation and dissemination of new technologies: a stable framework of rules (law), linkages for the flow of technology from more advanced to relatively backward sectors of the economy, incentive mechanisms to encourage productivity and innovation, a price system capable of efficiently linking supply and demand, and, perhaps most important, a strong national consensus for modernization (implying a receptivity to foreign input).

Current Chinese efforts at technology acquisition must be seen in the light of previous attempts to achieve S & T modernization via infusions of foreign technology. Shannon Brown charts the shifting course and complete plant purchases from the West from the period of Soviet dependency to the post-Mao era. Especially important for understanding current Chinese attitudes are the lessons of the 1950s: (1) that technology imports can easily lead the country into unconscionably high debt (a lesson relearned in the early 1970s); (2) that such imports are often incompatible with Chinese factor proportions and needs; and, most importantly, (3) that they are capable of generating unexpected technological imperatives, independent of the desires of the political leadership. Against this background, China's caution in proceeding with large-scale technology imports is eminently understandable.

Today the Chinese repertory of technology transfer has been greatly augmented. Advocacy of complete plant imports is no longer stigmatized as evidence of a "slavish comprador mentality"; the inadequacy of reverse engineering for complex machinery (attempts to build prototypes based on a limited number of imported originals) is now largely recognized. Nonetheless, the importation of complete plants will represent a relatively small part of China's total modernization investment. Even in the duplication of sophisticated technologies, imports will be kept to a minimum. In China's planned purchase of a communications satellite from the United States, for example, most of the advanced technology will be embodied in the satellite itself. The antennae through which a multitude of ground stations will rebroadcast television programs locally will be a simple and inexpensive ten feet in diameter.[14]

To be sure, it is helpful to differentiate between industries for which the technology can be purchased "out of a box," and those for which the requirements of absorption are much more complex. For example, the Chinese have been able to manufacture simple types of machine tools without much difficulty and are even able to export them to many nations at competitive prices. Advanced computer technology, on the other hand, is much more resistant to simple copying. The gap between the acquisition of advanced technology and the production of a prototype can be five to seven years, as the Chinese have learned. Even then, the prototype may signify little more than a superior "arts-and-crafts" achievement. Another gap, perhaps just as long, may precede serial production. Thus, the translation of technology into mass production may involve at least two quantum leaps; the import-prototype and prototype-production gaps cannot be easily eliminated in many sectors.

Today, a much more sophisticated approach to technology absorption has been put into motion: Licensing agreements, the invitation of experts to China to give technical seminars, the sending of thousands of students abroad, direct requests for foreign assistance—both technical and financial—and new forms of industrial cooperation with Japan and the West are all a part of this new approach. Less direct methods, such as the prolongation of technical contract negotiations with the maximum number of foreign companies—only one of which will eventually get the sale it is after—also play a part in the education of Chinese planners and technicians. In the future, the Chinese will place much less emphasis on the importation of products and much more on management systems, processes, and service contracts for systems development—recipes for putting indigenous and imported inputs together in the most efficient manner. As Ralph Miller perceptively observed, what the Chinese need now are not prototypes to copy; they need the tolerances, routing sheets, and factory floor-level expertise to orchestrate production so that millions of operations can come together to make a truck.

The Chinese outlook on S & T transfer seems to have come a long way from such concepts as buying technology "out of a box" and reverse engineering. But new problems, having to do with the phasing of technology acquisition, have arisen. Much of the technological progress made in China over the last twenty years has been based on the spread of technology acquired from the Soviets in the 1950s. Thus, the vanguard of China's future skilled labor force is now cutting its teeth on what are in many cases obsolete technologies. In the industrial city of Wuhan, the future labor force of what is hoped will be a state-of-the-art plant, the Wuhan No. 1 Automotive Plant, is currently undergoing its apprenticeship training at an outmoded 10,000-truck capacity plant; this plant is designed to produce copies of Russian trucks, which were brought in during the 1950s.[15]

Not only must trained manpower and imported technology be phased into production with some precision, but materials, too, must come on stream at the correct moment if costly bottlenecks are to be kept at a minimum. When the Chinese purchased Spey engine technology from the British in the early 1970s, they miscalculated their metallurgical capabilities so that, even after the knowledge had been acquired, some of the alloys needed to produce the finished product were missing.

Another side of the problem of phasing is illustrated by the fact that today China's existing steel works are producing at under capacity levels because of energy shortfalls and the lack of complementary modern oxygen plant technology to bring them up to full capacity.

Beyond problems of phasing lies the danger of taking a "catch-up mentality" too far, to the point where foreign technology becomes so attractive that it is adopted regardless of its suitability to Chinese factor endowments. Many of the technologies developed during the Great Leap Forward were extremely simple in technical terms, yet they serve rural areas better than their expensive alternatives, or better than nothing at all. Thus, Vaclav Smil observes that small, relatively uneconomical coal mines fill an important need. Small hydroelectric plants, which produce a low and wavering voltage of electric power, fill a similar need, as do small biogas digesters. Here the challenge to Chinese S & T policy, rather than being the importation of the latest in mining equipment or turbogenerators, will lie in maintaining systematic interconnections between the more advanced and the more backward sectors of the economy to stimulate a flow of technology between sectors.

After technology has been acquired and assimilated, a whole new set of difficulties faces China's centralized economy. What is to prompt the entrenched plant manager to experiment with cost-cutting innovations? From whence will come a "technology pull" to define the need for incremental improvements in the mode of production and to stimulate solutions to specific problems? What planning mechanisms will prevent provincial workshops from needlessly duplicating one another's research, ad infinitum, perpetually reinventing the wheel? In a capitalist economy, the market does the work of the state planning apparatus; the marginal utilities of alternative techniques are precisely ranked by the price system. Many Western analysts, comparing China to Japan in the 1920s and the 1930s, are pessimistic about the ability of the Chinese system simultaneously to thrive on dualism while gradually eliminating it, and to use the energies of rural industry in the service of modernization. The reason for their pessimism is that lacking the market mechanism, the Chinese have been slow to develop the institutional equivalent of the Japanese *zaibatsu*, or the ability to link entrepreneurs and financiers so as to create and channel investment in the most efficient fashion.[16]

What have the Chinese been doing to foster technology dissemination? Quite a bit, particularly by way of "administrative," i.e., bureaucratic, mechanisms. Currently, the most important efforts in this area have been in the covening of national conferences in specific fields. No fewer than sixteen such conferences on science, planetary physics, education, elementary particles, geology, and other S & T-related areas were convened within one year of the demise of the Gang of Four. These symposia are organized and directed by the center and are attended by representatives from all over China. They have continued throughout 1978 and early 1979 to focus new Chinese interest in such areas as high-energy physics and activation analysis.

The major institutional reforms discussed in the following section—in particular, the revival of the State Scientific and Technological Commission and many of the societies of the Chinese Science and Technology Association—come under the heading of "administrative" mechanisms as well. All of these represent "technology push" efforts of the center to disseminate S & T from the top. Beyond these very centralized efforts, the diffusion of technology downward at the provincial level has also been encouraged.

In contrast to these administrative measures, there have been "economic" moves, such as the tightening of direct contract linkages between urban and rural industry. These linkages create profit incentives for localities to act as supply bases for large-scale urban industry, recalling the Japanese model of development. In this connection, the People's Bank of China may grow into the major monitoring—even controlling—force that national banks have become in other developing countries. Finally, there have been recent signs that the Chinese are willing to try enclave and perhaps even concessions approaches where these are deemed the most rapid paths to S & T modernization. Perhaps the best example to date of the use of the enclave approach is in the planned 6 million metric ton steel plant at Paoshan, near Shanghai. Its location dictated purely by economic factors, the Paoshan plant will be modeled exactly on the Japanese Kimitsu plant and will be constructed with the aid of 1,000 resident Japanese technicians. It promises to be very much in the pattern of enclaves of advanced technology common in many other developing countries.

Organizing for Science and Technology

Two of the principal issues under discussion in this volume have been the inducement of innovation and the dissemination of technology in China. Success in both of these areas will hinge, to a large extent, on Chinese skill in preparing the organizational matrix within which these activities will take place.

As Richard Suttmeier has pointed out, like the Soviet system on which it was originally modeled, Chinese organization of R & D is based on the premise that technological innovation can be rationalized and planned in the service of the state and that technology can be effectively disseminated through a centralized state bureaucracy. The crucial question raised by Suttmeier is: How effective can a highly bureaucratized organizational structure be in encouraging innovation and disseminating technology in the absence of entrepreneurship? How, when the organs of R & D are rigidly segregated into three sectors (the Chinese Academy of Science and its component institutes, the ministerial institutes, and the research organs associated with institutions of higher education), can severe problems of intersectoral collaboration and communication be avoided? In this regard, Dean seriously questions the efficacy of "administrative" mechanisms in filling the roles performed by "economic" mechanisms in a capitalist economy. With the expansion of the contract system among enterprises and expanded bonuses for innovators, Chinese R & D may yet achieve an increased measure of responsiveness to the needs of the economy. Certainly a period of testing lies ahead.

The Cultural Revolution was the Woodstock of Chinese R & D: the destruction of institutional barriers, the breakdown of centralization, and the creation of "open-door research" all served to bring about an intimate association between theory and practice, research and production. Along the way, basic research traditions were often completely destroyed. In their wake, the Cultural Revolution left what Suttmeier refers to as an "Edisonian" approach to research, characterized by a still close alignment of production and research and what amounts to a trial-and-error type of methodology. While the stong linkages between production and research inherited from the Cultural Revolution are clearly desirable from the point of view of S & T modernization, "Edisonianism" will have to yield to a more profound understanding of basic scientific principles at the production level if Chinese design and R & D capabilities are to advance to world levels.

On the other hand, Volti fears that the current trend back toward a more structured, centralized R & D establishment may lead to a tendency to "discount the potentials existing at the basic levels of Chinese society."[17] He points out, moreover, that Soviet-style concentration on the development of selected industries and technologies will lead to the "encapsulation" of those technologies and the consequent neglect of the technological development of the economy at large.

A Question of Values

> *While learning advanced science and technology, China will on no account import the capitalist system, which is built on the exploitation of man by man, or its decadent ideology and way of life*
>
> —*Jen-min jih-pao*, April 19, 1979

In late 1977, it became clear that the new Chinese leadership was about to embark on a vast program of economic development. Most of the directions embodied in the new program were not new, but their scope, the speed at which they are being carried out, and the probable extent of Western S & T input have all been unprecedented.

The acquisition, absorption, and dissemination of S & T have become something of an obsession with the Chinese leadership. New approaches, new models—both socialist and capitalist—are being tried. Yet many of the attitudes of the individuals who will be called upon to implement the plans are seemingly right out of the late Ch'ing Dynasty.

Despite Hu Ch'iao-mu's exhortations to follow the objective economic laws of development, Teng Hsiao-p'ing's (now largely superseded) calls for more democracy, and Fang Yi's exoneration of the intellectuals, the editorial cited above serves as a potent reminder that the nineteenth century *"t'i-yung"* dichotomy referred to by Volti and Brown retains potency today. Chinese essence, transmuted by Mao, remains a powerful restraint on the future progress of S & T modernization in China. The programs of technologically minded reformers, from Li Hung-chang through Chou En-lai and Teng Hsiao-p'ing, have never met with smooth sailing. Nor is there any reason to assume that the lines of battle have been obscured today.

In the past, the *t'i-yung* argument was phrased in cultural terms. Today it continues in the jargon of dialectical materialism. At the National Science Conference in March 1978, Teng Hsiao-p'ing "refuted the Maoist notion that science is a part of the cultural superstructure of society and thus properly the object of political struggle,"[18] while Hua Kuo-feng continued to show at least as much concern with the relations of production—the Marxist substructure—as with the productive forces themselves.

Ultimately, most issues of Chinese S & T policy boil down to several interrelated questions of values. How much Chinese "essence" can the leadership safely sacrifice to the efficiencies of foreign organizational, managerial, and technological modes? To what extent does it dare to sacrifice mass involvement for elitism in industry and education? To what extent will the Party be willing to yield its managerial prerogatives to the corps of technocrats now being trained at Oxford and MIT? Regardless of who mans the Politburo, these questions will be asked for some time to come. Right now the only certainty is that technological change will eventually invade almost every corner of Chinese life if the planners in Peking have their way. From the classroom to the laboratory to the rice paddy, to the factory floor, the socio-cultural implications of the modernization of Chinese S & T will be enormous.

Having to a large extent modified the Gang of Four's rigid stance on the acquisition of foreign S & T, the current leadership now confronts enormous technical, financial, social, and cultural problems in absorbing and assimilating acquired technologies. It may be possible to restrict most of the foreign businessmen in China to the confines of a fifty-story foreign-trade center, but the broader cultural consequences of their presence—their institutions, their ideology, and their way of life—will be much less easy to contain. As a *Jen-min jih-pao* editorial of April 19, 1979, stated:

> With increased contacts with the outside world, the influence of bourgeois ideas and the bourgeois way of life will grow; and some people in society will invariably spread thoughts sceptical of or opposed to [our] fundamental principles.[19]

Solving this problem is said to be a "long-term task" that will require "intensive political and ideological work." Significantly, however, no firm clues have yet been offered as to just how the work of restricting and detoxifying bourgeois ideas is to proceed. Caveat Emptor!

Notes

1. *Miami Herald*, February 2, 1979.
2. Ibid.
3. Hua Kuo-feng, "Government Work Report," February 26, 1978, in Foreign Broadcast Information Service [hereafter FBIS] *Daily Report—P.R.C.*, March 7, 1978, p. D18; and Teng Hsiao-p'ing, "Report to the National Science Conference," March 18, 1978, in FBIS, March 21, 1978, p. E5. Also see Fang Yi, "Report to the Standing Committee of the CPPCC," December 27, 1977, in FBIS, December 30, 1977, p. E6; and "Central Committee Circular on the National Science Conference," September 18, 1977, in FBIS, September 23, 1977, p. E6.
4. Hua, "Government Work Report," p. D22.
5. FBIS, February 9, 1978, p. E5.
6. *American Banker*, April 9, 1979.
7. Editorial, *Jen-min jih-pao* [People's daily, hereafter *JMJP*], February 29, 1979, quoted in *Far Eastern Economic Review* 103, no. 3 (January 16, 1979).
8. See Chapter 4 of this volume.
9. See Richard Baum, "*Diabolus ex Machina:* Technological Development and Social Change in Chinese Industry," in Frederick Fleron, ed., *Technology and Communist Culture* (New York: Praeger, 1977), pp. 315–56.
10. Jon Sigurdson, "Technology and Science—Some Issues in

China's Modernization," in U.S., Congress, Joint Economic Committee, *Chinese Economy Post-Mao*, 95th Cong., 2d sess., 1978, p. 533.

11. See Chapter 5 of this volume; also see Richard P. Suttmeier et al., in *Science and Technology in the People's Republic of China* (Paris: Organization for Economic Cooperation and Development, 1977).

12. Pierre Perrolle, "Engineering Education in China" (Paper delivered at the Bermuda Workshop on "The Development of Industrial Science and Technology in the P.R.C.," January 1979), p. 8.

13. Ibid., Thomas Fingar, in discussion at the workshop.

14. *New York Times*, February 6, 1979.

15. Hans Heymann, in discussion at the January 1979 Bermuda Workshop (see supra note 12).

16. Lucian Pye, ibid.

17. See Chapter 7 of this volume.

18. James Reardon-Anderson, "Science and Technology in Post-Mao China," *Contemporary China* 2, no. 4 (Winter 1978).

19. *JMJP*, April 19, 1979; also *Beijing Review*, no. 19 (May 11, 1979), pp. 13–14.

Workshop Participants

Betsy Ancker-Johnson
Argonne National Laboratory

Robert E. Armstrong
The Henry Luce Foundation

Jack Baranson
Developing World Industry and Technology, Inc.

A. Doak Barnett
The Brookings Institution

Richard Baum
Department of Political Science
University of California, Los Angeles

Shannon R. Brown
Department of Economics
University of Maryland, Baltimore County

Mary Brown Bullock
Committee on Scholarly Communication with the People's Republic of China
National Academy of Sciences

B. T. Chao
Department of Industrial Engineering
University of Illinois

Kan Chen
Department of Electrical Engineering
University of Michigan

Robert G. Chollar
The Charles F. Kettering Foundation

William Clarke
Bureau of East-West Trade
U.S. Department of Commerce

Jack Craig
Central Intelligence Agency

Genevieve C. Dean
U.S.-China Relations Program
Stanford University

Robert F. Dernberger
Department of Economics
University of Michigan

Arthur Downey
Sutherland, Asbill, and Brennen, Attorneys-at-law

Nils Ekblad
Office of the Scientific and Technical Attache
Swedish Embassy, Peking

Robert M. Field
Central Intelligence Agency

Thomas Fingar
U.S.-China Relations Program
Stanford University

John P. Hardt
Congressional Research Service
U.S. Library of Congress

Hans Heymann, Jr.
Central Intelligence Agency

Roy Hofheinz, Jr.
Fairbank Center for
East Asian Research
Harvard University

John Holmfeld
Committee on Science
and Technology
U.S. House of Representatives

Benjamin Huberman
National Security Council/
White House Office of Science
and Technology Policy

Bruce Hunter
Defense Intelligence Agency

Sydney Jammes
Central Intelligence Agency

Roman Kolkowicz
Department of Political Science
University of California,
Los Angeles

David M. Lampton
Department of Political Science
The Ohio State University

Nicholas Lardy
Department of Economics
Yale University

Rennselaer Lee, III
Mathematica, Inc.

Stanley B. Lubman
Heller, Ehrman, White,
and McAuliffe,
Attorneys-at-law

Nicholas Ludlow
National Council for U.S.-
China Trade

John Mallon
Defense Intelligence Agency

Hugh Miller
National Academy of
Engineering

Ralph Miller
General Motors, Inc.

C.H.G. Oldham
Science Policy Research Unit
University of Sussex

Leo A. Orleans
Library of Congress/
Committee on Scholarly
Communication with the
People's Republic of China

J. Ray Pace
Baker Tool Company

Pierre Perrolle
Committee on Scholarly
Communication with the
People's Republic of China

Michael Pillsbury
Washington, D.C.

Jonathan Pollack
The Rand Corporation

Lucian W. Pye
Department of Political Science
Massachusetts Institute of Technology

Carl A. Riskin
Department of Economics
Queens College

Almon R. Roth
Central Intelligence Agency

Jeffrey Schultz
Chase Pacific Trade Advisors

Jon Sigurdson
Research Policy Program
University of Lund

Vaclav Smil
Department of Geography
University of Manitoba

Richard Sorich
New York

Richard P. Suttmeier
Department of Government
Hamilton College

Bohdan Szuprowicz
21st Century Research

Anne Thurston
Joint Committee on Contemporary China
Social Science Research Council

C. L. Tien
Department of Mechanical Engineering
University of California, Berkeley

Alfred H. Usack, Jr.
Central Intelligence Agency

Rudi Volti
Department of Sociology
Pitzer College

Martha Wallace
The Henry Luce Foundation

K. P. Wang
Bureau of Mines
U.S. Department of the Interior

Thomas B. Wiens
Mathematica, Inc.

K. C. Yeh
The Rand Corporation

Index